Y0-AAG-475

# Japanese Economic Policies and Growth

## Implications for Businesses in Canada and North America

*Masao Nakamura and Ilan Vertinsky*

**Japanese Economic Policies and Growth**
Implications for Businesses in Canada and North America

# Japanese Economic Policies and Growth

Implications for Businesses in Canada and North America

*Masao Nakamura and Ilan Vertinsky*

The University of Aberta Press

First published by
The University of Alberta Press
Athabasca Hall
Edmonton, Alberta, Canada T6G 2E8


ISBN 0–88864–264–4

**Canadian Cataloguing in Publication Data**

Nakamura, Masao.
Japanese economic policies and growth

Includes bibliographical references and index.
ISBN 0–88864–264–4

1. Japan—Economic conditions—1945– 2. Japan—Economic policy—1945– 3. Canada—Commerce—Japan. 4. Japan—Commerce—Canada. I. Vertinsky, I. II. Title.
HC462.9.N34 1994 338.952 C95–910034–2



Printed on acid-free paper. ∞

Printed and bound by
Quality Color Press Inc.,
Edmonton, Alberta, Canada

COMMITTED TO THE DEVELOPMENT OF CULTURE AND THE ARTS

## *Contents*

## *Tables*

## *Figures*

# Preface

Focusing on the economic policies and growth of Japan since World War II, *Japanese Economic Policies and Growth: Implications for Businesses in Canada and North America* describes and analyzes the policies and practices that moulded the Japanese economy and its linkages with other economies. While several books describe and attempt to explain the phenomenal economic growth of Japan between 1960 and 1990, there are few that have chosen a Canadian perspective for their investigation. This Canadian perspective allowed us to focus on the Japanese economic system and the dynamics that are either important to the understanding of the bilateral relationships of Japan and Canada or provide a basis of comparison from which Canadian policies and practices can be reassessed in view of the Japanese experience.

Understanding Japan is critical for Canadian governments and business. The fate of Japan has a great impact on the opportunities and threats facing Canada in this decade. Japan is the second largest economy in the world. Its relationship with the U.S. may affect Canada's prospects in its two most important markets. Japan is also the dominant player in the Asia-Pacific, with a great influence on the other economies of the region. The Asia-Pacific, with its expected unprecedented economic growth, provides Canada with its most significant opportunity in this decade to diversify its exports and reduce its dependence on the U.S. Thus the significant structural changes that the Japanese economy will undergo in the coming years may have an influence upon Canadian economic interests far beyond the direct linkages of the two economies in trade, investment, and technology flows. At present Canada is not well positioned to adapt to these structural changes in Japan. We hope that this book can contribute to the understanding of the changes as they relate to the Canadian economy and bring about appropriate responses from both businesses and governments. This book was written with two purposes in mind: to provides information and analysis to business persons and public officials who contemplate pursuing economic opportunities in Japan; and to provides a fundamental survey and analysis for public and private sector decision makers who would like to draw lessons for Canada from the Japanese economic experience.

Divided into two interrelated parts, the first part focuses on the Japanese economy and its dynamics with special attention to the role of government policies and business practices in stimulating and sustaining economic growth. The second part focuses specifically on the linkages between the Canadian and Japanese economies and the lessons that Canada may derive from the Japanese experience.

Part I, An Analysis of Japanese Economic Growth examines Japanese economic growth from a macro perspective; Japanese business practices in industrial relations, corporate groups and corporate control; government policy on industry and technology; and foreign trade and direct investment. Japanese firm behaviour (business practices) and government policy are considered by many analysts to be the essential factors which spurred Japan's rapid economic growth since World War II. How these behaviours and policies affected Japan and how they act as deterrents which stop newcomers from having easy access to various markets in Japan including labour markets, markets for goods and services and the market for corporate control are discussed. Implications for foreign firms' operations in Japan are also analyzed.

Part II, Canada and Japan examines the determinants of Japan's competitiveness and its implications for Canada; bilateral economic relationships between Canada and Japan; and Canadian policies towards Japan. Important influences on Japanese economic growth—long-term business practices, government policy and the aging of the Japanese population—are related to the shaping of Canada-Japan bilateral economic relationships and Canadian policies towards Japan.

Any attempt to provide a relatively brief overview of complex processes and systems must suffer from some degree of oversimplification, a high degree of judgment and some speculation. This may not suit some readers for, as Bertrand Russell observed, what men really want is not knowledge and informed judgment but certainty. But knowledge and judgment can enhance opportunity by reducing and defining the realms of uncertainty. Our conclusions and recommendations are based on our judgment and intuition developed on the basis of a three-year broad study of different aspects of Japanese competitiveness funded by the Social Sciences and Humanities Research Council of Canada (SSHRC).

The original manuscript for this book was prepared as part of a Canadian International Development Agency (CIDA) funded project on Canada and the Asia-Pacific Rim that was initiated under the supervision of the Economic Council of Canada and later under Queen's University. We are especially indebted to Tony Lemprière who researched the sections focusing on the bilateral trade relations of Canada and Japan, and Louise Hebert and Mabel Yee who prepared the manuscript for publication. We gratefully acknowledge the comments and suggestions we received on earlier versions of this manuscript from Jon Swanson, Terry Ursacki, Neil Swan, Donald J. Daly, Frank Flatters, and Alice Nakamura as well as two anonymous readers. We are, of course, responsible for all remaining shortcomings.

## ***Introduction***

*Japanese Economic Growth and Implications for Canada-Japan Economic Relations*

Economic growth is a complex phenomenon, although a growing body of empirical literature attempts to explain it. In the neoclassical growth models (Solow, 1956; Cass, 1965; Koopmans, 1965) it was hypothesized that levels of per capita income converge across countries—thus poorer countries are likely to grow at a faster rate than richer countries. Nelson and Phelps (1966) have emphasized that the ability to catch up depends on the ability of a country to absorb the new technologies and knowledge developed elsewhere. Abramovitz (1986) suggests that three factors may control the ability of a country to catch up, what he terms its "social capabilities" to develop. These are:

(1) The facilities for diffusion of knowledge—for example, channels of international technical communication, multinational corporations, the state of international trade and of direct investment.

(2) Conditions facilitating or hindering structural change in the composition of output, in the occupational and industrial distribution of the workforce, and in the geographical location of industry and population.

(3) Macroeconomic and monetary conditions encouraging and sustaining capital investment and the level and growth of effective demand (p. 390).

Barro (1991) studied 98 countries in the period 1960–1985 and found that the growth rate of real per capita GDP is positively related to initial human capital and negatively related to the initial level of real per capita GDP. "Thus, poor countries tend to catch up with rich countries if the poor countries have high human capital per person (in relation to their level of per capita GDP), but not otherwise." Countries with high human capital have low fertility rates and high ratios of physical investment to GDP. Other findings of this study show that economic growth is inversely related to the share of government consumption in GDP, but insignificantly related to the share of public investment. Barro interpreted this to signify that government consumption introduces distortions, such as high tax rates, but does not provide an offsetting stimulus to investment and growth. He also found that a proxy for price distortions is negatively related to growth. Finally, his findings indicate that growth is positively related to measures of political stability.

Dowrick (1992), in a study of technological catchup and divergence of income from 1960–1988, focused on the exceptional growth rates of five rapidly growing Asian economies. He concluded that half of their exceptional performance could be attributed to faster than average growth in factor inputs relative to population. He also commented that "It is particularly interesting to note that employment deepening, i.e., raising the ratio of workforce to the population, has been relatively more important than capital deepening in three of these five countries. It is only in Japan that capital deepening has substantially outweighed the employment deepening effect" (p. 606).

Grier and Tullock (1989) considered 113 countries in the 1951–1986 period and assessed the impact of the following variables on economic growth: (1) initial conditions (convergence), (2) population growth, (3) inflation, (4) standard deviation of inflation, (5) standard deviation of income growth and (6) the size of government. They found that coefficient values in their estimated models varied widely across identifiable groups of countries. They concluded that "these results demonstrate that we do not have a single empirical model of secular growth that applies around the world." They argue that the idiosyncratic variations in what Abramovitz calls "social capabilities" appear to be much more important than some of the common variables explaining economic growth.

The story of Japanese economic growth, focused on in Part I, confirms some of the findings of the empirical cross-country analysis of growth but also shows how combinations of factors may alter the predicted impacts of single factors. It is a story that emphasizes the importance of "social capabilities" in bringing about economic growth and demonstrates the role of government and business practices in developing these capabilities. It is also a story that, while confirming the importance of "small government," shows how a small government need not be a passive government.

The first chapter, "Japanese Economic Growth—A Macro Perspective," describes and analyzes Japanese economic growth from an historical overview. Particular attention is paid to certain macro-economic variables (e.g., foreign exchange) that played important policy roles historically. Three distinct stages of economic growth are identified: from 1950 to the late 1960s, from the late 1960s to the late 1970s, and the 1980s up to the recent burst of a speculative bubble in the early 1990s. Different factors played important roles for Japanese economic development in these stages. Active government policy intervention and regulations characterized institutional settings for Japanese firms from the 1950s to the late 1970s. As market mechanisms became more important in policy decisions by the early 1970s, Japanese business practices in industrial relations, corporate groups and corporate control, which evolved slowly from the early 1950s to the late 1960s, started to become important parts of the Japanese "social capability" and a source of international competitiveness for Japanese firms in technology-based manufacturing industries.

The 1980s marked attempts in Japan to shift from economic growth based mainly on exports to a more balanced condition where domestic growth plays a significant role. This period is characterized by some of the dysfunctional symptoms of rapid domestic growth including inflation in domestic asset prices—what is described as a bubble economy. The distortions that the speculative bubble created, combined with some of the dysfunctional attributes of the business practices that served Japan so well in the preceding periods, explain to a large extent the difficulties that Japan faces in the early 1990s in its attempts to adjust to the "post bubble" economy.

Three key elements of Japanese business practices that have defined in part Japan's "social capability" to catch up to other industrialized countries and then emerge as a leader are focused on in chapter 2, "Japanese Business

Practices: Industrial Relations, Corporate Groups And Corporate Control." The first is an "industrial relations" system that facilitated change, encouraged productivity growth through human capital investment, eliminated conflict and provided for a flexible deployment of the workforce. The system also has some important dysfunctional attributes that inhibit labour mobility, prevented the evolution of competitive labour markets and constrained the ability of some segments of the population (in particular women) from participating fully in the economy. A second important contributor to the Japanese "social capability" has been the presence of corporate groups linked with the public sector. The system of inter-firm linkages and the system of linkages between the private and public sector provided the economy with efficient mechanisms for coordination and information diffusion, mechanisms for risk sharing and mechanisms which provide opportunities for firms to enjoy economies of network and scale without enduring some of the costs associated with size.

A complex system of interrelationships is usually resistant to change. The Japanese system of industrial organization, however, appeared to be able to adjust and adapt and assume new structural equilibria. Dore (1973) attributed this capacity to adjust to the dualism of Japan's industrial structure. For example, large firms coexist with many smaller firms, and the smaller firms provide the flexibility and bear most of the burden of adjustment. Another type of duality is one that encourages simultaneously some forms of both competition and cooperation. Clark (1979) identified four characteristic tendencies of the Japanese company: (1) it tends to be a clearly defined cell of industrial and commercial activity; (2) its activities are narrowly specialized; (3) it has a clearly recognizable standing in a hierarchy in the industry, a standing related to size, and it seeks to improve standing; and (4) it is associated with other companies in some form of group. "The first three characteristics enhance myopic competition and consequently a sensitive response to the immediate environment. The fourth characteristic provides a mechanism for the balancing component of behavioral control—a collective core inducing cooperation" (Vertinsky, 1986, p. 47). The balance between competition and cooperation and between the short-run and long-run vision is a key characteristic of the Japanese industrial organization that maintains stability but allows for change and adaptation.

The third feature of Japanese business practices focussed on is the structure of corporate control. In this structure large fractions of outstanding shares of Japanese listed firms are held by stable shareholders such as other companies, banks and other financial institutions who are not expected to behave in an opportunistic manner. This facilitates a long-term orientation to business decision making. This is done without completely insulating firms (and their managers) from market realities. Financial distress triggers intervention and management replacement, typically in the form of direct intervention by the main bank of the firm which is likely also to be one of its shareholders. A long-term vision of business encourages innovation and experimentation, important attributes in sustaining industrial leadership.

The role of government in Japan and its relationship to the business sector is perhaps the most important factor that enhanced Japan's "social capabilities" first to converge, and then to lead and sustain its leadership. Japan provides an example of a government that has spent a relatively small share of Gross National Product (GNP) yet nevertheless has exercised great influence on the economy. It is a government that is an active player with a vision, yet it is not a government that is dominant in the economy. It is a government that provided a long-term framework for competition of powerful private firms. The government agencies and their advisory committees have done so by issuing plans and forecasts, by developing hybrid combinations of public and private enterprises (the "third sector") and by utilizing formal and informal channels of influence to mould corporate behaviour. Johnson (1983), commenting on planning in industrial policy, observed that by planning one means consistent, long-term government policies that are known and publicized, so that private sector actors in the economy know what the government is going to do and adjust to it. "The Japanese government's industrial policy is published. Any citizen can buy it at the corner newsstand. What is called the Economic Planning Agency in Japan is, in fact, an Economic Propaganda Agency, a hortatory body if you will" (p. 38). The efforts of the bureaucracy to coordinate, however, do not result in a loss of information from the system about options and consequences. The maintenance of alternative sources of information seems to be an important objective of the bureaucracy. "Indeed, the goal of the government's own planning oriented research contracts is not to increase control over information generation, rather, it is aimed at maintaining the diversity of independent information sources" (Vertinsky, 1986, p. 53). Similarly the use of "third sector" enterprises was typically geared to generating and maintaining new technological options and diffusing information about them widely, without constraining or competing with private sector research and development (R&D) (Johnson, 1983). In addition to its roles in the generation and dissemination of information, and in the articulation of a broad economic vision, the Japanese government enhanced the "social capabilities" of the nation by facilitating change and adjustment.

The role that specific industrial and technology policies have played in promoting change and adjustment in an effort to foster economic growth are discussed in chapters 3 and 4. Specifically, the policies to promote investment in social capital, policies aimed at promotion of strategically important industries and policies to deal with industrial decline are examined. The more active interventionist role the Japanese government played until the late 1960s using the allocation of limited resources to what were considered essential factors of production (e.g., allocating scarce foreign exchange to the purchase of foreign technologies for certain manufacturing industries) also are examined. The Japanese government recognized that international competitive advantage could be deliberately created by pushing broad sets of industries toward sectors of the world economy characterized by growth and technological change (Wade, 1990). The benefits of such active interventions were, however, often accompanied by significant costs.

An important objective of government policy has been to foster technological change. Chapter 4, "The Role of Government-Technology Policy," discusses how Japan attempted to ensure that the process of convergence would not prevent it from assuming a role of technological leadership. The chapter also examines the mechanisms that were used to encourage private-sector investment in research and development and how private sector pursuit of scale economies was encouraged.

Neoclassical economic theory prescribes opening of a domestic market to foreign trade and investment flows to achieve the optimal economic performance. However, Krugman (1986) and others recognized that, in conditions of increasing returns to scale and imperfect international markets, growth may be encouraged by activist trade and industrial policies. In Chapter 5, "Foreign Trade And Direct Investment," Japanese trade and foreign direct investment policies as well as the international strategies and management practices of Japanese firms are focussed on. The story that emerges is not consistent with neoclassical theory and policy prescriptions. How Japanese firm behaviour and activist trade and industrial policies caused shifts in comparative advantage is shown and how the adjustment to these shifts resulted in significant increases in the outward flow of direct investment and the internationalization of Japanese industry is examined. Japanese policies over the years encouraged the importation of technologies but restricted foreign direct investment, thus creating endogenous technological capabilities without sacrificing the opportunities to use foreign technology. It protected domestic markets while fostering internal competition, thus offering Japanese firms the growth required to capture economies of scale without removing the incentives to increase productivity and innovate that competitive markets produce. Under international pressure Japan has removed many of the formal barriers to trade and investment but informal barriers and some government practices continue to provide Japanese firms with significant advantages over their foreign rivals in the domestic market.

The first part of the book examines Japanese government policies that successfully developed social capabilities, which are considered prerequisites for sustained economic growth. The government, though small in size, played an active role in formulating public policies that facilitated private sector development of certain business practices. These practices helped create comparative advantages in the global market.

The chapters in Part II, Canada and Japan, are devoted to the discussion of Japanese economic performance in relation to other countries and in particular to the discussion of Canada-Japan bilateral economic relations.

In Chapter 6, "The Determinants of Japan's Competitive Position," international comparisons of various social and economic performance measures in analyzing the role of government are made. This analysis is begun by considering the role of the government in providing a stable macroeconomic environment. This is viewed as essential for private-sector firms to develop global competitiveness. The role of the Japanese government in correcting market failures is then assessed. This is followed by a discussion of the government role in adopting "industrial policies" in order to create new comparative advantages for Japanese industries.

Of particular interest are the conditions that underlie the successes of these policies and in identifying the conditions that prevent "government failures." The methods the Japanese government employed in an attempt to increase the probability that the government would support winners, not buttress losers are also examined.

The institutional structures underlying Japan's economic system are analyzed in the later part of Chapter 6. By identifying those institutional characteristics that encourage synergistic relationships among government, industry and other elements of the economy for economic growth, the preconditions for successful government intervention that existed in Japan are explored and contrasted with the Canadian condition.

The chapter concludes by examining the appropriateness for Canada of various Japanese government polices and institutional approaches and comparing the preconditions for successful government interventions in Japan with the Canadian situations.

Chapter 7 examines in detail bilateral economic relations between Canada and Japan. The patterns of foreign trade between Canada and Japan at both macro and micro levels are discussed. Particular attention is paid to the impediments to trade resulting from government policies and business practices, among other factors. Bilateral relations in portfolio investment, foreign direct investment and technology development and transfer are also discussed.

The implications for Canada of trade frictions between the U.S. and Japan are explored; alternative Canadian strategies for dealing with impediments and opportunities found in the Japanese markets for various Canadian goods are also discussed.

Based on the examination of bilateral relationships in Chapter 7, Chapter 8 explores Canadian policies towards Japan in three areas: trade, direct investment and technology. Japan's role in these three areas is important for both private and public sector decision making in Canada. How Canadian firms can take advantage of Japanese markets, direct investments and technologies is an important theme for Canadian public policies.

The final chapter, "Lessons and Opportunities for Canada" contains a summary of the book and our policy and recommendations for Canada in dealing with its economic relations with Japan.

# Part I

## An Analysis of Japanese Economic Growth

1

# Japanese Economic Growth—
## A Macro Perspective

### Introduction

The Japanese economy has experienced considerable growth over the four decades since the 1950s. The period from 1950 to the late 1960s was characterized by active government intervention to develop certain key industries and promote the diffusion of technology among Japanese firms. Promoting exports was particularly important since the expansion of the Japanese economy was often limited by a lack of foreign exchange. Government industrial and technology policies directed resources toward targeted industries through government control over scarce foreign exchange resources.

As industries gained international competitiveness, the foreign exchange constraint became less binding. In the period from the late 1960s to the late 1970s, Japanese government industrial policies became more consistent with market mechanisms. Many restrictive laws regarding foreign exchange, foreign ownership and capital markets were liberalized. Despite downturns due to the oil price shocks, economic growth was strong through the 1970s, largely due to growing exports.

Beginning in the mid 1980s, the upward revaluation of the Japanese currency combined with government policies to emphasize domestic growth began to transform the export-driven economy into one dominated by imports, domestic consumption and investment (including foreign invest-

**Fig. 1.1** Growth in Real GNP and Capital Investment: Year-to-Year Change, 1955–1992

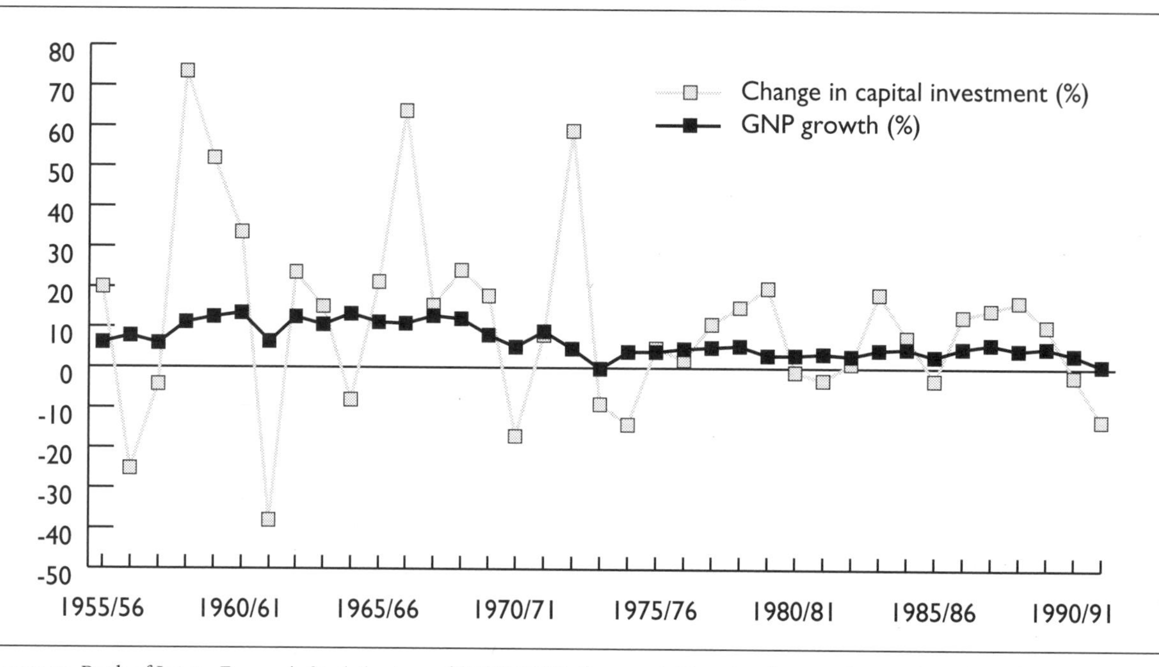


SOURCE: Bank of Japan, *Economic Statistics Annual* (1977, 1992); Economic Planning Agency, *Economic Statistics* (1981, 1993).

ment) activity. After the mid 1980s, speculation and excess liquidity led to the formation of a bubble in the Japanese economy (a major departure of asset prices from their fundamental values). For example, the Tokyo commercial land price index rose from 127 in 1985 (1983 = 100) to 341 in 1991 while GNP grew by only 42% during the same period. The bubble burst in 1990, resulting in a decline of the Nikkei 225 stock average index from 38,915 in January 1989 to 23,848 in February 1990 to almost 14,000 in August 1992. The index was still around 18,000 as of January 1994. During the same period, land prices fell for the first time since World War II. A serious recession in the first half of the 1990s followed the collapse of the bubble.

Demographic change has been, and will continue to be, an important source of change in the Japanese economy. The Japanese population is expected to age rapidly in the next 20–30 years, while the size of the working-age population group is expected to shrink substantially. It is anticipated that serious effects on labour supply and public finance will result.

**Fig. 1.2** Current Balance and Inventory Cycle, 1955–1982

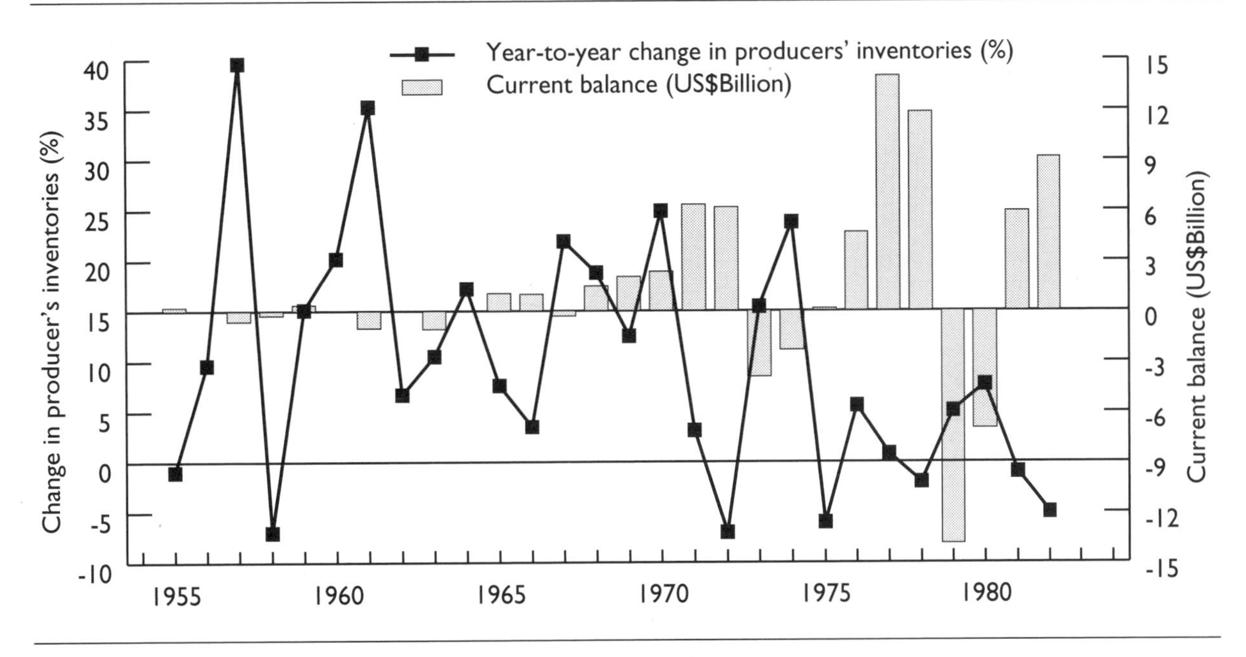


SOURCE: Economic Planning Agency, *White Paper on the Economy* (1993).

The long-term economic forecasts that these predictions of labour shortages are based are explored later in this chapter.

## The Period from 1950 to the Late 1960s

The Japanese economy underwent striking changes, both domestically and in its relationship with the world economy, from the early 1950s through the late 1960s (i.e., the period between the Korean War and the first oil price shock). Figure 1.1 depicts growth in real GNP and real investment in plant and equipment since 1955. For the period covering the 1950s and 1960s, the average annual growth of 22% in investment in plant and equipment was the driving force behind an average annual growth rate of 10% in GNP. While GNP grew at a relatively constant rate, considerable fluctuations in real investment were observed (see Figure 1.1). Similar fluctuations occurred also in producers' inventories, as can be seen in Figure 1.2. Foreign exchange shortages are believed to

**Table 1.1** Export Price Indexes, 1960–1979 (1975 = 100)

| | JAPAN | U.S. | CANADA | U.K. | FRANCE | WEST GERMANY | ITALY | SWEDEN |
|---|---|---|---|---|---|---|---|---|
| *1960* | 65 | 46 | 46 | 37 | 50 | 69 | 46 | 46 |
| *1965* | 59 | 49 | 50 | 40 | 53 | 74 | 46 | 49 |
| *1968* | 61 | 52 | 55 | 46 | 54 | 72 | 45 | 50 |
| *1970* | 68 | 56 | 58 | 51 | 64 | 76 | 49 | 56 |
| *1971* | 68 | 58 | 58 | 53 | 67 | 74 | 53 | 60 |
| *1972* | 67 | 60 | 60 | 56 | 69 | 76 | 53 | 61 |
| *1973* | 72 | 70 | 68 | 64 | 75 | 79 | 61 | 68 |
| *1974* | 98 | 89 | 90 | 82 | 95 | 92 | 87 | 87 |
| *1975* | 100 | 100 | 100 | 100 | 00 | 100 | 100 | 100 |
| *1976* | 99 | 103 | 102 | 120 | 109 | 104 | 122 | 108 |
| *1977* | 98 | 107 | 109 | 142 | 120 | 105 | 146 | 117 |
| *1978* | 92 | 114 | 118 | 156 | 126 | 105 | 156 | 126 |
| *1979* | 104 | 130 | 143 | 172 | 138 | 108 | 184 | 142 |

SOURCE: United Nations, *Statistical Yearbook* (1979).

be one cause of the observed fluctuations in inventory and, in turn, in investment. The patterns evident in Figure 1.2 are consistent with the following hypothesized chain of causation. As production expanded, inventories decreased and exports increased, resulting in an improvement in the current account. The increase in exports stimulated investment and increased imports leading to deficits in the current account. With declining foreign reserves, the monetary authorities imposed tight money measures. This in turn increased inventory, decreased investment, and led goods to be diverted to export markets. Increased exports increased foreign reserves and accelerated production. In the 1950s and 1960s, the constraint on foreign exchange availability made these sorts of business cycles inevitable. Increased foreign exchange reserves after the late 1960s led to considerable reductions in the fluctuations in inventories and capital investment (Figures 1.1 and 1.2).

While the Japanese economy grew at an annual average rate of 10%, the average growth rate for global domestic production was 5%. During this period (1955–1970) world trade tripled in volume, with an average growth rate of 7.6% per annum. Active participation in this expansion of international trade is believed to be part of the explanation for the high growth rate

**Table 1.2** Composition of Imports and Exports: Japan and Western Europe[a], 1955–1975 (Percent)

IMPORTS

| | Food | | Raw Materials | | Fuel | | Chemical Products | | Machinery and Transp. Equipment | | Other Industrial Products | | Value of Imports (US$100 million) | |
|---|---|---|---|---|---|---|---|---|---|---|---|---|---|---|
| | *Japan* | *W.E.* | *Japan* | *W.E.* | *Japan* | *W.E.* | *Japan* | *W.E.* | *Japan* | *W.E.* | *Japan* | *W.E.* | *Japan* | *W.E.* |
| *1955* | 26.4 | 23.5 | 50.5 | 23.6 | 9.7 | 11.0 | 4.7 | 4.8 | 5.2 | 13.1 | 3.4 | 24.0 | 24.7 | 407.2 |
| *1960* | 13.6 | 20.0 | 49.5 | 19.8 | 14.1 | 10.0 | 6.4 | 6.0 | 9.0 | 17.5 | 7.4 | 26.7 | 44.9 | 571.1 |
| *1965* | 19.3 | 17.9 | 36.5 | 14.6 | 19.0 | 9.8 | 5.2 | 6.7 | 9.6 | 21.4 | 10.3 | 29.6 | 84.5 | 807.9 |
| *1970* | 13.6 | 14.0 | 35.4 | 11.1 | 20.7 | 9.3 | 5.3 | 7.5 | 11.4 | 25.1 | 12.2 | 31.3 | 193.2 | 1405.1 |
| *1975* | 15.2 | 11.4[b] | 20.1 | 9.9[b] | 44.3 | 20.3[b] | 3.6 | 8.5[b] | 6.6 | 21.0[b] | 9.7 | 27.9b | 557.5 | 3451.5[b] |

EXPORTS

| | Food | | Fuel and Raw Materials | | Chemical Products | | Machinery and Transp. Equipment | | Other Industrial Products | | Value of Exports (US$100 million) | |
|---|---|---|---|---|---|---|---|---|---|---|---|---|
| | *Japan* | *W.E.* | *Japan* | *W.E.* | *Japan* | *W.E.* | *Japan* | *W.E.* | *Japan* | *W.E.* | *Japan* | *W.E.* |
| *1955* | 6.8 | 13.5 | 6.1 | 16.4 | 4.7 | 7.6 | 12.3 | 24.7 | 70.0 | 36.2 | 20.1 | 350.2 |
| *1960* | 6.7 | 11.8 | 4.2 | 13.1 | 4.2 | 8.4 | 23.2 | 30.0 | 62.0 | 35.4 | 40.6 | 515.1 |
| *1965* | 4.1 | 11.7 | 3.3 | 10.9 | 6.5 | 9.2 | 31.2 | 31.9 | 54.3 | 34.9 | 81.7 | 915.5 |
| *1970* | 3.4 | 10.2 | 2.1 | 9.2 | 6.4 | 9.7 | 40.5 | 34.3 | 46.8 | 35.3 | 188.8 | 1542.5 |
| *1975* | 1.4 | 10.3 | 2.0 | 9.5 | 7.0 | 10.5 | 49.2 | 35.5 | 39.2 | 33.0 | 578.6 | 4038.7 |

SOURCE: Bank of Japan, *International Statistics* (1978).

[a] Western Europe (W.E.) includes E.C. (West Germany, France, Italy, Belgium, the Netherlands, Luxembourg, Denmark, Ireland, and Britain), EFTA (Austria, Norway, Portugal, Sweden, and Switzerland) and Greece, Spain, Yugoslavia.

[b] Numbers based on 1974 data.

for the Japanese economy. During this period, Japan, along with (West) Germany, attained international competitiveness in manufacturing. From 1965 on, increases in Japanese and West German export price indexes have been among the lowest in the developed world (see Table 1.1).

The easing of foreign exchange shortages in the late 1960s was both a consequence and an indication of Japan's newly achieved international competitiveness. The international competitiveness that Japan gained during this period is also evident from the changes in the composition of exports and imports. Table 1.2 shows the shift in Japan's foreign trade

**Table 1.3** U.S. and Canadian Trade with Japan[a], 1969–1992 (US$million)

| | U.S. | | CANADA[b] | |
|---|---|---|---|---|
| | Imports from Japan | Exports to Japan | Imports from Japan | Exports to Japan |
| *1960* | 1,102 | 1,553 | 119 | 204 |
| *1961* | 1,067 | 2,096 | 117 | 266 |
| *1962* | 1,400 | 1,809 | 126 | 255 |
| *1963* | 1,507 | 2,077 | 125 | 319 |
| *1964* | 1,841 | 2,336 | 166 | 379 |
| *1965* | 2,479 | 2,366 | 214 | 357 |
| *1966* | 2,969 | 2,658 | 256 | 451 |
| *1967* | 3,012 | 3,212 | 274 | 633 |
| *1968* | 4,086 | 3,527 | 346 | 660 |
| *1969* | 4,958 | 4,090 | 481 | 669 |
| *1970* | 5,940 | 5,560 | 563 | 928 |
| *1971* | 7,495 | 4,978 | 876 | 1,004 |
| *1972* | 8,848 | 5,852 | 1,104 | 1,149 |
| *1973* | 9,449 | 9,269 | 999 | 2,015 |
| *1974* | 12,799 | 12,682 | 1,587 | 2,676 |
| *1975* | 11,149 | 11,608 | 1,151 | 2,499 |
| *1976* | 15,689 | 11,809 | 1,552 | 2,715 |
| *1977* | 19,717 | 12,396 | 1,708 | 2,881 |
| *1978* | 24,914 | 14,790 | 1,871 | 3,191 |
| *1979* | 26,402 | 20,431 | 1,738 | 4,105 |
| *1980* | 31,367 | 24,408 | 2,437 | 4,724 |
| *1981* | 38,609 | 25,297 | 3,399 | 4,464 |
| *1982* | 36,330 | 24,179 | 2,861 | 4,441 |
| *1983* | 42,829 | 24,647 | 3,625 | 4,430 |
| *1984* | 59,937 | 26,862 | 4,297 | 4,945 |
| *1985* | 65,278 | 25,793 | 4,520 | 4,773 |
| *1986* | 80,456 | 29,054 | 5,526 | 4,895 |
| *1987* | 83,580 | 31,490 | 5,611 | 6,073 |
| *1988* | 89,634 | 42,037 | 6,424 | 8,308 |
| *1989* | 93,188 | 48,246 | 6,807 | 8,645 |
| *1990* | 90,322 | 50,369 | 6,726 | 8,392 |
| *1991* | 91,538 | 53,317 | 7,251 | 7,698 |
| *1992* | 95,793 | 52,230 | | |

SOURCE: Japanese Economic Planning Agency, *Summary of Economic Statistics* (various years).

[a] Import figures are based on CIF prices (including the costs of goods, insurance and freight) measured at Japanese ports. Export figures are based on FOB (free-on-board) prices (including the costs of goods and delivery onto a carrier) at the point of shipment.

[b] Note that these data, as reported by the Japan Economic Planning Agency, differ from those reported by Statistics Canada because of different methods of measurement and because of discrepancies created by trade which is routed through U.S. ports.

**Table 1.4** Growth in Wholesale and Consumer Prices, 1970–1978 (Year-to-year percent change)

| | JAPAN | | U.S. | | CANADA | | U.K. | | WEST GERMANY | | FRANCE | | ITALY | |
|---|---|---|---|---|---|---|---|---|---|---|---|---|---|---|
| | W[a] | C[b] | W | C | W | C | W | C | W | C | W | C | W | C |
| *1970* | 3.7 | 9.7 | 3.6 | 5.9 | 2.4 | 3.3 | 7.1 | 6.4 | 4.9 | 3.4 | 7.3 | 5.9 | 5.0 | 5.0 |
| *1971* | –0.8 | 6.1 | 3.2 | 4.3 | 1.9 | 2.9 | 8.9 | 9.4 | 4.3 | 5.3 | 3.7 | 5.3 | 4.8 | 4.8 |
| *1972* | 0.8 | 4.5 | 4.6 | 3.3 | 4.4 | 4.8 | 5.3 | 7.1 | 2.6 | 5.5 | 5.9 | 6.1 | 5.7 | 5.7 |
| *1973* | 15.8 | 11.7 | 13.1 | 6.2 | 11.2 | 7.5 | 33.1 | 9.1 | 6.6 | 6.9 | 12.7 | 7.3 | 10.8 | 10.8 |
| *1974* | 31.4 | 24.5 | 18.9 | 11.0 | 19.0 | 11.0 | 22.6 | 16.0 | 13.4 | 7.0 | 23.7 | 13.7 | 19.1 | 19.1 |
| *1975* | 3.0 | 11.8 | 9.2 | 9.1 | 11.3 | 10.8 | 22.2 | 24.3 | 4.7 | 6.0 | 0.9 | 11.7 | 17.0 | 17.0 |
| *1976* | 5.0 | 9.3 | 4.7 | 5.8 | 5.0 | 7.5 | 17.3 | 16.5 | 3.9 | 4.5 | 10.4 | 9.7 | 16.8 | 16.8 |
| *1977* | 1.9 | 8.1 | 6.1 | 6.5 | 7.7 | 8.0 | 19.8 | 15.9 | 2.6 | 3.9 | 6.7 | 9.5 | 18.4 | 18.4 |
| *1978* | –2.5 | 3.8 | 7.8 | 7.6 | 8.0 | 8.9 | 9.1 | 8.3 | 1.2 | 2.6 | 4.6 | 9.3 | 12.1 | 12.1 |

SOURCE: Japanese Economic Planning Agency, *Summary of Economic Statistics* (1983).

[a] Wholesale Price Index.
[b] Consumer Price Index.

towards the export of highly processed, high value-added goods using high technology and low-cost raw material imports.

## The Period from the Late 1960s to the Late 1970s

Following a minor deficit in the balance of payments in 1967, Japan enjoyed a balance of payments surplus until the first oil price shock at the end of 1972 .(Figure 1.2). During this period, Japan's exports grew at an average annual rate of more than 20%, rising from US$10.4 billion in 1967 to US$24 billion in 1972, while the price level remained stable. This period also marked the beginning of Japan's persistent trade surplus with the United States (Table 1.3) that continued after the two oil price shocks and the upward revaluations of the yen in the 1970s and 1980s.

Following years of stable prices, the 1973 oil price shock resulted in a sharp rise in Japan's import price index and severe inflation followed. The increase in the Japanese consumer price index in 1973–1974 was the largest among the seven major industrial countries, while the increase in the wholesale price index was second only to that of Great Britain (Table 1.4). In addition to the exogenous oil price increase, the reduction in the official discount rate in June 1972 and the excess money supply policy adopted by the Bank of Japan for the period 1972–1973 is believed to have contributed to the 1973/74 inflation (Komiya, 1988). Restrictive fiscal and monetary policies, self-imposed wage restraint on the part of labour unions, and the efforts of firms to achieve productive efficiency are believed to be the primary factors which eventually brought this inflation down again to a relatively low level. For example, the official discount rate was increased from 4.25% in early 1973 to 9% by December 1973.

The business downturns caused by the tight fiscal and monetary policies during the 1970s are also seen in Figures 1.1 and 1.2. After the 1972–1973 period, investment in plant and equipment declined and inventories increased substantially. The unemployment rate rose and the production index fell significantly. Similar declines were also observed in Japan's exports, the export price index, and the balance of payments (Figure 1.1). The overall trade balance turned negative, and the foreign exchange constraint became binding again. Despite these downturns, however, the Japanese economy grew consistently throughout the 1970s.

The first oil price crisis changed the energy requirements of the Japanese manufacturing industries (Table 1.5), which in turn affected growth patterns for Japanese industry as a whole. Within manufacturing, the machinery category, which utilizes relatively little energy, recorded the largest growth.

Japan's real per capita GDP and investment in plant and equipment also registered downturns after the first oil price crisis, but appear to have been only slightly affected by the second oil crisis in the early 1980s (Figure 1.1). In comparative terms, the United States and Canada experienced more serious downturns than Japan did after the second oil price shock in these macro indicators.

## The 1980s and the Burst of a Bubble

In the high growth period from the mid 1960s to the first oil price shock in 1973, imports sometimes exceeded exports and the contribution to real GNP growth of net foreign trade (exports minus imports) was sometimes negative. After the first oil price shock, the annual GNP growth rate fell from an average of 9.9% to 3.3%. Reduced domestic production activities resulted in no growth in imports,

**Table 1.5** Trends in Energy Inputs in Japanese Manufacturing Industries, 1973 and 1978

| | Total Manufacturing | Fuel Products | Textiles | Pulp and Paper | Chemicals | Petroleum and Coal Products | Non-Metallic Mineral Products | Steel | Non-Ferrous Metals | Metal Products and Machinery | Other |
|---|---|---|---|---|---|---|---|---|---|---|---|
| *Actual Energy Consumption ($10^{25}$ kcal.)* | | | | | | | | | | | |
| *1973* | 208 | 6.4 | 8.5 | 9.7 | 51.3 | 12.9 | 17.0 | 66.5 | 9.5 | 12.6 | 13.4 |
| *1978* | 199 | 6.8 | 8.5 | 9.6 | 47.4 | 14.6 | 17.2 | 55.8 | 8.9 | 13.2 | 17.1 |
| *Production Indexes by Industry (1970 = 100)* | | | | | | | | | | | |
| *1973* | 127.8 | 119.2 | 110.5 | 123.3 | 127.5 | 135.0 | 125.7 | 129.4 | 140.1 | 133.2 | 110.9 |
| *1978* | 135.4 | 119.7 | 90.4 | 125.6 | 146.5 | 130.1 | 120.9 | 122.2 | 144.7 | 151.9 | 122.2 |
| *Amount of Energy Consumed per Production Index Point ($10^{10}$ kcal.)* | | | | | | | | | | | |
| *1973* | 1627 | 54 | 77 | 79 | 402 | 96 | 135 | 514 | 68 | 95 | 123 |
| *1978* | 1471 | 57 | 94 | 77 | 324 | 112 | 142 | 456 | 61 | 87 | 140 |

SOURCE: Japanese Energy Economics Research Institute, *Nihon no Enerugi Baransu no Shisutemu to Enerugi Matorikkusu no Hikaku* (1979).

while the contributions of exports to GNP continued to grow (Figure 1.3). Japanese economic growth started to become export-driven around this time. This situation continued until the late 1980s, when Japanese policies to spur domestic economic growth started to take effect.

From the first columns in Tables 1.6 and 1.7, a substantially greater increase for total imports (59.3%) than for total exports (14.8%) is evident during the period of 1985 to 1990. The substantial drop in 1986 in the import unit value indexes (see Table 1.7) was largely due to the appreciation in the value of the Japanese currency after the 1985 Plaza Accord. Yen-based export prices (see the Unit Value Indexes in Table 1.6) also went down in 1986, suggesting that Japanese exporters absorbed considerable portions of the exchange losses by reducing their export prices in yen. Yet even after taking into account the drop in the Unit Value Indexes, Japanese policies to expand domestic economic activities led to significant increases in imports,

**Fig. 1.3** Ratios of Exports and Imports to GNP, 1955–1992

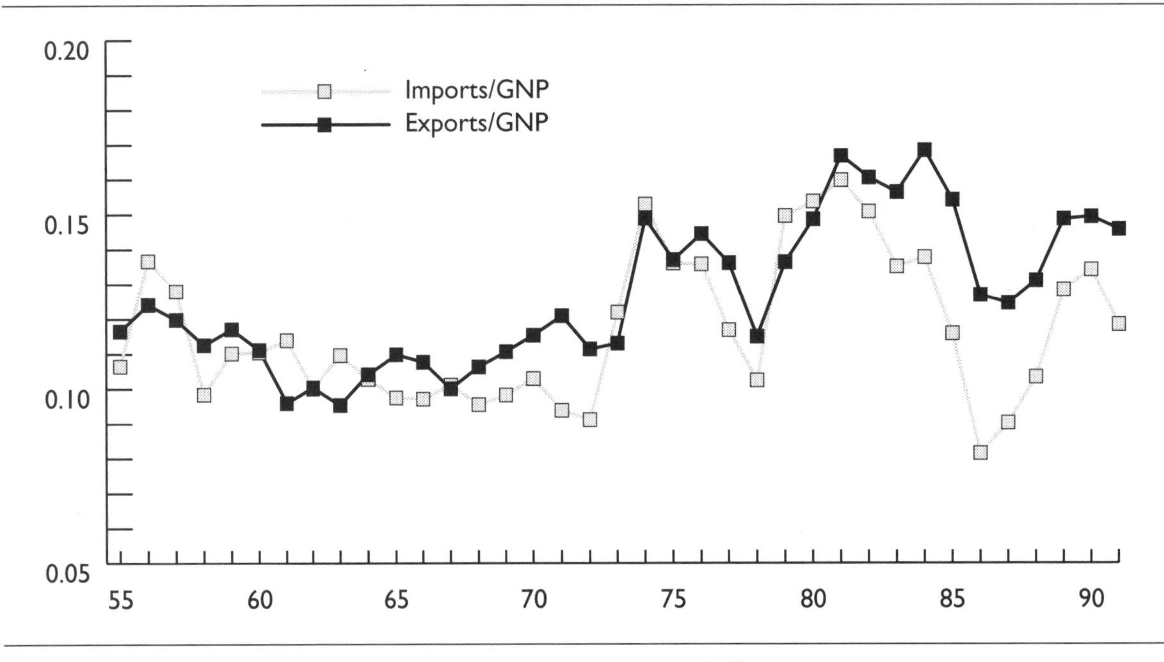


SOURCE: Economic Planning Agency, *Summary of Economic Statistics* (1982–1993).

and helped shift the sources of economic growth from export-oriented activities to the domestic economy.

*A Bubble in the Late 1980s*

Japanese asset prices, stock and land prices in particular, increased at extraordinary rates in the latter half of the 1980s and departed significantly from their underlying values (rational prices). However, they then fell sharply in the early 1990s as the bubble burst. For example, the Nikkei Stock Price Index increased from 7,682 in 1981 (year-end price) to 9,894 in 1983, 13,113 in 1985, 21,564 in 1987 and 38,916 in 1989. It subsequently dropped sharply to 23,849 in 1990, and to 16,925 by the end of 1992. At the same time the land price index for the six largest Japanese cities (1990 = 100) increased from 34 in 1985 to 48 in 1987, 77 in 1989 and 103 by March 1991. It then fell to 87 by March 1992. The Nikkei Index seems to lead land prices (Ziemba and Schwartz, 1991).

**Table 1.6** Indexes of Japanese Foreign Trade: Exports[a], 1980–1991 (1985 = 100)

| | QUANTUM INDEXES[b] | | | | UNIT VALUE INDEXES | | | |
|---|---|---|---|---|---|---|---|---|
| | All Commodities | Foodstuff | Raw Materials | Manufactured Goods | All Commodities | Foodstuff | Raw Materials | Manufactured Goods |
| *1980* | 70.6 | 131.3 | 93.3 | 69.8 | 99.2 | 86.9 | 110.9 | 99.3 |
| *1981* | 78.0 | 135.5 | 93.0 | 77.4 | 102.2 | 90.0 | 108.1 | 102.5 |
| *1982* | 76.3 | 120.9 | 85.7 | 75.7 | 107.6 | 91.9 | 111.9 | 108.1 |
| *1983* | 82.3 | 120.3 | 93.1 | 82.2 | 101.0 | 87.2 | 103.7 | 100.9 |
| *1984* | 95.6 | 137.8 | 97.0 | 95.5 | 100.5 | 78.8 | 105.8 | 100.6 |
| *1985* | 100.0 | 100.0 | 100.0 | 100.0 | 100.0 | 100.0 | 100.0 | 100.0 |
| *1986* | 99.4 | 96.4 | 110.1 | 99.2 | 84.6 | 82.1 | 71.4 | 84.9 |
| *1987* | 99.7 | 93.1 | 109.2 | 99.4 | 79.7 | 76.7 | 65.0 | 80.0 |
| *1988* | 104.8 | 91.8 | 112.8 | 104.3 | 77.2 | 75.0 | 65.2 | 77.5 |
| *1989* | 108.8 | 94.4 | 109.3 | 108.3 | 82.8 | 78.0 | 71.8 | 83.0 |
| *1990* | 114.8 | 89.0 | 109.6 | 114.0 | 86.0 | 84.4 | 75.6 | 86.3 |
| *1991* | 118.2 | 89.2 | 106.5 | 117.3 | 85.4 | 86.8 | 74.6 | 85.7 |

SOURCE: Japanese Economic Planning Agency, *Summary of Economic Statistics* (various years).

[a] Customs clearance basis; based on yen (1985 average = 100).

[b] Quantum Indexes = $\frac{\text{Value Indexes}}{\text{Unit Value Indexes}}$

Many factors helped develop the bubble, including the excess liquidity resulting from high corporate profits; the Bank of Japan's low official discount rate policy which started in 1980 (an historically low rate of 2.5% was implemented from February 1987 to May 1987); two public expenditure programs (one in 1986, another in 1987) to stimulate the economy during a recession caused by the appreciation of the yen; the banks' preference for using highly priced assets as collaterals for loans; and speculative investment behaviour by households and firms.

In contrast to asset prices, both the Consumer Price Index (CPI) and wage levels remained relatively constant: the CPI (1985 = 100) rose gradually to 112 by 1992 while the wage index (1985 = 100) rose to 124 by 1992. The relatively small increase in consumer prices is generally attributed to a massive increase in imported goods in the economy resulting from the appreciation of the yen. During this period the import price index fell from

**Table 1.7** Indexes of Japanese Foreign Trade: Imports[a], 1980–1991 (1985 = 100)

| | QUANTUM INDEXES[b] | | | | | UNIT VALUE INDEXES | | | | |
|---|---|---|---|---|---|---|---|---|---|---|
| | All Commodities | Foodstuff | Raw Materials | Mineral Fuels | Manufactured Goods | All Commodities | Foodstuff | Raw Materials | Mineral Fuels | Manufactured Goods |
| *1980* | 91.2 | 79.4 | 101.0 | 106.7 | 70.4 | 112.8 | 112.7 | 123.8 | 111.5 | 109.2 |
| *1981* | 89.9 | 83.2 | 89.3 | 99.6 | 79.2 | 112.5 | 113.1 | 113.4 | 119.5 | 101.5 |
| *1982* | 89.4 | 86.8 | 92.8 | 96.1 | 79.7 | 117.5 | 112.0 | 116.0 | 126.3 | 107.1 |
| *1983* | 90.1 | 89.6 | 92.9 | 96.0 | 81.7 | 107.1 | 106.2 | 107.2 | 108.9 | 104.9 |
| *1984* | 99.6 | 96.2 | 96.5 | 103.7 | 98.2 | 104.4 | 106.1 | 110.2 | 102.9 | 103.1 |
| *1985* | 100.0 | 100.0 | 100.0 | 100.0 | 100.0 | 100.0 | 100.0 | 100.0 | 100.0 | 100.0 |
| *1986* | 109.5 | 111.7 | 99.4 | 101.3 | 122.6 | 63.3 | 77.8 | 69.2 | 47.5 | 76.1 |
| *1987* | 119.7 | 128.1 | 107.7 | 105.2 | 137.9 | 58.4 | 68.3 | 68.5 | 40.5 | 73.0 |
| *1988* | 139.7 | 143.0 | 110.8 | 113.0 | 180.0 | 55.3 | 70.1 | 73.7 | 32.4 | 69.4 |
| *1989* | 150.6 | 148.2 | 114.1 | 119.6 | 202.1 | 61.9 | 77.3 | 83.6 | 36.9 | 76.8 |
| *1990* | 159.3 | 154.3 | 109.8 | 125.5 | 223.0 | 68.4 | 79.5 | 85.2 | 48.1 | 81.3 |
| *1991* | 164.0 | 165.6 | 109.7 | 126.3 | 230.8 | 62.6 | 75.3 | 75.3 | 43.6 | 74.7 |

SOURCE: Japanese Economic Planning Agency, *Summary of Economic Statistics* (various years).

[a] Customs clearance basis; based on yen (1985 average = 100).

[b] $\text{Quantum Indexes} = \dfrac{\text{Value Indexes}}{\text{Unit Value Indexes}}$

100 in 1985 to about 50 in 1986. Cheap imported goods had no impact, however, on Japanese asset prices during this period (Economic Planning Agency, 1993).

The rapid rise in the Bank of Japan's official discount rate from its historical low in May 1989 of 2.5% to 6% within 15 months ending in August 1990 decisively increased the long-term interest rate and led stock prices to fall by 40% by the end of 1990. A fall in land prices followed. Because speculative behaviour based on expectations of long-term increases in stock and land prices was prevalent among many households, firms and banks and other financial institutions, the burst of the bubble has had a serious impact on many aspects of the real economy.

While the bubble was forming in the late 1980s, adverse effects were observed for income and wealth distributions among households, firms' allocation of resources among competing economic uses and household budgeting. The collapse of stock and land prices which followed the burst of the bubble has led to a serious deterioration in the balance sheets at both corporate and household levels. In particular, incorrect investment decisions made during the bubble period (including direct overseas investments decisions) have resulted in unfavourable performance for many manufacturing and real estate firms. Performance measures for banks and financial institutions which financed many of these capital investments, both at firm and household levels, are also not encouraging. The Japanese Economic Planning Agency (1993) estimates that it will take at least another year or two before the economic distortions the bubble brought to the Japanese economy will be corrected.

An important policy issue being debated during the post-bubble recession in Japan is the future of the business practices. It is argued that changes may be needed. In part this is a response to criticisms that some practices (e.g., employment practices) make it difficult for Japanese firms to recover profitability quickly, and in part it is a response to rapidly internationalizing manufacturing operations of Japanese firms needing new forms of management that can exploit firms' multinationality more fully than can the present form.

## Long-Term Forecasts: The Impacts of Changing Demographics

In making long-term forecasts for the Japanese economy, both the Japanese private sector and government policy makers consider the changing demographics of Japan to be one of the most important supply-side factors. Because of low birth and death rates, the percentage of persons in the 15–24 age group is expected to decline from 20.8% in 1985 to 17.9% in 2010, while the percentage for the 55–64 age group is expected to increase from 15% to 22.1%. Furthermore, the total number of workers, which increased an average of 1.1% per year over the period of 1975–1988, is expected to increase by only 0.2% per year over the period of 1988–2010, assuming 1988 participation rates by age and sex (Ministry of Labour, 1989).

If a long-run economic growth rate of even 2–4% a year is to be achieved over the next decade or two, labour supply would have to increase by more than the projected 0.2% per year. To cope with potential labour shortages, the Japanese government and firms are planning to resort to the following policy initiatives: (1) attracting and retaining workers from outside the traditional source population (prime-aged men), such as female, older and foreign workers; and (2) fostering labour saving technical progress. Whether or not such labour shortages materialize, policy discussions on the implications of predictable demographic changes are deemed quite appropriate by both public and private sector decision makers.

The multi-sector econometric model of the Ministry of Labour (Japanese Ministry of Labour, 1987) provides the latest available forecasts of the impacts of long-run demographic changes on economic growth and sectoral employment patterns. Its usefulness for shorter term prediction, however, is limited. Other short comings of the model are that it does not take into account the production input of foreign workers, the numbers of whom are small relative to the domestic population, and the fact that technical progress is treated as an exogenous variable rather than an endogenous outcome. The predictions of the model are conditional on expectations incorporated into it about demographic changes, labour force participation patterns, certain aspects of public policy, and external economic conditions.

(1) Population Forecasts

In the Ministry of Labour model, it is assumed that the Japanese population will rise slowly to 131 million by the year 2000, 134 million by 2005, and 136 million by 2013. After 2013, the population is expected to decrease. The size of the working age group (15–64) is expected to be at its peak about now and is then expected to decline fairly rapidly over the period of 1995–2005. The 65+ age group is predicted to keep increasing (see Figure 1.4).

(2) Labour Force Participation Rates

A variety of policy measures have been implemented to induce women to enter and remain in the labour force, including the Equal Employment Opportunity Law of 1986, the relaxation of aspects of the Labour Standards Law, and measures to improve day care facilities (see Chapter 2 and Nakamura, 1993 for a further discussion of the difficulties associated with the Equal Employment Opportunity Law.) In the Ministry of Labour model it is assumed that changing public policies and attitudes will result in large increases in labour force participation rates for women aged 20–39. For men it is assumed that the most

**Fig. 1.4** Age Structure of the Japanese Population, 1936–2025 (Percent)

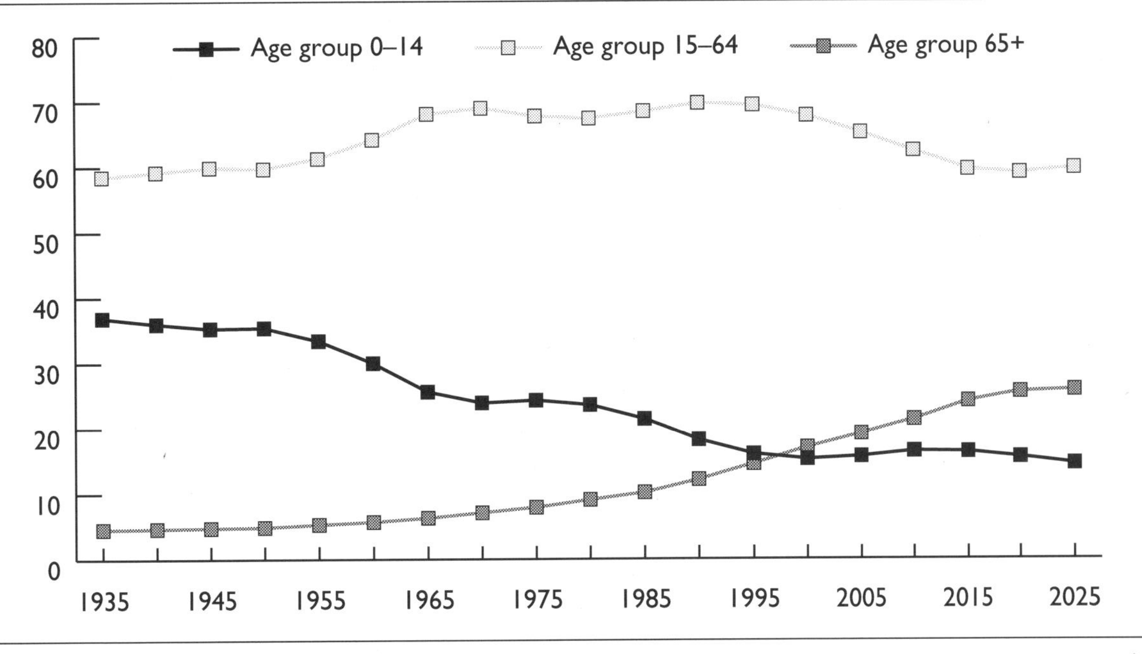


SOURCE: Economic Planning Agency, *Summary of Economic Statistics* (1976–1993).

important increase in participation rates will be for the 60–64 age group. The presumption is that firms will raise the age of mandatory retirement to 65 and that there will be a gradual rise in the minimum pensionable age to 65.

(3) Government Purchases, Investment in Housing, Government Public Investment, Exports, and the Exchange Rate (yen/U.S. dollar)

These variables are treated as exogenous to the Ministry of Labour model and are assigned forecasted values (see Table 1.8). Basic policy assumptions underlying these forecasted values include the following:

(a) The Ministry of Construction estimates that Japan will need to invest 340,000 billion yen during the period of 1986–2000 in public infrastructure in order to achieve the desired standard of living by the year 2000. This amounts to an average annual increase of 4.4% in public investment.

(b) The increase in government purchases is assumed to be 2.6% per year, the amount observed for 1985–86.

(c) Government policies to promote domestic consumption are expected to result in substantial increases in housing investment: 4.9% per year for 1985–1995 followed by 3.8% per year for 1996–2005. The growth rate for housing investment is expected to fall in the latter period because of lower population growth.

(d) Because of government policy emphasis on domestic consumption, exports are assumed to grow annually at a relatively low level of 3% to 3.4%.

(e) Economic performance considerations, the balance of payments and political pressure from the U.S. government are the factors underlying the assumption that the yen/U.S. dollar exchange rate will fall gradually from 160 yen in 1986 to 125 yen by 1995, 105 yen by 2000, and 100 yen by 2005. (The exchange rate had already attained the range of 95–105 yen per U.S. dollar by 1994, however.)

Different conditioning assumptions could alter subsequent forecasts based on the Ministry of Labour model. This should be kept in mind in considering the forecasts for key economic variables that are shown in Table 1.8 for the years 1990–2005. According to these forecasts, a GNP growth rate of more than 3% per year over the period 1990–2005 is possible. The driving forces behind this growth include expanded domestic consumption, and investment embodying labour-saving technical progress. The current trade surplus is predicted to vanish by the year 2000. The model also predicts that the Japanese savings rate will gradually decline from 13.3% in 1985 to 11.3% in 2005, because of the aging of the population.

Another set of model outputs are employment figures by industry for different demographic groups. Total employment increases from 58 million workers in 1985 to 66 million in 2005. While a generally stable level of employment is predicted for the manufacturing industries (25% and 23% of total employment, respectively, in 1985 and in 2005), the retail, wholesale, restaurant and enterprise service industries are expected to be sources of employment growth over the 1985 and 2005 period. Tertiary industries are predicted to provide 63% (42 million workers) of total employment by

**Table 1.8** Macro Model Projections[a], 1985–2005

| | | 1985–1995 | 1995–2005 | 1985–2005 |
|---|---|---|---|---|
| GNP | (real growth %) | 3.9 | 3.5 | 3.7 |
| Consumer expenditure | (real growth %) | 4.5 | 3.8 | 4.1 |
| Government expenditure* | (real growth %) | 2.6 | 2.6 | 2.6 |
| Private investment | (real growth %) | 3.5 | 3.7 | 3.6 |
| Housing investment* | (real growth %) | 4.9 | 3.8 | 4.3 |
| Government investment* | (real growth %) | 4.4 | 4.4 | 4.4 |
| Inventory investment | (real growth %) | 2.0 | 2.5 | 2.3 |
| Exports* | (real growth %) | 3.0 | 3.4 | 3.2 |
| Imports | (real growth %) | 4.6 | 4.9 | 4.7 |
| GDP | (real growth %) | 4.0 | 3.7 | 3.8 |
| Exchange rate* | (yen/US$) | 160–125 | 125–100 | – |
| Current balance | (nominal, $100 mill.) | 852 (1995) | 271 (2005) | – |
| Current balance/GDP | (%) | 2.00 (1995) | 0.03 (2005) | – |
| Budget balance | (nominal, bill.yen) | 6913.9 (1995) | 4961.4 (2005) | – |
| Working age population | (growth rate %) | 1.05 | 0.20 | 0.62 |
| Workers | (growth rate %) | 1.02 | 0.20 | 0.61 |
| Employed workers | (growth rate %) | 0.96 | 0.33 | 0.65 |
| Unemployment rate | (%) | 2.9 (1995) | 2.9 (2005) | – |
| Labour productivity | (real growth %) | 2.9 | 3.5 | 3.2 |
| Employment Income | (nominal growth %) | 3.9 | 4.7 | 4.3 |
| Average wages | (nominal growth %) | 3.9 | 4.6 | 4.3 |
| CPI | (growth rate %) | 1.9 | 1.9 | 1.9 |
| GDP deflator | (growth rate %) | 1.3 | 1.7 | 1.5 |
| Part time/Full time workers | (%) | 13.2 (1995) | 17.2 (2005) | – |
| Hours of work* | (per worker/year)* | 1925 (1995) | 1720 (2005) | – |
| Hours of work | (per full-time worker/year) | 1962 (1995) | 1737 (2005) | – |

SOURCE: Japanese Ministry of Labour (1987).

[a] Variables with asterisks are exogenously given to the model.

2005, compared to 56% (33 million) in 1985. Within the manufacturing sector, employment is expected to decline in steel, oil, coal, metal, and other materials.

The predicted proportions of female workers by industry are not expected to change much between 1985 and 2005. However, there will be substantial increases in female part-time workers in proportion to all workers in manufacturing (an increase of 0.57 million female part-time workers between 1985 and 2005), and in the wholesale/retail/restaurant and service industries (an increase of 2.38 million female part-time workers). Projected unemployment rates for male and female workers by age are predicted to remain relatively constant over the period of 1985–2005, except for the male age groups of 15–19 and 60–64. For these groups, unemployment rates are predicted to rise by more than 1% (from 8.9% in 1985 to 10.3% in 2005 for males 15–19, and from 7.8% to 9.3% for males 60–64).

Projected labour productivity by industry suggests that among the present-day low productivity industries, only the agriculture/fishing, construction, and transportation/communication industries are predicted to achieve significant gains in labour productivity. Despite the adoption of information technology, the remaining low productivity industries (that is, the wholesale/retail/restaurants and service industries) are not expected to be able to improve much by 2005 (by conventional measures, at least) because of the ever increasing demand for better services. Steady improvement in productivity is expected for manufacturing industries.

Finally, real wages are predicted to increase by 70% between 1985 and 2005 and the average household monthly income is predicted to rise from the 445,000 yen (of which 8% is wife's earnings) observed in 1985 to 746,000 (1985) yen (of which 11% is wife's earnings) by 2005. Disposable monthly household income increases from 374,000 yen (84% of household income) in 1985 to 604,000 yen (81% of household income) in 2005. These predicted increases in real wages and household incomes are much less than the past experience from 1980 to 1985. Nonconsumption monthly expenditure including taxes also increases, from 71,000 yen (16% of household income) in 1985 to 142,000 yen (19% of household income) in 2005.

Substantial increases in disposable income, combined with the greying of the Japanese population over the next few decades, will change the patterns of demand for, among other things, travel, personal services, adult education, health and medical services and equipment, and housing and retirement homes. Judicious marketing of Canadian goods and services tailored for a growing market for the aging Japanese population will likely be handsomely rewarded.

# 2

## Japanese Business Practices

### Industrial Relations, Corporate Groups and Corporate Control

### Introduction

While many aspects of firm behaviour are common for both North American and Japanese firms, there are certain types of business practices which distinguish Japanese firms from North American firms. These practices of Japanese firms sometimes lead to predictable differences in outcome for Japanese firms compared to North American firms.

For example, long-term risk sharing among corporations and incentive mechanisms for personnel management which favour long-term employment, combined with long-term stable shareholding, often allow Japanese firms to undertake projects they consider essential for their survival in the long run without worries about quarter-to-quarter changes in earnings or stock prices. Long-term business relationships among firms in Japan also imply sharing between a supplier and an assembler of the cost of unexpected price increases in the raw material for the supplier from whom the assembler firm purchases intermediate goods, even though the presence of a price contract between them means that, in a strictly legal sense, the supplier must absorb all the cost of the price increases. Similarly, the supplier is expected to absorb some of the cost reduction the manufacturer deems necessary to regain the competitiveness of the final product in the global market that it has lost for unforeseen reasons (e.g., a significant appreciation of the Japanese currency). This is in contrast to the standard Western notion that "a contract is a contract."

Another example is the practice of long-term employment which is particularly prevalent among large firms. It would be difficult, if not impossible, to implement layoffs in Japan to the extent that they are implemented in North America. North American firms which enter business relationships with Japanese firms are advised to be aware of these and other differences in business practices.

Japan's relatively low unemployment rates throughout the stages of the business cycle are the direct consequence of long-term employment practices in both the private and public sectors. Such employment practices and associated industrial relations issues are discussed in the next section. The different types of corporate groups (keiretsu) that are the prevalent form of inter-firm relationship in Japan are explained later in the chapter. The implications of Japanese industrial relations and inter-firm structures from the perspective of corporate control are assessed. The implications of these business practices for economic growth and market access are explored and a discussion of the impact of the post-bubble recession and of internationalization on these practices conclude this chapter.

## Industrial Relations

In Japan, firm managers are constrained by "three sacred treasures" of industrial relations:* lifetime (or long-term) employment, the nenko (length-of-service reward) wage system, and enterprise unionism. These contemporary industrial relations practices developed over time as a result of the conscious effort by both firm management and workers to avoid the types of serious labour disputes that took place between the early 1900s and the 1950s (Fruin, 1983). These three pertinent features of industrial relations practices are observed primarily for jobs that have traditionally been filled by prime-aged men. Many women, older workers, and foreign workers are in jobs where this is not the case.

As it is understood in Japan, lifetime employment usually means extended and secure long-term employment from the time of appointment after school graduation to an early retirement age of 55 to 60. Large firms and banks often move some older employees (as early as age 40) to their

---

* For a more detailed analysis of this topic see Nakamura (1993).

smaller affiliated firms. Many of the rotated out workers do not return to their original employment.

The length-of-service reward wage system consists of those wage components which steadily rise with age and others (ability pay, incentive pay, etc.) which do not. Recently, a trend towards faster growth in the latter components relative to the former has been observed. As workers grow older, cohort-specific pay differentials also increase.

Enterprise unionism is still prevalent for relatively large firms, but unionization rates vary among sectors. In 1992 these rates were: 29% for manufacturing, 48% for forestry, 25% for mining, 19% for construction, 67% for utilities, 45% for transportation and communication, 49% for real estate and service firms, 15% for service, 10% for wholesale and retail and 67% for the public sector (Japanese Ministry of Labour, 1993). About 40% of nonunionized workers are employed in establishments where there are formal joint consultation mechanisms between firm management and the workers (Japanese Ministry of Labour, 1991). Japanese industrial relations practices discussed later in this chapter apply to varying degrees to a large but not an overwhelming fraction of Japanese workers.

### *Benefits Associated with Japanese Industrial Relations Practices*

Certain benefits are commonly attributed to each of the three distinguishing features of Japanese industrial relations practices. These can be summarized as follows:

(1) Lifetime Employment
- (a) Because firms and employees can count on long-term employment relationships, both are willing to invest in employees' human capital. On-the-job training and formal job-related educational training are much more common in Japan than in North America.
- (b) Long-term employment allows firms to use job rotations to develop workers' multi-task skills and to expose workers to different aspects of business and production operations. There are few job classifications. As a consequence, firms can deploy personnel flexibly and effectively.
- (c) New productivity-enhancing technologies can be introduced with minimal worker opposition or concern about job losses.

(2) Nenko (length-of-service) Reward Wage System
   (a) Workers are assessed based on their career advancements. Hence workers have more incentive to perform in the long run.
   (b) Workers are assessed by many supervisors over a long period of time throughout their careers. Hence there is less room for incorrect judgments in personnel decisions (e.g., promotions).

(3) Enterprise Unionism
   (a) Because of the long-term commitments to a firm by workers, enterprise unions can demand a fair share of firm profits more effectively than otherwise.
   (b) Full-time positions at enterprise unions are often part of career tracks for potential managers of firms. Firms are able to share information on firm performance, problems and opportunities with enterprise unions.
   (c) Because of the information sharing and feelings of trust and shared objectives fostered by enterprise unionism, workers and managers alike accept rollbacks of bonus payments in tough times without threats to leave or morale deterioration of the sort that endangers production efficiency and product quality.

*Success Stories*

Evidence of the benefits of the Japanese industrial relations system is largely anecdotal. The nature of this evidence is most easily conveyed by examining some of these success stories (e.g., Krafcik, 1988). In the automobile industry, for example, Toyota perfected its production system (sometimes called the just-in-time (JIT), or Kanban, production system) by the early 1970s and then disseminated it to other Japanese competitors by the late 1970s. Two important aspects of the Toyota production system are that (1) in-process inventories are minimized by the use of JIT inventory management, which requires that all needed parts and/or semi-products are delivered to where they are needed as they are needed in the quantities needed; and (2) production flow is set up so that cars of various specifications are produced in sequence according to demand fluctuations. It is often the case that two successive cars produced on a production line are of different types. (Japanese firms' inventory levels, however, are not always lower than those for U.S. firms according to Nakamura and Nakamura, 1989).

JIT inventory management, as implemented by Toyota and its parts suppliers, requires close-to-zero defect rates in all stages of the production process in order for the system to run smoothly. To this end, production line workers actively participate, often in teams, in solving local production problems. Separate repair and maintenance positions are eliminated. This cooperation is possible because the workers are familiar with many aspects of the production process and view co-operation in production management as essential for their own long-term goals.

The multi-task capabilities of workers are also relied on in combining production of cars of different types. Producing a passenger car of type A followed by, say, a station wagon of type B on the same production line requires retooling press machines in a very short time. Workers skilled in a variety of tasks make it possible to design a production line where cars of different types are produced in accord with the time-varying demand distributions for these types of cars. Flexible manufacturing of this sort contributes to high capacity utilization rates that, in turn, lead to high productivity gains compared to North American companies (Fuss and Waverman, 1990).

Job rotations and on-the-job training combined with long-term employment security allow firms and workers to make long run investments in workers' human capital; it can take as long as ten years of experience to master some skills. Fewer job classifications are conducive to the multi-skill development of workers. It is generally the case that the number of job classifications for Japanese auto plants are smaller compared to the number in the traditional Big Three plants. For example, in the mid 1980s a Honda U.S.A. plant had three different job types—team leader, production, and maintenance, while a typical GM plant had 95 job types (U.S. General Accounting Office, 1988). A substantial amount of research and development takes place in Japanese auto plants to design production facilities that fully utilize multi-task production workers. The resulting advances in Japanese automobile production technologies are reflected in the technology trade figures for manufacturing industries. In 1991, the auto industry exported technology worth 99.5 billion yen (48.0 billion yen to North America; 33.4 billion yen to Asia; 12.2 billion yen to Europe), and imported technology worth only 8.0 billion yen (4.1 billion yen from North America and 3.7 billion yen from Europe).

Japanese firms do not lay off workers except under extreme circumstances. U.S. employment indexes, for example, follow production indexes much more closely than is the case in Japan. Job security helps workers to accept new production technologies. This may partially explain why Japanese factories are now equipped with large numbers of industrial robots relative to their Western counterparts. In 1989 the estimated numbers of operating industrial robots (excluding fixed sequence robots) were: 219,700 for Japan, 37,000 for the U.S., 22,395 for (West) Germany, 7,063 for France, 7,463 for Sweden, and 5,908 for the United Kingdom.

### *Mechanisms for Adjusting the Wage Bill*

Japanese firms, like the firms of other nations, must deal with business cycle fluctuations. In downturns, Japanese firms need ways of adjusting the total wage bill without layoffs. These methods include wage adjustments, adjustments of hours through overtime work and nonregular worker employment, and the flexible deployment of the workforce.

WAGE ADJUSTMENTS Japanese workers are paid regular monthly (fixed contract) earnings as well as bonus payments. The amounts of the bonuses are not prespecified but generally range between four to six months worth of regular contract earnings. The amounts of regular wages and bonus payments are both decided annually in negotiations between firms and labour unions: regular wages are settled in the spring offensive, and bonus payments are negotiated somewhat later but before summer. Both regular wage and bonus pay settlements at the firm level reflect, among other things, the general economic conditions and specific firm performance for the previous 12 months. By this means, a firm's total wage bill adjusts reasonably frequently to the firm's changing economic fortunes.

Japanese labour code prohibits a labour contract to extend beyond one year. The annual wage adjustments in Japan conform to this labour law. In contrast, the lengths of union wage contracts in Canada and the U.S. are as long as five years, with the average being around two and a half years. With standard Cost-of-Living-Adjustment (COLA) clauses, these long-term contracts act to secure the purchasing power of workers' wages, but at the potential cost of employment security.

Unlike bonuses in North America which are mostly paid to managers and executives, bonuses in Japan are used as part of the compensation package for most workers regardless of their rank, age or sex. The ratio of bonuses to total annual pay increases as worker qualifications rise, suggesting that the bonus fractions are correlated with the amounts of managerial and difficult-to-observe tasks involved in workers' jobs. (See Nakamura and Hübler, 1993 for empirical evidence on this.) Year-to-year changes are much greater for bonuses than for regular wages. In this way, business fluctuation risk is shared without resorting to employment layoffs. (See Nakamura and Nakamura, 1991, for a discussion of risk sharing aspects of bonus payments.) Firms also use bonuses as short-run incentive schemes for individual workers and groups of workers, through the allocation mechanisms for individual workers. Bonuses are by no means the only incentive scheme used by firms. In fact, promotions, strategic job assignments and regular pay increases are among Japanese firms' standard tools to maintain their workers' long-term incentives.

ADJUSTMENTS OF OVERTIME HOURS AND NONREGULAR WORKER EMPLOYMENT More so than in North American firms, overtime hours for regular workers are used to meet changes in demand conditions. (This may be partly because the legal overtime wage premiums are about 25%: half of the North American rate.) Because regular workers' employment is protected to a large extent, adjustments in a firm's wage bill may also require the layoff of nonregular workers, such as part-time workers. When demand conditions improve, firms will first use increased overtime and part-time worker hours to meet the increased demand. New regular workers will be hired when additional increases in overtime and part-time hours are not feasible or would not be profitable.

FLEXIBLE DEPLOYMENT OF WORKFORCE When facing business downturns, Japanese firms deploy workers in the areas where they are needed most. Geographical relocations and changes in work tasks may be required. For example, in September 1992, Mazda moved about 100 young workers from their head office to Mazda dealerships all over Japan in response to a continuing decline in domestic sales of Mazda cars. The deployment of a firm's workers across production and sales jobs, or in other related or even unrelated firms, is not unusual in serious business downturns.

One enabling factor for flexible deployment of the Japanese workforce is that wages are usually assigned to individual workers rather than to the specific tasks that workers perform. This explains why wage differentials by job task or firm size at initial appointment are small in Japan compared to those in the U.S. (Shimada, 1981). However, wages rise steeply in Japan as workers accumulate experience.

### *The Problems Associated with Japanese Industrial Relations Practices*

Because of their industrial relations policies, personnel development in Japanese firms is carried out primarily through internal labour market policies. Managers and workers cooperate to develop employee skills through job rotations, on-the-job training, and formal employer-supplied training. This is the case not only for production (blue-collar) workers but also for office (white-collar) workers. This system is believed to have helped Japan achieve the national goal of macro economic growth, with the rewards of this growth being shared by workers, shareholders, and other stakeholders of firms. Now that this macro goal has been largely achieved, however, some analysts fear that cooperation between employers and workers may begin to erode. Diversions in their respective goals could manifest themselves in a number of ways. These include conflicts between male workers (the traditional permanent workers) and women (the main secondary source of labour); the growing number of workers who want to change jobs; and the problems engendered by Japanese firms' internationalization.

FEMALE WORKERS High-paying jobs are generally available only to those workers with long seniority who have been given increasingly challenging assignments. It is expected that women will have intermittent career patterns, to allow for child bearing and rearing. As a consequence, female workers interested in pursuing demanding careers are likely to be subject to statistical discrimination by employers. (See Nakamura and Nakamura, 1985a, 1985b, 1985c, 1992 for discussion of related issues for U.S. and Canadian female workers, and evidence that individual work histories are a valuable source of information on the degree of career attachment; this insight could help reduce statistical discrimination in Japan as well as in North America.)

There has been little improvement in the workplace situation of women in Japan compared with North America. In response to the Japanese Equal

Employment Opportunity Law enacted in 1986, it is true that some large Japanese firms did open their general managerial career paths to female university graduates. With rare exceptions, these career paths were only available to men before 1986. Yet most women still do not choose this option. They continue to choose career paths that do not require geographic relocations and that lead to positions as lower-rank managers or specialists. If this current trend continues, most upper level managerial positions in Japanese firms will continue to be occupied by men and the gap between male and female wages will continue to widen, contrary to what was hoped for when the Equal Employment Opportunity Law was enacted. It should be noted that this law has no enforcement provisions. In implementing major hiring cutbacks in 1992 and 1993, firms openly chose to offer a reduced proportion of the available positions to women in comparison with previous years. The cutbacks for women were particularly severe for the general managerial career paths. Many view this as evidence of the continuing marginal position of women in the Japanese workforce.

Goldin (1988) reports that, before the 1950s, many U.S. firms had rules requiring female workers to resign at the time of marriage or the first birth. As labour supply tightened during the 1950s, such employment practices began to disappear. Because of expected labour shortages, some speculate that Japanese firms may also begin to aggressively recruit female workers. As of yet, however, there is no rush in Japan to adopt North American equal employment policies for women.

SECONDARY LABOUR MARKETS It is customary for most Japanese firms to hire workers at the time they graduate from school. While Japanese firms do hire workers in various stages of their careers, the fraction of workers hired in mid-career is quite small compared with North American practices. Furthermore, the probability of a male worker changing his job is considerably smaller for Japan than for Canada or the United States. This also implies that secondary labour markets in Japan are relatively thin compared with the primary labour market for new graduates. These patterns are consistent with the longer lengths of service with single employers observed for Japanese workers compared with U.S. and Canadian workers.

An obvious implication of the thin secondary labour market in Japan is that it is difficult, if not impossible, for workers to adjust their employment to changes in their own tastes, preferences, qualifications, and personal life cycle planning without substantial wage loss. Also, training not provided or encouraged by the employer may not be rewarded within a firm's internal labour market. Yet workers who have obtained additional education or training on their own may not be able to find other positions where their efforts would be rewarded.

The lack of an adequate secondary labour market is a particularly serious problem for Japanese women who often have to drop out of regular career positions to have children. These women have great difficulty locating new jobs with pay commensurate with their qualifications. Nakamura (1993) shows that (1) the separation rates for female workers are somewhat higher for the U.S. than for Japan; (2) the labour force participation rates of continuing and intermittent female workers are similar for both the U.S. and Japan (continuing workers are defined here as those who have held work without having experienced being out of work for more than one year, and intermittent workers are those who have experienced being out of work for more than one year); and (3) the years of work for intermittent female workers are much higher for the U.S. than for Japan while the years of work for continuing female workers are similar for U.S. white women and Japanese women. The lack of adequate secondary markets in Japan for intermittent female workers is a likely cause of these patterns.

FIRM-SIZE EFFECT Many of the Japanese industrial relations practices discussed are implemented to varying degrees by Japanese firms of different sizes. Generally, the smaller a firm is, the less rigidity there is concerning adherence to long-term employment practices, the length-of-service reward wage system, and enterprise unionism. It is also the case, as in the U.S. and Canada (Oi, 1983), that smaller firms pay lower wages than larger firms. In fact, what appears to be pure firm-size wage differentials are a much more prominent feature of the Japanese than the U.S. labour market. Workers' differing levels of education and experience explain up to one-third of the firm-size wage differential for the U.S. but only about 10% of the differential for Japan (Rebick, 1993).

Smaller firms hire more mid-career workers partly because they cannot hire as many new graduates as they want. Large firms, on the other hand, still rely primarily on recruiting new graduates. As a result, the secondary labour market for experienced workers operates most actively for smaller firms. It is quite common for a mid-career worker who resigns from a large firm (voluntarily or involuntarily) to find employment with a smaller firm for much less pay. Female workers' job opportunities are also more abundant in the segment of the labour market involving smaller firms. The reliance on bonus payments also declines as firm size decreases (Nakamura and Nakamura, 1991). It is important to recognize the role of small firms in the Japanese economy—firms with fewer than 500 workers employed about 85% of the 44 million regular workers in the Japanese labour force in 1991. Yet larger companies dominate the export market.

It is possible that the large firm-small firm mix of the Japanese economy contributes significantly to Japanese economic growth and productivity.

JAPANESE INDUSTRIAL RELATIONS PRACTICES AND JAPANESE MACROECONOMIC PERFORMANCE Japanese flexible wages and enterprise unionism, among other factors, may have helped prevent a vicious spiralling circle involving high inflation and real wage rates from taking place during the first and second oil price shock periods in 1973–1982. However, causal relationships that run from corporate practices to macro performance at the national level are difficult to prove empirically. Komiya (1988), for example, argues that Japanese flexible wages backed by cooperative relations between firms and unions have allowed tight monetary policies to be very effective in an inflationary period, because enterprise unions under such circumstances see the negative implications of excessive wage increases for firm performance and hence do not demand them. Another factor which limits inflationary trends in Japan is the productivity gain at the aggregate level resulting from the competition among firms, each of which implements new technologies and flexible job assignments of its workers with the cooperation of its enterprise union. Helliwell (1989, p. 68) also confirms "the long-established Japanese practice of stabilizing employment, at least in the larger enterprises, in the face of cyclical changes in output. Employment growth, but not output growth, is more stable in Japan than in North America, and this shows up as very damped responses of employment to changes in output."

In chapter 1 we noted that Japan may face a possible labour shortage in a decade or two because of the rapidly increasing older population and a low birth rate. Relaxing the present rigid corporate employment policy emphasizing lifetime learning of skills with a single employer without career interruptions will likely increase the supply of female labour and mid-career workers, significantly reducing the possibility of such a labour shortage. The potential long-run economic growth rate would also likely increase.

## Corporate Groups

There are two main types of corporate groups in Japan. They are production-based corporate groups (capital keiretsu) and bank-based corporate groups (financial keiretsu). The membership of these corporate groups usually includes a number of foreign-affiliated firms. A production-based corporate group often consists of a major manufacturer and its supplier subcontractors. The relationships between the manufacturer and suppliers are based on economic transactions (e.g., supplying parts) and are often quasi-permanent; the terms of transacting conditions (including prices) are often influenced by the relative bargaining power that the selling and buying firms have in bilateral negotiations (Nagatani, 1993). (Firm groups of this type exist in the U.S. auto industry but at a much smaller scale than in the Japanese auto industry.)

For example, it was estimated that Toyota had direct relations with 122 first-tier suppliers and indirect relations with 5,437 second-tier suppliers and 41,703 third-tier suppliers in the late 1970s. The quasi-permanent nature of the Toyota group is illustrated by the fact that, between 1973 and 1984, only three firms ceased to be members of the association of Toyota's first-tier suppliers while 21 firms joined the association (Aoki, 1988). Comparing the auto industry in Japan and the U.S., it is often said that Toyota buys 80% of its parts from outside while GM makes 80% inside.

### *Capital Keiretsu (Production-Based Corporate Groups)*

The production-based corporate group is often characterized by the following factors: (1) ownership by the prime manufacturer (or the dominant company in the centre of a group) of small fractions of its subsidiaries or suppliers (typically 10–20% of the total outstanding shares of first-tier suppliers); (2) long-run business associations based on vertical technological relations; (3) sub-contractors who often do business with other production-based corporate group companies (in fact, the prime manufacturer sometimes encourages its group suppliers to retain orders from firms outside the group for the purpose of attaining scale economies in production); (4) supplier firms that are usually smaller than the prime manufacturer, but remain as independent companies; and (5) some group firms that are spin-off subsidiaries of the prime manufacturer (Hitachi Ltd., for example, has spun off many divisions which are now separately listed firms). Provided that common long-term business goals and risk sharing arrangements are agreed upon between a prime manufacturer and its supplier firms, a production-based corporate group can be an efficient producer of complex, assembly-based products such as cars and electric equipment.

The strengths of a production-based corporate group, compared to a vertically-integrated company, include: (1) the size of each firm in the group, including supplier firms and the prime manufacturer firm, is kept small and hence easier to manage; (2) incentives for corporate performance are less likely to be lost in small separate firms; and (3) small firms pay lower wages. Long-term business relationships also allow the supplier and the prime manufacturer to cooperate on activities such as developing parts for new products. But, it is not difficult to imagine that if the long-run goals of a prime manufacturer and supplier firms are not well aligned in terms of incentive and risk sharing schemes, then the corporate group may not function as well as a vertically integrated firm would. Japanese firms have accumulated substantial know-how in dealing with inter-firm business relationships (see Fruin, 1992). Aoki (1988) discusses some types of inter-firm contracts used in production-based groups.

It is not yet well understood under what kinds of conditions the production-based group approach to production is superior to the more vertically integrated firm-based production traditionally found in the U.S. So far these production-based corporate groups in Japan have been quite successful in the global market in the auto and electronics industries and other manufacturing industries.

### *Financial Keiretsu (Bank-Based Corporate Groups)*

There are six major bank-based corporate groups in Japan. They are the Mitsubishi, Mitsui, Sumitomo, Fuji, Dai-Ichi Kangyo and Sanwa groups. The members of the Presidents' Clubs for these groups regularly meet for exchanging information. Each group typically consists of (at least) one city bank, one trust bank, one general trading firm (Sogo Syosha) and firms in noncompeting lines of business. (Table 2.1 gives members of the Presidents' Clubs for the six bank-based corporate groups.) There are, however, exceptions to this general rule on group membership. A number of companies belong to several groups. (For example, Hitachi Ltd. belongs to three groups; Nissho Iwai and Nippon Express each belong to two groups.) Both the Mitsubishi and Mitsui groups have several group firms competing in chemical and petrochemical industries.

Most listed Japanese firms, both independent (nongroup) and group, have a main bank. (The main bank is not a legal term.) The main bank of a (client) firm is usually the largest bank shareholder of the client firm as well as its largest bank lender. It is profitable for a bank to be the main bank of an industrial firm, since the main bank can charge interest on loans to firms in its group at interest rates which are above the market rate and it also retains the business accounts of these firms which often carry no interest (Caves and Uekusa, 1976; Aoki, 1988).

When a client firm faces financial distress, however, its main bank is expected to take part in the management of the troubled firm on behalf of the syndicate of financial institutions involved with the firm, including other banks, and it is expected to absorb more than its proportional share of losses if necessary. For example, the Sumitomo Bank wrote off 113.2 billion yen in 1977 when Ataka Industries failed because of, among other things, a major investment loss in a Newfoundland oil refinery. Nippon Light Metal, Alcan's listed subsidiary in Japan, also received substantial subsidies from its main and sub-main banks (the Daiichi Kangyo Bank and the Industrial Bank of Japan) during the 1970s and 1980s when the Japanese aluminum industry went through restructuring (Sheard, 1991).

Generally the main bank for bank-based corporate group firms is the bank in the centre of the group. The group bank and other financial institutions act as major, but not exclusive, financial intermediaries for group firms. Although holding companies are illegal in Japan, banks are allowed to hold up to 5% of equity in industrial firms and they often hold this upper limit in each group firm, while group firms hold equity in the bank as well. (However, nongroup firms and other banks also act as stable shareholders of group banks and firms.)

In the U.S., bank holding firms are also allowed to hold up to a 5% of the equity in any industrial firm, but by law, bank holding firms in the U.S. are not permitted to be active shareholders involved in board decision making for the firms of which they own portions. Because of this legal constraint, very few U.S. banks have an interest in holding equity in industrial firms. In Japan, banks are allowed to be active participants in company board decision making processes. Japanese banks do take full advantage of their position as large institutional shareholders when they deem it in their interests to do so.

Because of their horizontal nature covering many industries, bank-based corporate groups are often suspected of having and exercising considerable market power. However, others believe that the presence of independent competitors, as well as competitors in other bank-based groups, provides sufficient competition to keep bank-based group firms' profitability low relative to independent firms (Caves and Uekusa, 1976; Nakatani, 1984). Caves and Uekusa (1976) failed to find any monopsonic or monopoly power exercised by firms in bank-based corporate groups. While some preferential intra-group transactions seem to take place between, for example, general trading firms and steel producers, some of the strong product producers in the automotive, electronics and other industries have chosen not to rely on general trading firms in distributing their products in domestic or overseas markets. Group firms' continuous profit maximization processes may not always lead to the preferential use of existing group firms. This seems consistent with the findings by Caves and Uekusa.

This is not to say, however, that bank-based group firms are never involved in activities which violate Japanese anti-monopoly (anti-trust) laws. It is sometimes suspected, for example, that bank-based group firms in certain established industries (e.g., chemicals, metals and construction), as well as nongroup firms, do violate the anti-monopoly laws. There is also some anecdotal evidence suggesting that, in addition to exchanging information, member firms of the Presidents' Clubs for bank-based corporate groups cooperate in setting up joint ventures in emerging, but potentially risky, lines of business. Although bank-based group firms' profitability may be somewhat lower, risk-sharing activities and a secure demand for their products from other group firms probably make profits more stable over time than is the case for independent companies. This sort of risk sharing or insurance aspect of a corporate group does not necessarily, in itself, make group firms more competitive.

Another function that both production-based and bank-based groups

**Table 2.1** Members of President's Clubs: Bank-Based Corporate Groups, 1990

| *INDUSTRY* | MITSUI | MITSUBISHI | SUMITOMO | FUYO | SANWA | DAIICHI-KANGYO |
|---|---|---|---|---|---|---|
| *City bank* | Sakura Bank[1] | Mitsubishi Bank | Sumitomo Bank | Fuji Bank | Sanwa Bank | Daiichi-Kangyo Bank |
| *Trust bank* | Mitsui Trust | Mitsubishi Trust | Sumitomo Trust | Yasuda Trust | Toyo Trust | |
| *Life insurance* | Mitsui Life | Meiji Life | Sumitomo Life | Yasuda Life | Nippon Life | Asahi Life<br>Fukoku Life |
| *Casualty insurance* | Mitsui F&M | Tokio F&M | Sumitomo F&M | Yasuda F&M | | Taisei F&M<br>Nissan F&M |
| *General Trading* | Mitsui & Co. | Mitsubishi Corp. | Sumitomo Corp. | Marubeni | Nissho Iwai[3]<br>Nichimen<br>Iwatani | Itochu<br>Nissho Iwai[3]<br>Kanematsu<br>Kawasho |
| *Forestry/Mining* | Mitsui Mining<br>Hokkaido Coal[2] | | Sumitomo Coal | | | |
| *Construction* | Mitsui Constr.<br>Sanki Engnr. | Mitsubishi Constr. | Sumitomo Constr. | Taisei | Ohbayashi<br>Toyo Constr.<br>Sekisui House<br>Zenitaka | Shimizu |
| *Food* | Nippon Flour | Kirin Brewery | | Nisshin Flour<br>Sapporo Breweries<br>Nichirei | Ito Ham<br>Suntory | |
| *Fibres & textiles* | Toray | Mitsubishi Rayon | | Toho Rayon<br>Nisshin Spinning | Unitica<br>Teijin | Asahi Chemical |
| *Paper* | Oji Paper | Mitsubishi Paper | | Sanyo-Kokusaku | | Honshu Paper |
| *Chemicals* | Mitsui Toatsu<br>Mitsui Petro-chemical<br>Denki Kagaku[7] | Mitsubishi Kasei*<br>Mitsubishi Petro-chemical[10]*<br>Mitsubishi Gas Chem.<br>Mitsubishi Plastics | Sumitomo Chemical<br>Sumitono Bakelite | Showa Denko<br>Nippon O&F<br>Kureha Chemical | Sekisui Chemica<br>Ube Industries<br>Hitachi Chemical<br>Fujisawa<br>Kansai Paint<br>Tokuyama Soda<br>Tanabe Seiyaku | Denki Kagaku[7]<br>Nippon Zeon<br>Sankyo<br>Shiseido<br>Lion<br>Asahi Denka<br>Kyowa Hakko |
| *Oil* | | Mitsubishi Oil | | Tonen[11] | Cosmo Oil | Showa Shell[12] |
| *Rubber* | | | | | Toyo Rubber | Yokohama Rubber |

SOURCE: Toyo Keizai Kigyo Keiretsu (various years).

| INDUSTRY | MITSUI | MITSUBISHI | SUMITOMO | FUYO | SANWA | DAIICHI-KANGYO |
|---|---|---|---|---|---|---|
| *Glass & cement* | Onoda Cement** | Asahi Glass<br>M. Mining & Cement | Nippon Sheet Glass<br>Sumitomo Cement | Nihon Cement | Osaka Cement | Chichibu Cement** |
| *Steel* | Japan Steel Works | Mitsubishi Steel | Sumitomo Metal Ind. | NKK | Kobe Steel[4]<br>Nakayama Steel<br>Hitachi Metals<br>Nisshin Steel | Kawasaki Steel<br>Kobe Steel[4]<br>Japan M&C |
| *Nonferrous metals* | Mitsui M&S | Mitsubishi Material<br>Mitsubishi Aluminum<br>Mitsubishi Cable<br>Mitsubishi Copper | Sumitomo M&M<br>Sumitomo Electric<br>Sumitomo Light Metal | | Hitachi Cable<br>Furukawa Co. | Nippon Light Metal[13]<br>Furukawa Electric |
| *General machinery* | | Mitsubishi Kakoki | Sumitomo Heavy Ind. | Kubota<br>Nippon P.M. | NTN | Niigata Engrg.<br>Iseki<br>Ebara |
| *Electric machinery* | Toshiba | Mitsubishi Electric | NEC | Hitachi, Ltd.[5]<br>Oki Electric<br>Yokogawa Elec. | Hitachi, Ltd.[5]<br>Iwasaki Elec.<br>Sharp<br>Nitto Electric<br>Kyocera | Hitachi, Ltd.[5]<br>Fujitsu<br>Fuji Electric<br>Yasukawa Electric<br>Nippon Columbia |
| *Transportation machinery* | Toyota Motor[9]<br>Mitsui Eng. & Shipblg.<br>IHI[8] | Mitsubishi Heavy Ind.<br>Mitsubishi Motors | | Nissan Motor | Hitachi Zosen<br>Shin Meiwa<br>Daihatsu | Kawasaki Heavy Ind.<br>IHI[8]<br>Isuzu Motors[14] |
| *Precision* | | Nikon | | Canon | Hoya | Asahi Optical |
| *Department stores* | Mitsukoshi | | | | Takashimaya | Seibu Dept. Store |
| *Finance* | | | | | Orix | Orient Corp.<br>Kankaku Secur. |
| *Real estate* | Mitsui Real Est. | Mitsubishi Estate | Sumitomo Realty | Tokyo Tatemono | | |
| *Transportation & warehousing* | Mitsui-OSK Lines<br>Mitsui W. | Nippon Yusen<br>Mitsubishi W. | Sumitomo W. | Showa Kaiun<br>Tobu Railway<br>Keihin Railway | NABIX<br>Nippon Express[6]<br>Hankyu Railway | Kawasaki Kisen<br>Nippon Express[6]<br>Shibusawa W. |
| *Service* | | Mitsubishi Research | | | | Tokyo Dome |

1 Formerly Mitsui-Taiyo-Kobe Bank.
2 Hokkaido Coal is not an active member.
3, 4, 5, 6, 7, 8 Firms belonging to more than one group.
9 Toyota Motor is not an active member of the Mitsui group.

10, 11, 12, 13, 14 Firms partly owned by foreign companies; 10 (owned by Shell), 11 (Exxon, Mobil), 12 (Shell), 13 (Alcan), 14 (GM).

* Mitsubishi Kasei and Mitsubishi Petrochemical will merge to form the Mitsubishi Chemical Company on October 1, 1994.
**Onoda Cement and Chichibu Cement will also merge to form the Chichibu Onoda Company on October 1, 1994.

perform is to facilitate the movement of excess labour when, for instance, some group firms in declining industries must downsize their operations.

In addition to the two main types of corporate groups found in Japan, there are many other types of inter-firm relationships in Japan, and Japanese firms, regardless of their more formal keiretsu affiliations, participate in these inter-firm activities. Morgan and Morgan (1991, p. 171) note: "The Japanese are the masters of partnering, and any large company has many investors and partners, relationships and contracts, consortium activities and joint projects. Never discount Japanese flexibility and interest in new opportunities."

The corporate groups and partnerships prevalent in Japan implement risk sharing and incentive mechanisms have had a positive impact on long-run economic growth. Another, perhaps more important, contribution of the presence of corporate groups and possibilities for corporate alliances of different kinds in Japan is that this brings competition to markets where high monopoly rents are being earned. This competition among corporate groups was counted on in Japanese industrial policies in the 1960s. The potential difficulty posed by Japanese corporate grouping and alliance practices for access to the Japanese market by foreign firms will be discussed in Chapter 5.

## Corporate Control

One aspect of Japanese firm behaviour which is quite controversial is who really controls a Japanese firm. In the North American literature the standard model of control is that a firm's shareholders delegate the responsibility to run a firm to hired managers and executives who in turn work as the agents of the shareholders. The shareholders have the ultimate power for corporate control. When company management is not performing adequately, share prices are too low and management could be replaced, possibly after a hostile takeover, with a resulting increase in share prices. Corporate control mechanisms in Japan seem much more complex than this. The influences on the control mechanisms of a Japanese firm include workers on (implicit) long-term employment contracts, enterprise unions, other companies, banks and other financial institutions as stable (long-term) shareholders, the main bank and the management.

Workers on long-term employment contracts accumulate substantial firm-specific skills over time which are indispensable to the firm. They also have a serious stake in the firm's long-run performance. These concerns are often effectively represented by their enterprise unions whose executive positions are usually part of the company ladder to future company executive positions.

Since large fractions (often up to 70%) of listed Japanese firms' outstanding shares are held by stable shareholders such as other companies, banks and other financial institutions that are expected not to behave in an opportunistic manner, individual and other investors who are hostile to the present management can be mostly ignored. A typical situation where a coalition of shareholders can effectively replace the present firm management is when the firm's main bank and other banks and institutional shareholders decide that the present management is not in the large shareholders' interests. This may occur, for example, when a firm is in financial distress. The role of the main bank is particularly important in replacing the (incompetent) management, since the main bank, being a large shareholder of the firm and also the largest bank lender, is expected to take a leading role in the management of their troubled client firm on behalf of the consortium of banks and other financial institutions which have outstanding loans to the firm. Morck and Nakamura (1983) present an empirical analysis of main banks' involvement in their troubled client firms and conclude that in Japan the market for corporate control has been replaced by banks' involvement in the management of troubled firms.

## Implications of Japanese Business Practices—A Summary

Many Japanese business practices are based on long-term relationships. These practices have helped to create a highly efficient production system in Japan. Another consequence is that the markets associated with such practices are often difficult for newcomers—foreign or Japanese—to crack.

Long-term employment practices make it difficult for mid-career job changers to locate new jobs since secondary labour markets are very thin, particularly for highly skilled workers from large firms. Most large Japanese firms are not yet set up to take advantage of available skills outside the firms.

Production-based corporate group firms tend to buy and sell goods more among themselves than through external markets. This characteristic would not be viewed as a market problem if the group supplier firms were owned by the prime manufacturer since then group transactions would simply become the prime manufacturer's intra-firm transactions. Since most group supplier firms are independent firms which transact with the group's prime manufacturer as well as other manufacturers on a long-term basis, there is a potential for an outsider to become one of the suppliers. Full vertical integration eliminates such potential. It is apparent that considerable effort is required on the part of a newcomer to be included in group transactions which are long-term based.

Large Japanese firms have long-term employees who have accumulated substantial firm-specific skills. This deters both friendly and hostile mergers between large firms because of the extreme difficulty in combining two firms with different firm-specific practices. Most listed Japanese firms also have stable shareholders (e.g., industrial firms, banks and other financial institutions) who own up to 70% of their outstanding shares. Such stable shareholding also deters mergers of any kind. These factors explain why there is no market for corporate control, at least for large firms, in Japan.

The lack of a substantial labour market for skilled, mid-career workers; the lack of a market for corporate control; and the closed nature of the markets for intermediate and final products because of production-based as well as distribution-based corporate groups all reflect special features of the Japanese business system.

There is considerable academic debate as to the extent to which Japanese corporate groups (and bank-based groups in particular) exercise their influence on business transactions in the Japanese economy. In particular, product market ties are very difficult to study because of data and methodological difficulties (Gerlach, 1992). Fruin (1992) points out that the coalitional networks that power Japanese firms and inter-firm relations on a day-to-day basis cannot be fully explained by firms' financial ties and interlocking directorates at the aggregate level. How production efficiency is related to Japanese corporate grouping, a yet-to-be explored research topic, is of practical importance for the increasing numbers of Japanese and foreign firms considering joint ventures.

Since the burst of the bubble, the profitability of Japanese firms has been persistently very low. This is in contrast to U.S. firms which recovered their profitability fairly quickly in the early 1990s after restructuring themselves to achieve cost reductions. The long-term employment practices and corporate group mechanisms have been blamed (e.g., Daly, 1993) as part of the reason why Japanese firms could not cut costs quickly enough and why Japanese firms could not change their product lines fast enough to capture market shares for newly emerging products.

Recognizing that massive layoffs are not socially acceptable unless active secondary labour markets exist, the Japanese Ministry of Labour (1992) and the Keidanren (1993), the Japan Federation of Economic Organizations, have both called for changes in Japanese business practices, including hiring practices. The Japanese Science and Technology Agency (1991) has called for improving the employment conditions of female, as well as older and foreign, researchers so that the expected labour shortage will not result in the undersupply of scientists and engineers. There is also considerable political pressure from the U.S. government and business firms on Japanese firms to change the closed nature of their business practices. The pressure for such a change also comes from the rapid internationalization of Japanese manufacturing operations.

There are different views among scholars, both within and outside of Japan, about the extent of the differences between the Japanese business (and economic) system and the Anglo-American system, and between Japanese and Anglo-American economic theories (e.g., Galbraith, 1987; MacLean, 1992). Many analysts agree that the present Japanese business system is in equilibrium. This means that, in order to bring about restructuring to achieve a better equilibrium, it is not sufficient simply to undertake marginal or unidimensional adjustments. Comprehensive changes would be needed and these will become possible only when the Japanese business system as a whole finds them in its own interest. It may require simultaneous radical change in many elements of the system.

3

# The Role of Government Industrial Policy

## Introduction

Industrial policies are usually justified as a means of preventing or compensating for market failures. Unfortunately, however, industrial policies can fail too. Industrial policy measures can be costly, and government intervention is not always successful. The Japanese government has put forward policy measures to deal with (perceived) market failures, due to economies of scale, the externalities of pollution, monopolistic conditions in international markets, infant industry situations, the public good nature of research and development and of infrastructure, economic uncertainties, and production factor price rigidities. Some market failures are particularly likely to occur at certain stages of a nation's economic development. For example, in the early phase of economic development, when only limited amounts of scientific and technical information are available as a public good for the use of R&D, underinvestment in research and development may be particularly likely.

The success of industrial policies discussed in this chapter depends in large measure on stable macroeconomic conditions that encourage firms to undertake forward-looking capital investments. Industrial policies such as these cannot succeed in isolation of successful macroeconomic policies.

There is a Japanese government ministry that is responsible for developing policy measures for each major sector of the economy. For example, the

Ministry of International Trade and Industry (MITI) is responsible for most manufacturing industries; the Ministry of Finance (MOF) is responsible for the finance-related industries; the Ministry of Transportation (MOT) is responsible for shipbuilding, ocean transport, airlines and all types of surface transport; and the Ministry of Agriculture (MOA) is responsible for food processing, agriculture, forestry and fishing.

Successful and unsuccessful industrial policies have been instituted by MITI, MOF and MOT, and other Japanese ministries. Despite some failures in firm level intervention, it is difficult to deny the positive contribution of ministry policies for certain key industries. The most valuable contributions of industrial policy may often be in stimulating market forces, in encouraging debate, and in providing new perspectives, rather than in moulding the economic paths for specific industries in Japan in accordance with bureaucratic vision. It is possible that what sometimes appear at first to be policy failures, in the sense that the specific plans of the policy makers were not realized, in fact may be successes in that dynamic processes of adjustment were triggered that resulted in economic growth.

## Policies for Promoting Industries

One of the implicit objectives of Japanese industrial policy in the growth era of the late 1950s and the 1960s was to limit competition by encouraging mergers and the formation of vertical and horizontal corporate groupings. It is generally believed that this objective reflected the preference of government bureaucrats for an industrial structure with less competition among domestic firms. One explanation sometimes given is that Japanese bureaucrats believed it would be easier to administer an economy with small numbers of large, internationally competitive firms with stable domestic market shares rather than cut-throat domestic competition with inevitable business failures and unemployment problems. MITI's industrial policy measures often came into conflict with government antitrust policies. In fact, the Japanese Fair Trade Commission's antitrust policies were simply overridden in many cases by the industrial policy measures of ministries such as MITI.

Despite their power, however, ministries including MITI, have faced a number of problems in their industrial structure planning efforts. One is that they have not always managed to encourage or force private companies to follow their policy directives. For example, MITI wanted to limit the number of Japanese passenger car makers to two (Toyota and Nissan). Yet MITI was unable to prevent Honda, then a motorcycle manufacturer, from entering the automobile market. Honda and Kawasaki Steel are only two of many Japanese firms that entered product markets that were new to them without the government's blessings and succeeded. As favourable market opportunities developed, there were always new entrants backed by banks or existing industrial groups. By the late 1960s, ministry officials had come to recognize vigorous competition, even in domestic markets, as a driving force of the Japanese economy and a legitimate determinant of the Japanese industrial structure.

A second problem is that mergers promoted by the ministries have not always resulted in the rationalization of productive capacities and personnel intended by ministry proponents. Private sector commitment to lifetime employment and related labour relations practices are part of the reason for this. Consider the merger between Yawata Iron and Steel and Fuji Iron and Steel, the largest and second largest steel producers in Japan. MITI encouraged this merger on the premise that there was undesirable excess capacity in the Japanese steel industry. The production capacity of this industry had more than quadrupled, from 22 million tons in 1960 to 93 million tons by 1970. However, in order to avoid personnel management problems, the merged company, the Nippon Steel Corporation, kept all 80,000 regular workers of Yawata and Fuji. Also, the top management of Nippon Steel was a carefully balanced combination of the top executives from Yawata and Fuji. And there were no significant shutdowns of the productive facilities of either Yawata or Fuji, contrary to MITI intentions in proposing the merger. Similarly the Dai-Ichi Kangyo Bank, which was created in 1968 by a MOF-promoted merger between the Dai-Ichi Bank and the Kangyo Bank, kept a personnel system for ten years in which the former employees of the Dai-Ichi and Kangyo Banks were managed separately, respecting the separate employment regulations of Dai-Ichi and Kangyo regarding job rotations, promotions and wage payments.

A third problem area has been the lack of foresight and effective policies on when to terminate government assistance to "infant" industries, as illustrated by the history of government assistance to the shipbuilding industry. Japanese plans to expand the shipbuilding industry started in the early

1950s and required enormous government spending every year. The objectives were to rebuild the merchant fleet, expand fleet capacity, save foreign exchange and improve the trade account balance. Assistance to the shipbuilding industry continued well into the 1960s, by which time all of the stated policy objectives had become less relevant. Not long after, in the 1970s, both the merchant fleet and the shipbuilding industry suffered major setbacks. This activated the government's Industrial Adjustment Policy, for helping with the downsizing of declining industries. It is not clear when the government policy of subsidizing the Japanese shipbuilding and merchant fleet industries turned from (1) providing public goods to the Japanese economy to (2) providing windfall profits to shipbuilders and marine fleet companies, and then to (3) minimizing the losses suffered by these industries due to the new international conditions which emerged in the mid 1970s.

The Japanese experience with the shipbuilding and merchant fleet industries also suggests the difficulty of prioritizing government policies when multiple market failures exist in an industry. Similar difficulties have been encountered in designing government policies for industries characterized by both scale economies and technical progress.

A fourth problem of the industrial structure planning efforts of ministries like MITI has been the choice of target industries. One criterion for choosing an industry as a target for industrial policy in this period was that, in global markets, foreign firms were enjoying monopolistic or oligopolistic profits. It was considered essential that Japanese firms enter such an industry so as to lower the economic rents received by foreign firms, and so as to reduce the currency reserves spent on procuring the goods and services of foreign firms. Other criteria that were used for choosing target industries included Japan's long-term comparative advantage (e.g., knowledge intensive industries), national prestige and the international and domestic news value of success in the industries. In accord with perceived public support, industries that have been objects of government policies and growth strategies since the 1950s include (in chronological order): iron and steel, shipbuilding, merchant marine, machinery, heavy electrical equipment, chemicals, automobiles, petrochemicals, nuclear power, computers and semiconductors.

Many industries in Japan developed impressive global export capabilities without government protection and/or promotion. Listed in chronological order, these include: sewing machines, cameras, bicycles, motorcycles, watches, pianos, zippers, transistor radios, colour televisions, tape recorders, magnetic recording tape, audio equipment, fishing gear, clocks, calculators, electric wire, machine tools, numerically controlled machine tools, textile machinery, agricultural machinery, insulators, communication equipment, ceramics and robots. Most of the firms which produce these products started as small-scale enterprises. Despite this initial small scale and despite the lack of government encouragement, the technological level achieved by some of these industries catering to civilian product markets often exceeded the performance and the reliability requirements of even the most advanced military equipment.

However, the question remains regarding the extent to which these successful private sector product developments benefitted from high quality material supplies, information on production technologies, and the availability of foreign exchange for export promotion activities—all of which share some public good properties and which may not have been as available without government intervention in the market place. In earlier periods, it has been noted, for example, that the lack of high quality steel supplies prevented Japanese auto manufacturers from producing vehicles comparable in quality to those of the U.S. auto companies.

Another important contribution of industrial policy was that it encouraged the dissemination of information relevant for economic growth at the national level. For example, the Ministry of Finance often chaired sessions in which the allocation of investment funds at the national level was determined. In these sessions the representatives of major industries with capital investment projects approved by MITI presented their desired amounts of borrowing to the representatives of major lending institutions. Then the latter were asked by the chair, the Minister of Finance, to disclose the amounts of funds they were willing to supply. Representatives from the Bank of Japan, academia and consumer groups, who were also present in these sessions, provided input as well. After a number of revised plans from both the suppliers and users of funds were exchanged, the total supply of funds was equated to the total demand at what those present (and particularly policy makers) deemed an optimal level and the session ended (Nagatani, 1991). Considerable information exchange took place among various government agencies and different parts of the private sector that often contributed to the effective implementation of government policy measures.

The Japanese government shifted its emphasis away from industrial targeting of the sort discussed above by the mid 1970s. This is also when active liberalization plans to allow more imports of mining and manufacturing products began (Patrick, 1977; Shinohara, 1982; Trezise, 1983).

## Policies for Industrial Adjustment

Japan has had its share of declining industries, including agriculture, mining and ocean transport, and also certain manufacturing industries such as textiles, nonferrous metal refining, and petrochemicals. Within Japan, it is sometimes argued that the Japanese government has devoted more policy attention and larger financial subsidies to dealing with uncompetitive, declining industries than to promoting and developing newly emerging industries. Typical market failures faced by declining industries include incorrect market expectations, the deviation of private discount rates from the social discount rate, incomplete resource mobility, and factor price rigidities. The most desirable (first best) solution would be to remove the sources of market failure, but this is not usually possible in practice. A second best practical solution is for the government to intervene in the market to hasten the reallocation of resources while minimizing adjustment problems.

The three phases in the evolution of Japanese industrial adjustment assistance policies for declining industries are: (1) the period before the implementation of the 1978 Law on Temporary Measures for Stabilization of Specified Depressed Industries (Industry Stabilization Law), (2) the period immediately following adoption of the Industry Stabilization Law (1978–1983), and (3) the period after 1983 when the Japanese adjustment assistance laws were reformed.

Before the Industry Stabilization Law came into effect in 1978, two groups of declining industries received policy attention. Short-term adjustment policies were applied to the first of these groups which included sulphur mining, coal mining and textiles. Long-term policies were applied to the second group which included agriculture, the leather industry, and small retailers. Summary statistics for these industries (except for the small retailers) are given in Table 3.1.

**Table 3.1** Examples of Japanese Adjustments, 1960–1980

| | | 1960 | 1965 | 1970 | 1975 | 1980 |
|---|---|---|---|---|---|---|
| Textile | Production[a] | 1,270.2 | 1,566.1 | 2,039.8 | 1,776.4 | 2,049.7 |
| | No. of Workers[b] | 1,103.4 | 1,153.4 | 1,097.8 | 884.3 | 676.8 |
| | Imports[a] | 3.0 | 62.5 | 131.4 | 277.8 | 667.2 |
| Coal Mining | Production[a] | 52,607 | 56,259 | 38,329 | 18,597 | 18,095 |
| | No. of Workers[b] | 238,274 | 111,360 | 50,262 | 36,073 | 30,070 |
| | Imports[a] | 8,595 | 16,936 | 50,950 | 62,339 | 72,711 |
| Leather | Production (tons) | 83,535 | 137,419 | 147,952 | 188,987 | 184,238 |
| | No. of Workers[b] | 22,708 | 31,401 | 31,202 | 35,845 | 32,212 |
| | Consumption of Imported Hides[a] | 67,476 | 125,521 | 146,460 | 176,149 | 148,319 |
| Sulfur | Production[a] | 248 | 213 | 261 | 103 | 17 |
| | No. of Workers[b] | 6,142 | 4,544 | 3,143 | n.a. | 170 |
| | Production through Petroleum[a] | n.a. | 37 | 76 | 239 | 483 |
| Citrus Fruits | Cultivated area (1,000 hectares) | 63.0 | 115.2 | 163.0 | 169.4 | 139.0 |
| | No. of Cultivating Farms (1,000) | 210.0 | n.a. | 371.0 | 353.4 | 302.3 |
| | Amount Harvested[a] | 893.6 | 1,317.0 | 2,552.0 | 3,665.0 | 2,892.0 |
| | Import of Grapefruit[a] | n.a. | n.a. | 2.3 | 146.7 | 135.2 |
| | Import of Lemons and Lime[a] | n.a. | 18.9 | 54.0 | 64.1 | 100.7 |

Source: Japanese Ministry of International Trade and Industry, *Yearbooks on Industries* (various years).

[a] 1,000 tons.
[b] 1,000 regular workers.

In 1978, the Law on Temporary Measures for Stabilization of Specified Depressed Industries was adopted. This law, in fact, consisted of the following four laws: (1) the Industry Stabilization Law dealing with the reduction of production capacity in depressed industries; (2) the Law on Temporary Measures for Those Unemployed in Specified Depressed Industries; (3) the Law on Temporary Measures for Those Unemployed in Specified Regions; and (4) the Law on Temporary Measures for Small and Medium Enterprises in Specified Depressed Regions (see Table 3.2). Tables 3.3 and 3.4 show the reductions in production capacity achieved under the Industry Stabilization Law during the period 1977–1981. Table 3.5 describes specific employ-

**Table 3.2** Japanese Temporary Policy Measures for Industrial Adjustment

| LAW ON: | INFORMATION DISSEMINATION | INCREASING ABILITY TO CHANGE | INTERINDUSTRY TRANSFER OF RESOURCES |
|---|---|---|---|
| Depressed Industries[1] (Jan.1978 - June 1983) | Employment intermediation placements by PESB.[5] | Training seminars, employment guidance. | Subsidy to firms employing workers carrying specially issued job seeker identifications; layoff and training cost allowances paid to firms for transferred workers. |
| Depressed Regions[2] (Nov. 1978 - June 1983) | Employment intermediation by PESB. | Training seminars, employment guidance. | Subsidy to firms employing specified job seekers of age 45–65; layoff and training cost allowance paid to firms for transferred workers. |
| Industry Stabilization[3] (May 1978 - April 1983) | Basic Stabilization plans for depressed industries formed in part in consultation with related councils. | Temporary applications of import control. | Use of the Specified Depressed Industries Trust Fund to finance depressed industries carrying out capacity reductions. |
| Small and Medium Enterprises[4] (Nov. 1978 - June 1983) | — | Financing at favorable rates for small and medium firms. | Subsidy to firms employing specified job seekers of age 45–65; favourable loan treatments, loan guarantees, loss carry over and accelerated depreciation. |

1 Law on Temporary Measures for Those Unemployed in Specified Depressed Industries.
2 Law on Temporary Measures for Those Unemployed in Specified Depressed Regions.
3 Industry Stabilization Law.
4 Law on Temporary Measures for Small and Medium Enterprises in Specified Depressed Regions.
5 Public Employment Stabilization Bureaus.

ment assistance measures implemented by these laws and the extent of their coverage.

In 1983, the Law on Temporary Measures for the Structural Improvement of Specified Industries replaced the Industry Stabilization Law (Law (1)) in 1983. Laws (2) and (3) were replaced by the Law on Special Measures Concerning the Stabilization of Employment in Specified Depressed Industries and in Specified Depressed Regions. Law (4) was replaced by the Law on Temporary Measures for Dealing with Regions Related to Specified Depressed Industries.

| STABILIZING REGIONAL ECONOMIES | COMPENSATING INCOME | OTHER |
|---|---|---|
| Promoting employment (up to 40%) of excess labour by public enterprises. | Employment insurance coverage period extended (to 90 days for those over 40; to 60 days for those under 40). | Depressed industries chosen by the Industry Stabilization Law, subject to review by the Ministry of Labour. |
| Promoting employment (up to 40%) of excess labour by public enterprises for those under 40. | Employment insurance coverage period extended (to 90 days for those over 40; to 60 days). | Depressed regions chosen by the Law on Small and Medium Size Enterprises in Specified Depressed Regions. |
| The governors of the prefectures which suffered major capacity reductions could make direct representations to the related ministries. | — | Firms in designated depressed industries were allowed to scrap excess capacity jointly; exempted from application of the anti-monopoly laws. |
| Incentives given to firms which relocate their factories in specified depressed areas. | Employment insurance coverage period extended (to 90 days for those over 40; to 60 days for those under 40). | Municipalities with high concentrations of designated depressed industries specified as depressed regions. |

There have been large employment reductions in depressed industries in Japan. For example, between 1977 and 1979, 44,000 jobs were eliminated in shipbuilding (Table 3.3). Production capacity was cut by more than 50% in the aluminum industry between 1978 and 1981 (Table 3.4). And employment in coal mining declined from 294,000 in 1958 to 40,000 in 1971. Comparative figures for some of Canada's depressed industries show relatively modest reductions in employment (in percentage terms) in comparison with the Japanese experience (Treibilock, 1989, p. 215). For example, employment for 1975 and 1982, respectively, for some Canadian manufac-

**Table 3.3** Economic Characteristics of Depressed Japanese Industries[1], 1977 and 1981

| | PRODUCTION[2] (RATE OF CAPACITY UTILIZATION, %) | | IMPORTS (IMPORT RATIO,[4] %) | | NUMBER OF WORKERS (NUMBER OF FIRMS, %) | |
|---|---|---|---|---|---|---|
| | 1977 | 1981 | 1977 | 1981 | 1977 | 1981 |
| Open Hearth and Electric Furnaces | 9,633.0 (62.7) | 11,283.0 (80.0) | 0.0 (–) | 0.0 (–) | 32,400.0 (69.0) | 31,300.0 (59.0) |
| Aluminium Refining | 1,188.0 (73.0) | 665.0 (58.5) | 472.0 (33.5) | 1,062.0 (66.0) | 7,642.0 (7.0) | 4,344.0 (6.0) |
| Continuous Nylon fibers | 287.6 (78.9) | 270.0 (88.5) | 7.7 (4.1) | 14.8 (7.2) | 71,021.0 (6.0) | 59,464.0 (6.0) |
| Discontinuous Acryl Fibers | 341.4 (80.2) | 327.1 (92.9) | 10.2 (6.0) | 25.0 (13.4) | 45,270.0 (6.0) | 39,408.0 (6.0) |
| Continuous Polyester | 271.8 (76.9) | 287.9 (86.2) | 13.7 (8.4) | 37.0 (19.4) | 81,330.0 (8.0) | 69,317.0 (9.0) |
| Discontinuous Polyester | 297.4 (76.6) | 321.1 (95.1) | 17.3 (11.7) | 24.8 (12.7) | 66,217.0 (7.0) | 55,841.0 (7.0) |
| Urea | 1,972.0 (50.1) | 1,311.0 (56.5) | 1.0 (0.1) | 10.0 (1.2) | 417.0 (12.0) | 300.0 (8.0) |
| Ammonia | 2,810.0 (61.7) | 2,102.0 (62.4) | 0.0 (–) | 0.0 (–) | 1,075.0 (18.0) | 790.0 (14.0) |
| Hydrous Phosphoric Acid | 542.0 (58.0) | 484.0 (63.6) | 56.0 (9.8) | 37.0 (7.2) | 467.0 (21.0) | 422.0 (16.0) |
| Cotton Spinning | 883.9 (70.1) | 946.4 (88.0) | 111.7 (14.1) | 220.9 (23.4) | 71,996.0 (n.a.) | 61,100.0 (193.0) |
| Worsted Yarn Spinning | 117.1 (64.3) | 115.0 (83.0) | 9.3 (8.3) | 12.7 (11.8) | 22,988.0 (142.0) | 15,273.0 (109.0) |
| Ferro-Silicon | 287.0 (55.4) | 220.0 (63.6) | 45.0 (13.7) | 208.0 (47.8) | 1,536.0 (16.0) | 1,022.0 (10.0) |
| Cardboard | 4,653.0 (62.9) | 4,459.0 (68.8) | 67.0 (1.5) | 272.0 (5.9) | 5,828.0 (88.0) | 5,960.0 (77.0) |
| Shipbuilding[3] | 943.0 (76.0) | 862.0 (79.0) | 0.0 (–) | 0.0 (–) | 164,000.0 (61.0) | 114,000.0 (44.0) |

SOURCE: Japanese Fair Trade Commission, *Bulletin* (Nov. 1982) and *Fair Trade Association.*

1 Depressed industries designated by the Industry Stabilization Law.
2 Figures for shipbuilding in 10,000 gross tons; other figures in 1,000 tons.
3 Includes firms with production capacity exceeding 5,000 tons.
4 Imports divided by the sum of production and imports minus exports.

**Table 3.4** Reductions in Production Capacity for Depressed Japanese Industries[1], 1977–1981

| | PRODUCTION CAPACITY BEFORE SCRAPPING | CAPACITY TARGETED FOR SCRAPPING | CAPACITY SCRAPPED BY THE END OF 1981 | TOTAL LOAN[2] GUARANTEES |
|---|---|---|---|---|
| *Industries exempted at least in part from the application of the antimonopoly laws* | | | | |
| Continuous Nylon Fibers | 366.7 | 71.5 | 72.9 | – |
| Discontinuous Acryl Fibers | 430.5 | 73.2 | 95.5 | 3.0 |
| Continuous Polyester Fibers | 349.8 | 36.8 | 36.6 | – |
| Discontinuous Polyester Fibers | 397.5 | 67.6 | 70.7 | – |
| Urea | 3,985.0 | 1,790.0 | 1,670.0 | 2.7 |
| Ammonia | 4,559.0 | 1,190.0 | 1,190.0 | – |
| Worsted Yarn Spinning | 181.7 | 18.3 | 17.6 | 1.2 |
| Cardboard | 7,549.0 | 1,147.0 | 1,083.0 | 2.1 |
| *Industries not exempted from the application of the antimonopoly laws* | | | | |
| Open Hearth and Electric Furnaces | 20,790.0 | 2,850.0 | 2,720.0 | – |
| Aluminum Refining | 1,642.0 | 530.0 | 899.0 | – |
| Shipbuilding | 9,770.0 | 3,420.0 | 3,580.0 | 14.2 |
| Ferro-Silicon | 487.0 | 100.0 | 100.0 | – |
| Hydrous Phosphoric Acid | 934.0 | 190.0 | 174.0 | – |
| Cotton Spinning | 1,204.0 | 67.1 | 52.3 | – |

SOURCE: Japanese Fair Trade Commission, *Bulletin* (Nov. 1982) and *Fair Trade Association.*

1 Production capacity figures in 1,000 tons per year.
2 Loan guarantee figures in billion yen.

turing industries are: 71,050 (for 1975) and 59,416 (for 1982) for textiles, 24,682 and 18,318 for knitting mills, 100,528 and 91,306 for clothing, 26,834 and 22,951 for leather products, and 16,344 and 16,128 for shipbuilding.

In response to the current severe recession, which was still continuing in 1993, the Ministry of Labour designated 151 industries as eligible for employment adjustment subsidies by June 1, 1993 and budgeted 50.9 billion yen for fiscal 1993 for various measures stipulated in the laws described in Table 3.5 (Ministry of Labour, 1993). These subsidies include furlough pay, retraining and relocation costs. By the end of 1992, 1069 firms applied

**Table 3.5** Japanese Employment Assistance Measures

| LAW ON: | CONDITIONS FOR IMPLEMENTATION | NUMBER OF APPLICABLE CASES | BUDGET |
|---|---|---|---|
| Depressed Industries[1] (Jan.1978 - June 1982) | Firms in depressed industries must get their employment adjustment (layoff) plans approved by the director of a local PESO[4] if they intend to lay off more than 30 workers in a single month or the total number of laid-off and transferred workers exceeds 100; upon approval both employers and workers will be eligible for special measures. | 40 industries were designated as depressed industries; about 6,600 plans were approved by November, 1982; 103,200 job-seeker identifications were issued; 10,760 workers received training; 68,200 got reemployed. | The Laws on depressed industries and depressed regions together required 10.4 billion yen; the new Employment Stabilization Law which replaced these two Laws in 1983 was budgeted 15.8 billion yen. |
| Depressed Regions[2] (Nov. 1978 - June 1983) | Firms and workers resided in depressed regions become eligible for special measures. | 44 areas were designated as depressed areas; on average 4,941 laid-off workers became eligible for extended employment insurance per month by November 1982; public enterprises provided 2,580,000 man-days of employment. | See above; also 3.6 billion yen spent on employment assistance; some additional subsidies to older workers. |
| Small and Medium Enterprises[3] (Nov. 1978 - June 1983) | Small and medium size firms facing adverse business conditions as a result of the closure of large firms' establishments become eligible for special measures upon approval from the head of the local municipality. | 35 municipalities and 7 industries designated as depressed by September 1982; 5,600 small and medium size firms became eligible by the end of 1981 for special measures. | 42.7 billion yen for emerging loans; 18.6 billion yen for increased loan guarantees; 2.4 billion yen for special tax reimbursements; 1.5 billion for attracting new firms into depressed areas; 0.17 billion yen for helping changes in lines of business. |

1 Law on Temporary Measures for Those Unemployed in Specified Depressed Industries.
2 Law on Temporary Measures for Those Unemployed in Specified Depressed Regions.
3 Law on Temporary Measures for Small and Medium Enterprises in Specified Depressed Regions.
4 Public Employment Stabilization Office.

for employment adjustment subsidies covering more than half a million workers. Of these firms, 392 were in the software, 194 in electronics, 83 in printed circuit manufacturing, 79 in tool and machinery, and 32 in steel ingot industries.

MITI's policies towards declining industries have been generally consistent in that no formal protection against foreign imports, such as voluntary export restraints, has been granted and the government has coordinated comprehensive plans to cut back plant capacity in structurally depressed industries. (See Okimoto, 1989 for a comparison of government policies in Japan and the U.S. towards declining industries.) These market-oriented policies by MITI are in contrast to more protective policies adopted by other branches of the Japanese government: the Ministry of Finance's policies towards the finance sector, the Ministry of Transport's policies towards air travel, the Ministry of Agriculture's policies towards rice and the Ministry of Construction's policies towards public projects.

One possible reason that Japan was able to relocate excess labour from depressed industries in a relatively short time is the presence of bank-based and other types of corporate groups. A worker whose job was eliminated because of capacity reductions under the Industry Stabilization Law might receive help in locating a new job from three sources: the firm he/she had worked for, different levels of government, and other firms in the corporate group that his or her firm belonged to. Bank-based corporate groups, for example, include firms from diverse industries, making it possible in many cases for them to absorb excess workers from group firms in depressed industries.

Group firms also become involved financially in reorganization processes. For instance, the parent firms (mostly in the chemical industry) of Japanese aluminum smelting firms wrote off 428 billion yen during the 1979–1986 period, while government subsidies to the aluminum smelting industry amounted to only 83 billion yen (Sheard, 1991). Private-sector losses are also shared by the banks that are at the centre of many corporate groups.

In the case of Nippon Light Metal (NLM), the largest producer of aluminum in Japan (of which Alcan owns 46.5%), three Japanese banks implemented an interest reduction program in 1978 which resulted in an annual interest subsidy of 900 million yen to the company. In 1983 the three banks and other large Japanese shareholders injected 7 billion yen into NLM's

**Table 3.6** Energy Consumption Index, 1970–1989 (1973 = 100)[a]

| | JAPAN | U.S. | U.K. | FRANCE | WEST GERMANY | U.S.S.R. | EASTERN EUROPE | CHINA |
|---|---|---|---|---|---|---|---|---|
| *1970* | 100.0 | 103.9 | 108.5 | 100.4 | 100.5 | 87.5 | – | 118.2 |
| *1971* | 101.6 | 103.5 | 105.4 | 98.2 | 98.1 | – | – | – |
| *1972* | 96.3 | 102.6 | 102.8 | 97.3 | 98.1 | – | – | – |
| *1973* | 100.0 | 100.0 | 100.0 | 100.0 | 100.0 | – | – | – |
| *1974* | 101.1 | 97.3 | 97.2 | 95.6 | 96.6 | – | – | – |
| *1975* | 94.1 | 96.1 | 93.3 | 88.4 | 92.8 | – | – | – |
| *1976* | 93.6 | 96.5 | 92.1 | 90.7 | 93.8 | – | – | – |
| *1977* | 89.8 | 94.3 | 91.9 | 89.3 | 91.3 | – | – | – |
| *1978* | 86.6 | 92.0 | 88.6 | 88.9 | 92.3 | – | – | – |
| *1979* | 86.1 | 90.5 | 90.5 | 86.7 | 94.2 | – | – | – |
| *1980* | 80.2 | 87.1 | 84.9 | 84.4 | 87.5 | 100.0 | 100.0 | 100.0 |
| *1981* | 75.9 | 83.5 | 82.8 | 82.7 | 83.7 | – | – | – |
| *1982* | 71.1 | 82.1 | 80.4 | 79.1 | 81.7 | – | – | – |
| *1983* | 69.0 | 79.1 | 77.8 | 78.7 | 80.3 | – | – | – |
| *1984* | 71.7 | 77.8 | 75.7 | 79.6 | 80.8 | 101.9 | 96.6 | 82.6 |
| *1985* | 68.4 | 74.9 | 76.5 | 79.1 | 81.7 | 104.8 | 98.1 | 78.0 |
| *1986* | 67.4 | 73.1 | 75.9 | 80.0 | 79.8 | 104.2 | 98.7 | 75.9 |
| *1987* | 64.7 | 73.2 | 72.2 | 79.6 | 78.4 | 105.0 | 99.6 | 71.2 |
| *1988* | 65.2 | 72.9 | 69.4 | 76.0 | 76.0 | 105.6 | 97.4 | 66.6 |
| *1989* | 64.2 | 72.3 | 66.5 | 75.1 | 71.2 | – | – | – |

SOURCE: Japanese Economic Planning Agency, *Summary of Economic Statistics* (various years).

[a] 1980 = 100 for U.S.S.R., Eastern Europe and China.

equity base. In addition these banks arranged for the private sale, at favorable prices, of the shares in banks and other firms that NLM held, providing NLM with a net capital gains profit of 30.4 billion yen over the period 1977–1986.

## Policies for Energy and the Environment

After the first oil price shock, Japan achieved much greater efficiency in energy consumption (Table 3.6). Nevertheless, among all developed countries Japan is still the least self-

**Table 3.7** Energy Self Sufficiency, 1974–1988 (Domestic energy production/ Energy consumption, Percent)

| | 1974 | 1980 | 1986 | 1987 | 1988 |
|---|---|---|---|---|---|
| West Germany | 47.1 | 45.4 | 47.8 | 47.7 | 47.5 |
| Canada | 115.4 | 106.2 | 118.3 | 120.4 | 123.6 |
| U.S. | 84.6 | 86.1 | 87.5 | 85.8 | 83.8 |
| France | 23.9 | 27.5 | 45.5 | 46.1 | 47.1 |
| Italy | 19.1 | 17.3 | 20.5 | 19.4 | 19.9 |
| Japan | 12.4 | 14.8 | 18.7 | 19.0 | 17.7 |
| U.K. | 48.3 | 98.3 | 119.2 | 115.8 | 110.9 |
| E.C. | 37.8 | 48.1 | 58.1 | 57.0 | 55.5 |

SOURCE: OECD, *Energy Balances of OECD Countries* (1990).

sufficient in energy (Table 3.7). Not surprisingly, therefore, Japan considers a stable supply of energy to be one of its most important security issues. The same concern with national security also underlies Japanese policies with respect to the supply of food, metals, and other raw materials for which Japan is almost entirely dependent on imported supplies. While the Middle East and Asia provide more than 95% of the oil Japan imports, their share of global oil reserves amounts to only about 70% of the total. Japan imports tin almost exclusively from Asia but Asia's tin reserve is less than 70% of the global total. Similarly, Japan imports wheat exclusively from North America and Oceania but their share of wheat production is less than 20% of the global total.

The tradeoffs between depending on long-term supply arrangements with countries with large excess capacities versus the security gains from diversification of supply sources have greatly influenced Japanese foreign investment decisions. In those countries with abundant supplies, the focus has been on investment in infrastructure. In the case of other countries with limited excess capacities but potential untapped reserves, Japan has invested in efforts to discover new sources of supply. The long run potential for Canadian exports of energy, grains and mineral resources to Japan needs to be assessed in this light.

As Table 3.8 shows, nuclear energy research has received a high priority

**Table 3.8** Japanese Research on Energy: Expenditures and Personnel, 1991[1] (Million yen and number of researchers)

| | ALL | INDUSTRY[2] | GOVERNMENT RESEARCH INSTITUTES | UNIVERSITIES | PRIVATE RESEARCH INSTITUTES |
|---|---|---|---|---|---|
| Fossil energy | 95,979 (1,933) | 51,383 (1,235) | 1,334 (96) | 1,900 (213) | 35,360 (389) |
| Oil | 54,423 (737) | 31,511 (505) | 171 (16) | 625 (66) | 22,116 (150) |
| Gas | 6,929 (256) | 6,707 (229) | 1 (0) | 195 (25) | 26 (2) |
| Coal | 29,210 (780) | 14,908 (389) | 1,162 (80) | 910 (100) | 12,230 (211) |
| Other | 5,417 (160) | 4,257 (112) | 0 (0) | 171 (22) | 989 (26) |
| Natural energy | 32,681 (1,587) | 15,968 (618) | 4,002 (238) | 5,223 (498) | 7,488 (233) |
| Geothermal | 3,807 (208) | 839 (38) | 1,476 (67) | 504 (56) | 998 (47) |
| Solar | 19,821 (782) | 11,526 (451) | 1,109 (53) | 1,922 (210) | 5,264 (68) |
| Marine | 1,073 (82) | 349 (16) | 203 (26) | 456 (31) | 65 (9) |
| Wind | 1,719 (62) | 1,244 (22) | 224 (13) | 251 (27) | 0 (0) |
| Biomas | 4,746 (319) | 1,688 (73) | 974 (77) | 1,876 (157) | 208 (12) |
| Other | 1,518 (134) | 332 (18) | 17 (2) | 214 (17) | 955 (97) |
| Nuclear energy | 435,835 (6,807) | 71,321 (1,883) | 295,425 (2,444) | 28,834 (1,874) | 40,255 (606) |
| Power generation | 178,444 (2,003) | 36,954 (943) | 112,950 (600) | 1,015 (109) | 27,525 (351) |
| Multipurpose | 13,746 (217) | 222 (21) | 13,175 (161) | 349 (35) | 0 (0) |
| Fuel cycle | 107,148 (1,379) | 19,526 (507) | 76,749 (611) | 653 (72) | 10,220 (189) |
| Fusion | 40,757 (916) | 4,072 (147) | 19,887 (294) | 16,789 (473) | 9 (2) |
| Other | 25,628 (501) | 3,706 (106) | 19,387 (308) | 1,038 (53) | 1,497 (34) |
| Ships | 1,452 (23) | 28 (3) | 1,419 (19) | 5 (1) | 0 (0) |
| Radiation use | 29,418 (1,312) | 6,317 (129) | 15,966 (251) | 6,690 (916) | 445 (16) |
| Radiation protection | 39,242 (456) | 497 (27) | 35,892 (200) | 2,294 (215) | 559 (14) |
| Energy conservation | 392,332 (9,963) | 213,466 (6,205) | 4,116 (267) | 6,115 (621) | 170,635 (2,870) |
| Industrial | 43,515 (1,707) | 38,220 (1,247) | 1,665 (124) | 1,552 (182) | 2,078 (154) |
| Household | 35,678 (1,635) | 33,691 (1,414) | 224 (20) | 757 (77) | 1,006 (124) |
| Transportation | 254,636 (4,671) | 94,215 (2,250) | 695 (39) | 915 (82) | 158,811 (2,300) |
| Power conversion/storage | 39,400 (1,147) | 31,784 (836) | 1,023 (52) | 1,504 (138) | 5,089 (121) |
| Hydrogen | 6,550 (286) | 5,121 (182) | 274 (17) | 906 (77) | 249 (10) |
| Other | 14,554 (517) | 10,436 (276) | 234 (15) | 481 (65) | 3,403 (161) |
| Other energy | 15,670 (489) | 9,503 (262) | 510 (7) | 646 (77) | 5,011 (143) |
| Total | 974,499 (20,779) | 367,641 (10,203) | 305,389 (3,052) | 42,719 (3,283) | 258,750 (4,241) |

SOURCE: Japanese Science and Technology Agency, *Indicators of Science and Technology* (1993).

1 Expenditures are for fiscal year 1991. Number of researchers given in parentheses are as of April 1, 1992.
2 Industry includes companies with capitalizations (book value) of at least 100 million yen.

in Japanese energy research policies. Unfortunately, these policy initiatives have not succeeded in their objective of ensuring alternative renewable energy sources, even though additional funds were raised for this purpose by the private sector to establish the New Energy Development Organization. One reason for this failure could be the lack of attention to promoting the demand for energy from new sources. This is in contrast to other more successful policy interventions which have encompassed both research subsidies and the generation of new demand, such as the combined development of shipbuilding and mercantile fleet industries in the 1950s and 1960s, and the development of semiconductor, computer and information-based industries since the 1960s.

One of the beliefs underlying Japanese environmental policies is that improving energy efficiency is the most effective means of dealing with many global environmental problems. As Table 3.9 shows, by international standards Japan is an efficient user of energy, as measured in terms of carbon dioxide ($CO_2$) per capita and per GNP. The Japanese currently believe that there is a potential for serious conflict between global environmental problems and economic growth in developing countries. Developing countries' total global share of $CO_2$ production is presently about 30%, which is not much larger than that of North America (20.5% for the U.S., 4.5% for Canada). However, economic growth in these countries is expected to drastically increase their share. A U.S. Environmental Protection Agency forecast states that, under the present production rate of $CO_2$, the amount produced by developing countries (including China and India) and by Eastern Europe (including the former U.S.S.R.) will increase by more than 400% and 300% between 1990 and 2100, respectively, while the amount of $CO_2$ production in OECD countries is expected to remain fairly constant over this period. It is not likely that debt-ridden Third World and East European countries will be able to invest in energy efficiency while maintaining a reasonable level of economic growth. The tradeoff between investing in capital for economic growth versus environmental protection remains the same whether the capital comes from foreign aid or business profits. In recent international policy discussions, Japan has indicated a willingness to transfer energy saving technology to developing countries through bilateral and multilateral programs. An example of this willingness is provided by a joint

**Table 3.9** Carbon Dioxide Exhaust from Fossil Fuels, 1987

| | $CO_2$ EXHAUST | | | |
|---|---|---|---|---|
| | Quantity (100 m. tons) | Share (percent) | Per GNP $CO_2$ Exhaust (g/US$1) | Per Capita $CO_2$ Exhaust (10 kg/US$1) |
| *OECD Countries* | | | | |
| North America | 15.0 | 24.9 | 304.3 | 556.2 |
| U.S. | (12.4) | (20.5) | (275.2) | (507.7) |
| OECD Europe | 8.8 | 14.6 | 158.5 | 215.5 |
| OECD Pacific | 3.2 | 5.3 | 121.8 | 226.0 |
| Japan | (2.4) | (4.0) | (102.6) | (199.7) |
| OECD All | 27.0 | 44.8 | 215.1 | 329.4 |
| *Non OECD Countries* | | | | |
| Asia | 6.3 | 10.4 | 512.6 | 37.6 |
| Latin America | 3.2 | 5.3 | 438.7 | 79.3 |
| Africa | 2.6 | 4.3 | 1148.9 | 45.9 |
| Communist Nations | 21.2 | 35.2 | 552.0 | 138.0 |
| USSR | (11.2) | (18.6) | (408.4) | (346.3) |
| E. Europe | (4.6) | (7.7) | (379.5) | (289.8) |
| China | (5.3) | (8.8) | (1802.6) | (49.5) |
| Non OECD All | 33.3 | 55.2 | 553.4 | 79.5 |
| World | 60.3 | 100.0 | 325.1 | 120.4 |

SOURCE: Japanese Economic Planning Agency, *White Paper on the Economy* (1990).

China-Japan research project that got underway recently in China for collecting data on air pollution. Mutual cooperation in this regard between Canada and Japan seems feasible and desirable.

Japanese policies view investment in cleaning the environment as one way of dealing with externalities caused by market failures. Another approach is taxation of the consumption of fossil fuels, which generates incentives for energy efficiency gains. Because of such taxes, Japanese petroleum product prices are up to twice as high as the corresponding prices in the U.S. although they are comparable to European prices for most petroleum products. In Japan, revenues from these taxation programs are currently used for developing new technologies related to energy conservation, methods of carbon dioxide removal, and new energy supplies. The success of these programs hinges, in part, on whether or not demand can be generated in the private sector for the new technologies that result.

4

# The Role of Government Technology Policy

## Introduction

Without government intervention, market failure in the sale of technologies can occur, since technologies often can be simply appropriated. This is why it is customary for governments to try to protect the property rights of the original developers of technical knowledge through patents or copyrights. The protection of property rights is considered essential in order to avoid under-investment by the private sector in research and development. Yet, in practice the full protection of an original developer's property rights is not possible. Hence it is possible that aggregate investment in R&D by private firms is less than the level that is socially desirable. Further government intervention, beyond patent and copyright protection, may be called for to overcome this type of market failure.

## Policies for Promoting Private Sector Research and Development Activities

Research and development activities in the private sector are affected by general macro (e.g., fiscal and monetary) policies, antimonopoly laws and other government regulations, the supply of workers trained in science-based disciplines, and policies directly targeted at specific R&D projects. Stable macroeconomic conditions are considered essential for Japanese technology policies, since relatively large fractions (25% in 1970, 17% in 1989) of Japanese total spendings on science and technology come from the private sector which depends on a good macroeconomic environment for solid performance. In comparison, government spending on R&D constitutes 46%, 32%, 50% and 37% of the total R&D spendings for the U.S. (in 1990), Germany (1990), France (1988) and the U.K. (1988), respectively.

Until the end of the 1960s the Japanese government made extensive use of the Foreign Capital Law and the Foreign Exchange Control Law for controlling the flow of imported technology. Another important use of these laws was to restrict the import of specific technologies to a few firms (but not just one) for fast adoption of the technologies on a competitive basis. This controlled approach to technology importation sometimes resulted in considerable savings in royalties and other costs of technology importation. For instance, Japanese royalty payments on an important oxidation process imported from Austria were held down to less than 1% of sales revenue due to an agreement between MITI and the industry, while U.S. firms paid up to 35% for the same imported technology. These laws were relaxed in 1967, and liberalization of foreign exchange took place in 1969.

There were about half a million full-time researchers in Japan in 1992. This compares with about 950,000, 165,000, 124,000 and 118,000 full-time researchers found in the U.S. (1989), West Germany (1987), France (1990) and the U.K. (1990), respectively. The supply of research personnel consists of university graduates with Bachelor's, Master's and Doctoral degrees. The numbers of graduates with these degrees in physical and biological sciences, engineering, agriculture, and health sciences for Japan in 1988 were respectively: Bachelor's degree (Sciences = 13,420; Engineering = 80,136; Agriculture = 14,297; Health = 22,132); Master's degree (S = 2,692; E = 11,913; A = 2,725; H = 1,126); and Doctorates (S = 881; E = 1,717; A = 746; H = 5,789). The numbers for the U.S. in 1987 were: Bachelor's degree (S = 70,425; E = 133,268; A = 14,222; H = 60,095); Master's degree (S = 13,919; E = 35,998;

A = 3,479; H = 18,523); and Doctorates (S = 8,158; E = 4,721; A = 1,142; H = 1,247). At the Bachelor's level, the U.S. produces more graduates in the fields of pure science and the health sciences compared to Japan, while Japan produces more graduates relative to the U.S. in the fields of engineering and agriculture. Japan's emphasis on engineering fields relative to pure science fields at the college level is historical and consistent with the Japanese government policy to secure a sufficient number of engineers for the widespread diffusion of technical innovations. (See, for example, Peck and Tamura, 1976, and Glazer, 1976 for the role of Japanese employment and education policies in economic growth.)

The ratio of one scientist per seven engineers among new university graduates has changed little since the early 1960s. The proportion of Japanese technical personnel trained at the graduate level is also small relative to the U.S. These differences suggest that Japan has an abundant supply of well-trained technical personnel but likely has a shortage of the scientists with graduate training and research leadership necessary for the original development of technically advanced products. Japanese firms have traditionally relied on in-house training of their key R&D personnel over their lifetime employment in order to meet the needs for such research leadership. Given the reasonable success in their R&D efforts in recent years, Japanese firms will likely continue, to a large extent, their practice of long-term, in-house training of potential R&D project leaders rather than relying on the external market supply of senior R&D project leaders. Despite pressures which encourage changing Japanese employment practices, Japanese manufacturing firms have been very protective of the employment security of their key R&D and technology personnel.

### *Government Support for Research and Development Activity*

Three types of direct government support for private-sector R&D activities are: (1) direct subsidies to R&D projects; (2) preferential tax measures; and (3) low-interest loans for R&D projects from government financial institutions. Total government support as a fraction of private-sector research spending plus payments for technology imports stayed at about 5% until the mid 1960s and then gradually decreased to less than 3% by 1980. For example, total government subsidies for R&D activities were 16.4 billion yen in 1965 (3.1 billion for direct subsidies and 13.3 billion for preferential tax measures) compared to 312 billion yen for private-sector R&D expenditures and technology imports combined. In 1980, these figures were 101 billion yen for government support (60.8 billion for direct support, 38 billion for preferential tax measures and 2.2 billion for low-interest loans) compared to 3,519 billion yen for private-sector R&D expenditures and technology imports combined.

Prior to 1965, government subsidies were used to accelerate R&D in areas where private-sector firms would have invested anyway. Starting in the mid 1960s, the emphasis shifted to promoting R&D in advanced technology areas. Table 4.1 shows the amount of major subsidies and commissions provided to private-sector R&D projects over the period of 1966–1982. Many of these projects took the form of Research Associations, which will be discussed in detail below.

Until 1965, various tax measures were actively used to facilitate the importation of foreign technologies. These tax measures included tariff exemptions for the import of important machinery and reductions in withholding taxes on fees for the use of foreign technology. After 1965, the emphasis shifted to tax measures to promote investment in indigenous R&D. These measures included accelerated depreciation and deferred payments on corporate taxes that depended on the amount of investment in R&D, tax deductions on experimental research expenditures, and special deductions on foreign technology transactions. Table 4.2 shows the cost of tax measures taken to promote investment in R&D.

The Japan Development Bank and the Small Business Finance Corporation provided public funds at interest rates below the market rate to promote commercialization of new technologies developed by R&D. Although these funds were not used for subsidizing the costs of R&D expenses, the presence of these funds reinforced firms' incentives to invest in R&D.

### *Mining and Manufacturing Technology Research Associations*

Government support of R&D projects has often taken the form of subsidization of Research Associations. The Mining and Manufacturing Technology Research Association Law was enacted in 1961 to allow the government to directly subsidize specific research projects jointly set up by private-sector firms. The underlying idea started in the United Kingdom and then spread to Europe. However, unlike the U.K. and European Research Associations which were set up to help small firms, the Japanese Research Associations

**Table 4.1** Japanese Government Support to Private-Sector R&D, 1966–1982 (100 million yen)

| | MINING MFG.[1] | IND. TECH.[2] | BASIC TECH.[3] | PUBLIC TRANSP.[4] | JET ENGINE[5] | COMPUTERS[6] | TECH.[7] | ENERGY[8] | ENERGY[9] |
|---|---|---|---|---|---|---|---|---|---|
| *1966* | 8 | 7 | – | – | – | – | – | – | – |
| *1967* | 9 | 20 | – | – | – | – | 1 | – | – |
| *1968* | 12 | 30 | – | 1 | – | – | 1 | – | – |
| *1969* | 13 | 39 | – | 2 | – | – | 1 | – | – |
| *1970* | 16 | 39 | – | 5 | – | – | 2 | – | – |
| *1971* | 19 | 43 | – | – | – | – | 2 | – | – |
| *1972* | 23 | 40 | – | 2 | – | 52 | 2 | – | – |
| *1973* | 33 | 60 | – | 7 | – | 173 | 3 | – | – |
| *1974* | 42 | 66 | – | 21 | – | 197 | 5 | – | 12 |
| *1975* | 42 | 87 | – | 20 | – | 135 | 5 | – | 19 |
| *1976* | 39 | 121 | – | 2 | – | 149 | 7 | – | 31 |
| *1977* | 33 | 117 | – | 11 | – | 84 | 8 | 1 | 37 |
| *1978* | 28 | 122 | – | 13 | – | 101 | 10 | 5 | 46 |
| *1979* | 28 | 118 | – | 53 | – | 69 | 10 | 5 | 65 |
| *1980* | 27 | 112 | – | 69 | 17 | 57 | 10 | 6 | 32 |
| *1981* | 26 | 116 | 25 | 24 | 47 | 62 | 11 | 6 | 28 |
| *1982* | 22 | 98 | 38 | 18 | 55 | 55 | 10 | 7 | 23 |

Source: Japanese Ministry of Finance, *Handbook on Subsidies* (various issues).

1 Mining and manufacturing technology (subsidies).
2 Large-scale industrial technology (commissioned research).
3 Next generation basic technology (commissioned research).
4 Public transport equipment (subsidies).
5 Jet engine for passenger aircraft (subsidies).
6 Promotion and development of computers (subsidies).
7 Technology improvement (subsidies).
8 Energy technology (subsidies).
9 Energy technology (commissioned research).

have been dominated by large firms. These Research Associations are set up to deal with specific research topics and are dissolved as soon as the objective is met. Large numbers of Research Associations have been established—64 were formed by 1983, and 45 of these are still active. Although the Japanese Research Association system has not always functioned efficiently, it is generally believed to have contributed to greater technological innovation and diffusion.

The economic rationale underlying Research Associations is the existence of externalities. By setting up a joint Research Association for a particular R&D activity involving all firms which would potentially benefit from the R&D activity, the problems of free riders and underinvestment are resolved. Individual firms share the costs and risks of research.

The following conditions are believed to be necessary for a Research Association to be successful:

(1) the selected research topics are of immediate interest to participating firms, but are not of interest to nonparticipating firms;

(2) the research topics are neither purely basic nor purely related to final (market) products; rather they have to do with essential intermediate steps in production processes which would be required regardless of the specific final products participating firms may want to produce;

(3) antimonopoly laws are drafted (or amended) to allow such research organizations; and

(4) these activities are backed up with government subsidies.

There is little cooperation among Japanese firms in R&D for final products, since the success of R&D at the final product level often determines the survival and relative success of a firm in an industry. The Japanese government has encouraged and subsidized joint research activities satisfying conditions (1) through (4) above, though the actual amounts of subsidies have been small compared to firms' research budgets.

Another important aspect of Japanese Research Associations is that they have functioned as a mechanism for technology diffusion. Firms send their researchers to Research Associations for a period of three to four years as part of their job rotation schemes. These researchers report back to their employers regularly, noting technological deficiencies of their firms versus other firms participating in the Research Association. This aspect of Research Associations is quite specific to Japanese firms, where lifetime employment is prevalent and hence researchers have little job mobility.

In contrast, the U.S. joint high-tech research consortium Microelectronics & Computer Technology Corporation (MCC), established in 1982 in Austin, Texas, hires many of its own employees. MCC has 400 researchers, only 36 of whom are on loan from participating firms. There are also other aspects of MCC that sharply distinguish it from Japanese Research Associations. For instance, MCC has many participating firms: 22 shareholding

**Table 4.2** Japanese Special Tax Measures as Private-Sector R&D Subsidies, 1952–1980 (100 million yen)

| | TOTAL | MACHINERY DEPRECIATION[1] | EXPERIMENTAL RESEARCH[2] | FOREIGN TRANSACTIONS[3] | FOREIGN TECHNOLOGY[4] | FOREIGN MACHINERY[5] |
|---|---|---|---|---|---|---|
| *1952* | 10 | – | – | – | – | 10 |
| *1953* | 20 | – | – | – | – | 20 |
| *1954* | 22 | – | – | – | 2 | 20 |
| *1955* | 26 | – | – | – | 6 | 20 |
| *1956* | 31 | – | – | – | 6 | 25 |
| *1957* | 38 | – | – | – | 8 | 30 |
| *1958* | 61 | 16 | – | – | 10 | 35 |
| *1959* | 79 | 15 | – | – | 14 | 50 |
| *1960* | 91 | 15 | – | – | 16 | 60 |
| *1961* | 124 | 25 | – | – | 5 | 94 |
| *1962* | 122 | 25 | – | – | 7 | 90 |
| *1963* | 123 | 25 | – | – | 8 | 90 |
| *1964* | 165 | 63 | – | 7 | 10 | 85 |
| *1965* | 133 | 45 | – | 11 | 8 | 59 |
| *1966* | 39 | – | 13 | 26 | – | – |
| *1967* | 115 | – | 87 | 28 | – | – |
| *1968* | 153 | – | 110 | 43 | – | – |
| *1969* | 162 | – | 122 | 40 | – | – |
| *1970* | 191 | – | 130 | 60 | – | – |
| *1971* | 215 | – | 158 | 57 | – | – |
| *1972* | 128 | – | 88 | 40 | – | – |
| *1973* | 243 | – | 198 | 45 | – | – |
| *1974* | 310 | – | 210 | 100 | – | – |
| *1975* | 330 | – | 210 | 120 | – | – |
| *1976* | 220 | – | 140 | 80 | – | – |
| *1977* | 290 | – | 170 | 120 | – | – |
| *1978* | 250 | – | 150 | 100 | – | – |
| *1979* | 340 | – | 210 | 130 | – | – |
| *1980* | 380 | – | 240 | 140 | – | – |

SOURCE: Japanese Tax System Research Council.

1 Accelerated depreciation for equipment used for experimental research and commercialization of new technology.
2 Special tax deductions for equipment used for experimental research.
3 Special tax deductions for foreign transactions including R&D activities.
4 Reductions in withholding taxes on payments to foreign owners of important technology.
5 Tariff exemptions for importing important foreign machinery.

firms and 51 associate members. MCC aims at commercializing new technologies: it has spun off two for-profit ventures in which it has an equity stake. MCC determines its own research and management strategies to a large extent; it dropped some research projects because they did not meet certain MCC timetable requirements. Also, the U.S. government seems to play little role in managing MCC. These differences may reflect basic differences in economic policies and the relationship between the private and government sectors in the United States versus Japan. For example, MCC may have opted to have many participating firms because the U.S. government antitrust policies prohibit having a few large oligopolistic firms as the equity holders.

The U.S. National Cooperative Research Act (NCRA) enacted in 1984 protects research consortia registered under this act from treble damages (but not from actual costs) in the antitrust lawsuits against them. MCC subsequently registered under this act in 1986. No research consortia registered under this act have been the subject of antitrust lawsuits to date. (Recall that the antitrust concerns of Japanese firms participating in Research Associations are minimal because Research Associations are explicitly permitted under the Mining and Manufacturing Technology Research Association Law and are strongly supported by MITI.)

Two Japanese Research Associations that are generally considered to have been successful are VLSI Research Association and Optics System Research Association. Established in 1976 by five semiconductor manufacturers, VLSI Research Association's purpose was to jointly develop the manufacturing technology for very large scale integrated circuits (one megabit chips). IBM was believed to be developing a similar technology. The time horizon was four years. The basic research, which constituted 20% of the project, was jointly conducted by about 100 researchers from the five semiconductor firms and the Electrotechnical Laboratory of the Agency of Industrial Science and Technology. The remaining 80% of the research was conducted by individual firms. This Research Association terminated its research activities in 1979 (as planned), although an office for administering the revenues from the resulting (some 1,000) patents was kept open until the end of 1987, by which time all the subsidies from the government had been paid back. After this, the patents reverted to the companies to which the inventions belonged.

Optics Application System Research Association was established jointly by the manufacturers of optical fibre and the MITI Industrial Technology Laboratory in 1979. The mission of this Research Association was to develop control mechanisms for fibre optics. It did this, and succeeded in developing infra-red fibre and image fibre as well. It was dissolved in 1985, by which time the total government subsidy had amounted to 15.7 billion yen (approximately US$110 million).

### *Detailed Statistics on Research and Development Activity by Industry*

Japanese firms' expenditures on R&D in 1991 amounted to 9,743 billion yen, a nominal increase of 50% from the 1987 level. About 76% of these expenditures were made by large firms capitalized at 10 billion yen or more, while 14% of the total private R&D expenditures came from firms with capitalizations of 1 to 10 billion yen (Table 4.3). Thus about 90% of the private-sector R&D expenditures in Japan are made by large corporations.

It is also the case that more than 90% of the total private R&D expenditures are made by manufacturing firms. In particular, in 1991, electrical machinery, chemicals, and transportation machinery firms accounted for 35% (3,383 billion yen), 16% (1,548 billion yen) and 15% (1,509 billion yen), respectively, of the total private R&D expenditures. R&D expenditures-to-sales ratios increased, on average, from 2.72% in 1989 to 2.78% in 1991, with larger firms achieving higher increases: from 1.77% in 1989 to 1.76% in 1991 for firms with 1–299 employees; from 1.59% to 1.72% for firms in the size range of 300–999 employees; from 2.02% to 1.97% for firms with 1,000–2,999 employees; from 2.68% to 2.70% for firms with 3,000–9,000 employees; and from 3.86% to 3.96% for firms with 10,000+ employees. For manufacturing industries, pharmaceuticals has the highest R&D expenditures-to-sales ratio (7.50% in 1989, 8.66% in 1991), followed by communication and electronics equipment (6.10%, 6.63%), electrical tools and equipment (5.47%, 5.66%), synthetic fibre (4.84%, 5.24%), automobiles (3.48%, 3.33%) and ceramics (2.75%, 3.00%).

The breakdown of R&D expenditures by project and by industry is given in Table 4.3. It is evident that most of the private-sector R&D budget is spent on new product development (71.1%). Applied basic research and basic research receive 22.2% and 6.8% of the budget, respectively, though there are large differences by industry. An extreme example is the pharma-

**Table 4.3** Japanese R&D Expenditures and Researches by Industry, 1991

| Industry | Expenditure (billion yen) | TYPE OF RESEARCH (%) Basic | Applied | Product Development | No. of Researchers[1] |
|---|---|---|---|---|---|
| All | 9,743 | 6.8 | 22.2 | 71.1 | 340,809 |
| Capitalization (million yen): | | | | | |
| 5–10 | 12 | 4.1 | 7.2 | 88.7 | 917 |
| 10–100 | 381 | 2.9 | 19.1 | 78.0 | 22,940 |
| 100–1,000 | 558 | 4.7 | 20.1 | 75.2 | 32,777 |
| 1,000–10,000 | 1,392 | 5.0 | 20.7 | 74.3 | 63,455 |
| 10,000+ | 7,373 | 7.4 | 22.8 | 69.8 | 220,298 |
| Public Corporations | 27 | 20.7 | 29.0 | 53.3 | 422 |
| Agriculture/Forestry/Fishing | 5 | 9.5 | 26.9 | 63.5 | 254 |
| Mining | 40 | 19.5 | 34.6 | 45.9 | 965 |
| Construction | 205 | 5.8 | 23.7 | 70.4 | 7,667 |
| Manufacturing | 9,195 | 6.8 | 21.7 | 71.5 | 325,838 |
| Food | 206 | 10.6 | 32.7 | 56.7 | 10,129 |
| Textiles | 92 | 9.5 | 33.4 | 57.1 | 4,300 |
| Pulp/Paper | 52 | 8.5 | 33.2 | 58.2 | 2,290 |
| Printing/Publishing | 39 | 5.2 | 35.2 | 59.6 | 1,380 |
| Chemicals | 1,547 | 14.0 | 29.2 | 56.8 | 55,592 |
| Industrial Chemicals/Synthetic Fibre | 612 | 9.0 | 33.3 | 57.8 | 21,371 |
| Oils and Prints | 154 | 7.8 | 34.1 | 58.1 | 8,218 |
| Pharmaceuticals | 590 | 22.0 | 27.4 | 50.6 | 16,892 |
| Other | 191 | 10.0 | 18.0 | 71.9 | 9,111 |
| Petro/Coal Products | 89 | 12.4 | 23.7 | 63.9 | 2,075 |
| Plastics | 126 | 3.9 | 22.9 | 73.2 | 4,795 |
| Rubber | 130 | 3.4 | 15.2 | 81.4 | 4,957 |
| Ceramics | 260 | 8.2 | 24.0 | 67.8 | 8,840 |
| Iron/Steel | 360 | 14.8 | 18.6 | 66.6 | 6,429 |
| Non-ferrous Metals | 149 | 6.6 | 25.6 | 67.8 | 5,070 |
| Fabricated Metal Products | 137 | 2.4 | 18.1 | 79.4 | 6,432 |
| General Machinery | 674 | 4.9 | 25.4 | 69.7 | 29,015 |
| Electrical Machinery | 3,383 | 4.3 | 20.2 | 75.6 | 129,310 |
| Electr. Tools/Equip. | 1,010 | 4.5 | 19.5 | 76.0 | 35,350 |
| Communication/Electronic Products | 2,373 | 4.2 | 20.4 | 75.4 | 93,960 |
| Transp. Machinery | 1,509 | 4.3 | 13.2 | 82.4 | 33,435 |
| Auto | 1,286 | 4.1 | 11.2 | 84.7 | 27,932 |
| Other | 222 | 5.6 | 24.9 | 69.5 | 5,503 |
| Precision Instruments | 314 | 4.4 | 23.0 | 72.5 | 14,841 |
| Other Manufacturing | 128 | 3.2 | 22.1 | 74.6 | 6,948 |
| Utilities/Transp./Communication | 297 | 6.0 | 33.2 | 60.8 | 6,085 |

SOURCE: Japanese Science and Technology Agency, *Indicators of Science and Technology* (1993).

1 Number of full-time researchers (as of April 1, 1992); does not include research assistants, technicians or clerical staff.

**Table 4.4** Japanese Technology Trade, 1971–1991 (Billion yen)

| | EXPORTS (RECEIPTS) | IMPORTS (PAYMENTS) | RECEIPTS/ PAYMENTS |
|---|---|---|---|
| | *All Cases* | | |
| *1971* | 27 | 134 | .20 |
| *1979* | 133 | 241 | .55 |
| *1984* | 277 | 281 | .99 |
| *1985* | 234 | 293 | .80 |
| *1986* | 224 | 260 | .86 |
| *1987* | 216 | 283 | .76 |
| *1988* | 246 | 312 | .79 |
| *1989* | 329 | 330 | 1.00 |
| *1990* | 339 | 371 | .91 |
| *1991* | 370 | 395 | .94 |
| | *New Cases* | | |
| *1971* | 11 | 16 | .71 |
| *1979* | 52 | 27 | 1.94 |
| *1984* | 91 | 32 | 2.85 |
| *1985* | 73 | 33 | 2.20 |
| *1986* | 52 | 34 | 1.54 |
| *1987* | 45 | 56 | .80 |
| *1988* | 47 | 55 | .87 |
| *1989* | 67 | 48 | 1.38 |
| *1990* | 58 | 73 | .80 |
| *1991* | 70 | 54 | 1.31 |

SOURCE: Japanese Science and Technology Agency, *Indicators of Science and Technology* (1993).

ceutical industry which spent close to half of its R&D budget on basic and applied basic research. Finally the numbers of researchers by industry are given in the last column of Table 4.3.

*Technology Trade*

The ratio between the payments received for technology exports and the payments for technology imports has increased from 0.20 in 1971 to close to one by 1989 (Table 4.4).

**Table 4.5** Japanese Technology Trade by Industry, 1991

| | EXPORTS | | IMPORTS | |
|---|---|---|---|---|
| Industry | Receipts per Item[1] | Total Receipts[2] | Payments per Item[1] | Total Payments[2] |
| All | 46 | 370 | 53 | 395 |
| Agriculture/Forestry/Fishery | 10 | 0.05 | 3 | 0.01 |
| Mining | 45 | 1 | 58 | 0.7 |
| Construction | 45 | 21 | 6 | 0.7 |
| Manufacturing | 46 | 348 | 54 | 393 |
| Food | 32 | 9 | 89 | 9 |
| Textiles | 26 | 4 | 67 | 6 |
| Pulp/Paper | 34 | 1 | 23 | 0.4 |
| Printing/Publishing | 12 | 0.4 | 22 | 2 |
| Chemicals | 40 | 59 | 60 | 67 |
| Ind. Chemicals/Synthetic Fibre | 39 | 25 | 50 | 25 |
| Oils and Prints | 11 | 3 | 17 | 5 |
| Pharmaceuticals | 71 | 28 | 108 | 29 |
| Other | 20 | 2 | 165 | 8 |
| Petro./Coal Products | 8 | 0.2 | 33 | 4 |
| Plastics | 14 | 2 | 23 | 2 |
| Rubber | 41 | 5 | 42 | 4 |
| Ceramics | 45 | 11 | 30 | 5 |
| Iron/Steel | 23 | 10 | 19 | 6 |
| Non-ferrous Metals | 16 | 4 | 51 | 10 |
| Fabricated Metal Products | 12 | 3 | 15 | 2 |
| General Machinery | 18 | 15 | 31 | 33 |
| Electrical Machinery | 57 | 106 | 73 | 161 |
| Electrical Tools/Equipment | 46 | 32 | 78 | 32 |
| Communication/Electronic Products | 64 | 73 | 72 | 129 |
| Transportation Machinery | 91 | 102 | 69 | 56 |
| Auto | 115 | 99 | 33 | 8 |
| Other | 10 | 3 | 85 | 48 |
| Precision | 64 | 12 | 31 | 13 |
| Other Manufacturing | 34 | 4 | 53 | 11 |
| Utilities/Transp./Communication | 12 | 0.3 | 5 | 0.05 |

SOURCE: Japanese Science and Technology Agency, *Indicators of Science and Technology* (1993).

1 Receipts and payments per item in million yen.
2 Total receipts and payments in billion yen.

The breakdown of technology trade by industry for 1991 is given in Table 4.5. The automobile and steel industries have high receipts/payments ratios while general machinery, electrical machinery, and other transport machinery (including airplanes) incurred deficits in technology trade.

The breakdown of technology trade by country is given in Table 4.6. In 1989, Japan incurred deficits in technology of about 100 and 50 billion yen with the U.S. and Europe, respectively. These deficits were offset, however, by surpluses from Asia, West Asia, South America, Africa, and Oceania of 129.0, 2.0, 4.6, 6.8 and 6.5 billions of yen, respectively. This situation did not change appreciably in 1991 except that Japan's deficit with the U.S. increased to 150 billion yen.

In 1991, Japan paid 1.2 billion yen to Canada in technology trade while Canada paid Japan 1.9 billion yen. These figures are quite small compared to the figures for the U.S.-Japan, Asia-Japan and Europe-Japan technology trade. The numbers of patents granted by Japan (and other industrialized countries) to Canadian nationals are also considerably below one tenth of those granted to U.S. nationals (see Table 4.7). This may be in part because a significant fraction of private-sector R&D investment in Canada is funded by U.S. firms which own the intellectual property rights for the results of their R&D investments. U.S. firms typically market their technologies overseas directly, regardless of the country of origin of such technologies.

### *Patents and Intellectual Property Rights in Japan*

Canada's Patent Act enacted in October 1989 replaced the old first-to-invent system with the first-to-file system. Patent applications are made public 18 months after they are filed. These rules are consistent with the patent laws of most countries including Japan, but not the U.S. which still uses the first-to-invent system. Despite this formal similarity between the patent laws of Canada and Japan, the Japanese patent procedure emphasizes the rapid and efficient dissemination and diffusion of technology while the Canadian and European systems (and also the U.S. system) emphasize protection and the rewarding of individual inventors. In Japan, MITI is authorized by law to compel a patent holder to cross-license a technology of national importance. (See External Affairs and International Trade Canada, 1991, for a practical comparison of Canadian and Japanese patent law procedures and coverage.)

**Table 4.6** Japanese Technology Trade by Country, 1979–1991 (Million Yen)

| | TOTAL | | ASIA | | WEST ASIA | | NORTH AMERICA | |
|---|---|---|---|---|---|---|---|---|
| | Receipt | Payment | Receipt | Payment | Receipt | Payment | Receipt | Payment |
| *1979* | 133,145 | 240,984 | 54,833 | 2,793 | 9,936 | x[a] | 23,021 | 156,073 |
| *1980* | 159,612 | 239,529 | 54,218 | 206 | 24,413 | – | 29,501 | 156,863 |
| *1981* | 175,106 | 259,632 | 67,904 | 890 | 10,157 | – | 38,326 | 173,901 |
| *1982* | 184,921 | 282,613 | 70,767 | 654 | 5,697 | – | 40,819 | 188,561 |
| *1983* | 240,887 | 297,280 | 101,920 | 180 | 17,300 | – | 60,034 | 194,000 |
| *1984* | 277,512 | 281,447 | 112,516 | 298 | 30,783 | x | 71,915 | 193,989 |
| *1985* | 234,220 | 293,173 | 87,523 | 864 | 14,113 | x | 58,740 | 210,279 |
| *1986* | 224,078 | 260,577 | 86,481 | 334 | 10,485 | x | 62,288 | 174,551 |
| *1987* | 215,575 | 283,245 | 86,435 | 90 | 1,588 | x | 72,502 | 179,251 |
| *1988* | 246,255 | 312,195 | 101,412 | 185 | 2,277 | – | 76,976 | 198,127 |
| *1989* | 329,348 | 329,925 | 128,862 | 257 | 2,360 | 63 | 115,136 | 210,741 |
| *1990* | 339,352 | 371,907 | 153,317 | – | 1,959 | – | 108,120 | 257,871 |
| *1991* | 370,552 | 394,661 | 170,546 | – | 3,669 | – | 117,147 | 275,168 |

SOURCE: Japanese Science and Technology Agency, *Indicators of Science and Technology* (1991, 1993).

[a] x means publication of figures is not permitted because of too few applicable cases.
[b] – means data are not yet available.

In theory, a patent system must accommodate both the dissemination aspect of new knowledge and incentives for R&D investments. In practice, though, implementation of patent laws may largely reflect the societal attitudes towards intellectual property rights and the historical stages of economic development in different countries. Ordover (1991) argues, for example, that those aspects of the Japanese patent system which emphasize the rapid dissemination of new knowledge are less well-designed to meet the intellectual property protection requirements of a technological leader, which Japan has become, as opposed to a technological borrower. He also argues, however, that the current U.S. policy stance, which advocates very strong intellectual property rights, may have gone too far in protecting the interests of the inventor. Japan has been implementing new procedures for protecting patents and other intellectual property rights. It will be interesting to observe how Japan's changed status as a generator of new industrial knowledge, and accompanying changes in social attitudes towards individ-

| SOUTH AMERICA | | EUROPE | | AFRICA | | OCEANIA | |
|---|---|---|---|---|---|---|---|
| Receipt | Payment | Receipt | Payment | Receipt | Payment | Receipt | Payment |
| 7,592 | –[b] | 22,197 | 80,963 | 12,825 | x | 2,741 | 1,124 |
| 10,842 | x | 29,046 | 82,127 | 8,372 | x | 3,220 | 300 |
| 11,770 | x | 32,149 | 84,425 | 9,561 | x | 5,239 | 309 |
| 10,803 | x | 38,963 | 92,662 | 12,356 | 331 | 5,515 | 402 |
| 10,068 | x | 37,053 | 84,499 | 9,181 | x | 5,332 | 357 |
| 3,654 | 25 | 40,707 | 86,698 | 12,845 | 35 | 5,091 | 282 |
| 8,740 | x | 45,461 | 81,567 | 6,623 | x | 13,021 | 345 |
| 5,161 | x | 43,598 | 85,137 | 9,479 | x | 6,586 | 389 |
| 4,460 | x | 40,261 | 103,417 | 5,037 | x | 5,292 | 341 |
| 4,443 | x | 49,262 | 113,602 | 5,999 | – | 5,886 | 269 |
| 4,580 | x | 65,067 | 118,163 | 6,817 | – | 6,526 | 700 |
| 2,949 | x | 61,466 | 112,762 | – | – | 46 | – |
| 3,065 | x | 67,091 | 118,613 | – | – | 47 | – |

ual rights, will affect Japan's implementation of patent and other intellectual property rights protection laws.

## Promoting Technical Progress Versus Scale Economies

In promoting emerging technology-based industries, the Japanese government has paid attention to technology diffusion, scale economies in production, and technical progress. It is helpful to analyze technology policies from these three perspectives. The policies adopted for promising infant industries are designed to promote the diffusion of technology among a number of potentially competing firms. Such policies have traditionally included facilitating import of foreign technologies and direct research subsidies to these firms. Often these technology diffusion policies have been supplemented and/or followed by policies to promote economies of scale in production. Examples include

**Table 4.7** Number of Patents by Nationality of Inventor, 1989

| | COUNTRY IN WHICH PATENTS WERE GRANTED | | | | | | | | |
|---|---|---|---|---|---|---|---|---|---|
| Country of Inventor | Japan | U.S. | Germany | France | U.K. | Canada | Switzerland | Netherlands | Foreign/ Domestic[b] |
| Japan | 54,743 | 20,168 | 6,888 | 4,294 | 5,440 | 2,084 | 1,060 | 1,532 | .93 |
| U.S. | 3,799 | 50,185 | 7,135 | 6,118 | 6,859 | 8,056 | 2,567 | 3,525 | 1.36 |
| Germany | 1,813 | 8,303 | 16,904 | 6,832 | 6,179 | 1,311 | 4,408 | 3,932 | 3.38 |
| France | 654 | 3,140 | 2,752 | 8,301 | 2,422 | 928 | 1,467 | 1,753 | 2.91 |
| U.K. | 432 | 3,100 | 1,637 | 1,471 | 4,234 | 867 | 788 | 1,026 | 4.05 |
| Canada | 74 | 1,959 | 204 | 169 | 226 | 1,069 | 94 | 121 | 3.55 |
| Switzerland | 461 | 1,363 | 66 | 1,291 | 1,214 | 373 | 2,916 | 758 | 4.49 |
| Netherlands | 342 | 1,060 | 1,140 | 940 | 879 | 279 | 472 | 842 | 10.68 |
| % Foreign[a] | 13 | 47 | 60 | 75 | 86 | 93 | 82 | 96 | |

SOURCE: Japanese Science and Technology Agency, *Indicators of Science and Technology.*

[a] Fraction (%) of total patents granted to foreign nationals including patents granted to inventors in countries not listed in this table.

[b] The ratio between the numbers of patents granted in foreign and home countries; foreign countries include countries not listed in this table.

policies to protect domestic firms from foreign competition, loans for investments in production facilities, and favourable tax provisions for capital investments. These policies have also included domestic purchase practices for government and subsidized loans to finance the purchase of domestic products by private sector firms. The importance of scale economies in lowering the marginal cost of production and promoting the accumulation of production skills in workers and managers (through learning by doing) cannot be overstated. (Significant scale economies were found in Japanese manufacturing industries by Yoshioka, Nakajima and Nakamura, 1993).

Scale economies, however, are not sufficient to guarantee the long run survival of firms in a developing industry. It is technical progress that enables firms to enjoy long-run productivity gains. Japanese government subsidies for developing new technologies are intended to spur long-run technical progress. In providing these subsidies, considerable attention has been paid to the needs of the potential consumers or users (often firms); that is, to the common good dimensions of technical progress.

Consider the mainframe computer industry. Because of its strategic importance, many countries formulated government policies to encourage development of a domestic computer industry. Virtually all of the important developments in the United States in computer technology during the period of 1945–1960 can be traced back to U.S. government-sponsored research projects. The British government started the Advanced Computer Technology Project in 1963. France started project Calcul in 1966, and West Germany's first promotion plan for the computer industry started in 1967. Notice that these policy initiatives got under way after the U.S. computer manufacturers had established a dominant global presence. (The largest French computer manufacturer, Machines Bull, was taken over in 1964 by General Electric when Bull could not survive the heavy burden of rental financing.)

In Japan, various early computers had already been developed during the 1952–1955 period by government research agencies and many universities. In particular, the computer technology developments at the Japanese Agency of Industrial Science and Technology were made available to all domestic firms. As technology diffusion began during the period 1957–1959, NEC, Hitachi, Fujitsu and Toshiba announced production of small-sized computers. The importation of U.S. computers into Japan also started in this period.

The Law on Temporary Measures for Promoting the Electronics Industry became effective in 1957 and was applied to computer hardware developments, although the primary aim of this law was the promotion of the domestic household appliances industries. Under the auspices of MITI, this law allowed computer manufacturers to receive R&D subsidies as well as low-interest financing from the Japan Development Bank (JDB). The amounts of financing made available in this way were small compared to company financing needs. The real importance of this financial aid lay in signalling that MITI considered the industry to have good growth potential. These Japanese government financing measures notwithstanding, by 1960 U.S. manufacturers' dominance in the Japanese market was evident (Table 4.8). In response to this, seven domestic manufacturers established the Japan Electronic Computer Company (JECC), a company set up to provide financing for domestic computer purchases.

JECC borrowed heavily from the Japan Development Bank (JDB) (523.5

billion yen by 1982) as well as from other major financial institutions. The fate of the Japanese computer manufacturers was uncertain and this had discouraged potential customers from buying Japanese computers. (Purchasers of mainframe computers were concerned about long-term maintenance arrangements and continuing software development.) The JDB financing to JECC was viewed by potential customers as government backing of the domestic industry. The resulting rise in confidence in the long run survival of the domestic computer firms generated a substantial demand for domestic computers. Preferential government procurement of domestic computers also added to this demand. Increased demand and tax incentives for capacity expansion resulted in substantial gains in scale economies for the domestic industry as a whole. The role of JECC declined significantly by around 1970 when domestic manufacturers became more competitive. Hitachi, for example, switched to its own rental arrangements with customers by the late 1970s.

MITI's first computer research project was initiated in 1961 under the Mining and Manufacturing R&D Association Law. An Electronic Computer R&D Association was established in 1962 by NEC, Fujitsu and Oki Electric for the purpose of developing large-scale computers (the Fontac project). This project received 350 million yen in government subsidies during the 1962–1964 period. Other government-sponsored research projects were begun thereafter, including the following which were designated as "large scale projects":

(1) Development of a super high performance computer (1966–1971, 10 billion yen).
(2) Development of pattern information processing (1971–1980, 22 billion yen).
(3) Development of an optimal measurement and control system (1979–1987, 18 billion yen).
(4) Development of a high speed computer system for science and technological uses (1981–1989, 23 billion yen).

The primary objective of these and other research projects was to foster long-run technical progress in the computer industry. The costs of this sort of effort can be high, and hard to fully tally. They include direct subsidies, tax exemptions, and productivity losses resulting from the use of inferior products due to protectionism.

**Table 4.8** Japanese Market for Mainframe Computers, 1957–1982

| | NEWLY PURCHASED UNITS | | | TOTAL UNITS IN OPERATION | | |
|---|---|---|---|---|---|---|
| | Number of Units | Total Value (billion yen) | Proportion of Foreign Makers' Share of Total Value (%) | Number of Units | Total Value (billion yen) | Proportion of Foreign Makers' Share of Total Value (%) |
| *1957* | 3 | 0.15 | 21.9 | – | – | – |
| *1958* | 8 | 1.01 | 92.9 | – | – | – |
| *1959* | 26 | 2.4 | 78.5 | – | – | – |
| *1960* | 66 | 6.7 | 72.7 | – | – | – |
| *1961* | 119 | 13.3 | 81.7 | – | – | – |
| *1962* | 228 | 22.1 | 66.8 | – | – | – |
| *1963* | 485 | 43.3 | 70.3 | – | – | – |
| *1964* | 562 | 41.6 | 57.2 | – | – | – |
| *1965* | 636 | 51.5 | 47.8 | 1,455 | 130.0 | 68.1 |
| *1966* | 844 | 66.8 | 46.4 | 1,937 | 174.2 | 63.1 |
| *1967* | 1,162 | 108.6 | 52.8 | 2,606 | 224.8 | 54.9 |
| *1968* | 1,568 | 161.4 | 43.5 | 3,546 | 301.2 | 52.0 |
| 1969 | 2,135 | 212.4 | 42.5 | 4,869 | 441.2 | 48.6 |
| *1970* | 3,287 | 330.9 | 40.4 | 6,718 | 617.2 | 44.7 |
| *1971* | 4,244 | 350.1 | 41.2 | 9,482 | 891.2 | 46.7 |
| *1972* | 5,973 | 418.7 | 47.0 | 12,809 | 1,136.2 | 45.2 |
| *1973* | 7,978 | 528.3 | 48.6 | 17,255 | 1,373.3 | 46.5 |
| *1974* | 8,535 | 640.8 | 48.4 | 23,443 | 1,601.9 | 45.7 |
| *1975* | 6,903 | 614.0 | 44.2 | 30,095 | 1,946.4 | 44.8 |
| *1976* | 7,533 | 731.5 | 43.3 | 35,305 | 2,258.3 | 43.1 |
| *1977* | 9,591 | 790.0 | – | 40,719 | 2,532.6 | 42.9 |
| *1978* | 13,043 | 798.3 | – | 48,132 | 2,820.7 | – |
| *1979* | 15,294 | 834.3 | – | 58,944 | 3,218.3 | – |
| *1980* | 18,373 | 970.3 | – | 72,108 | 3,623.9 | – |
| *1981* | 20,439 | 1,009.8 | – | 88,223 | 4,164.7 | – |
| *1982* | – | – | – | 106,344 | 4,716.4 | – |

SOURCE: Japan Electronic Computer Company, *Reports* (various years).

The Japanese experience with its computer industry shows that, after the initial government protection and subsidies, in the 1960s and 1970s competition among domestic firms (as well as between domestic and U.S. firms) helped domestic firms to achieve scale economies and technical progress. It also appears important, at least in the case of the Japanese computer industry, that the government showed its determination to develop the industry over the long run. Japanese government funding directed towards the industry was not large. However, it reassured customers about the long-run survival of the Japanese computer companies and also made it possible for these firms to raise or borrow funds.

## Japanese Industrial and Technology Policy—An Assessment

It is generally recognized that Japanese government industrial policies since the mid 1960s have become much less "interventionist" and more consistent with market forces and market mechanisms. This reflects a growing belief in Japan that successful industrial and technology policies must be based on and consistent with accurate predictions of long-term future market movements and Japan's long-term comparative advantage.

However, even policies designed to work in accord with market mechanisms do not always succeed. The technology policy adopted for the hardware manufacturing segment of the information industries was a success, while the policy adopted for computer software development was ineffective. This is despite the fact that MITI was undeniably correct in identifying software development as an important market area. The failure of the MITI Research Association approach in this area is particularly serious since the Japanese computer industry has invested relatively little in software development. There is some concern that Fujitsu and Hitachi, both of which have often opted for IBM compatible mainframes and pay significant amounts of user fees to IBM for using its software, will not be able to develop operating systems and other software that will be competitive in the long run with what IBM can offer.

Another industry which has not achieved international competitiveness despite significant amounts of public investment and policy attention is the Japanese chemical industry. Perhaps MITI-type industrial promotional policies are ineffective for an industry where major breakthroughs are found through basic research and large-scale experiments rather than by the accumulation of know-how from production experiences. There is general agreement that Japanese chemical firms are not yet in the same league with leading global competitors such as Dupont and Bayer in terms of original technological developments. For the same reasons, the prospects for a number of the Research Associations established in the biotechnology field may also be poor.

Yet there is no question that government policy accelerated technology diffusion, scale economies and technical progress in certain sectors of the economy such as the automobile and computer industries. This is interesting given that the actual amounts of government funds spent on Japanese R&D projects appear relatively modest by, for instance, the Canadian standards (McFetridge, 1985a, 1985b). Furthermore, the growth in these and other manufacturing industries made it easier to rapidly reabsorb resources being released from declining industries. Industrial adjustment policies helped to accelerate this process.

There has been considerable policy debate regarding the recent role of industrial adjustment subsidies to declining or weak industries. Many believe that industrial adjustment policies can only be effective when the growth in some sectors is rapid enough to facilitate absorption of resources from declining industries.

Our tentative conclusions with respect to Japanese industrial policy initiatives are summarized as follows.

(1) Policies designed to raise general standards in the quality of goods, services and information (all of which share public goods properties) were generally successful. Policy emphasis since the early 1970s has been to encourage long-term economic growth by investments in education, savings and capital investment, among other things. This is in contrast to policies emphasizing income redistribution based on, for example, transfer payments (Scott, 1985).

(2) As part of its policy to increase the general level of productivity, the Japanese government was instrumental in establishing the Japan Productivity Centre (JPC) in 1955 as a nonprofit, nongovernmental organization funded by firms, labour and the government, among other supporters. The three guiding principles of JPC are: (i) improvement in productivity will increase employment in the long run but, during the transition period before the employment effects of improved productivity become apparent, the government and workers must cooperate to provide suitable measures such as the transferring of surplus workers to areas where needed so as to prevent unemployment; (ii) labour and management must cooperate in discussing, studying and adopting measures to increase productivity; and (iii) the fruits of improved productivity, in correspondence with the conditions of the national economy, must be distributed fairly among management,

labour and the consumer. For decades, public lectures, consulting and other means have been used by the JPC headquarters and its branches all over Japan (and by other organizations such as the Japan Union of Scientists and Engineers) to disseminate up-to-date information to improve many aspects of the management of production activities, including quality control.

(3) Interventions at the industry level were often successful. Interventions at the firm level were not. Industrial policy seems most effective when government deals with industries while letting the marketplace select winning (and losing) firms within industries.

(4) The initiatives of independent firms as well as various bank-based corporate groups have often provided (excess) competition in a promising industry at the expense of required scale economies, given the size of the domestic market. In the case of industries thought to have outstanding growth potential, each bank-based group has sometimes wanted to have some presence. This potential for excess competition and Japanese firms' long-term employment practices are factors which have worked against successful government intervention at the firm level.

(5) The presence of corporate groups has been helpful in shifting excess labour from declining industries to growing ones.

(6) Many independent companies, like Sony and Honda, succeeded without any direct aid from Japanese industrial policies. However, some of these companies may have benefitted indirectly from a greater diffusion of technology, greater availability of qualified personnel and foreign exchange, and better quality intermediate materials, all of which are attributable to government industrial policies.

(7) Now that many Japanese firms in technology-based industries are large, have access to direct financing from global sources and can act independently of government support, more instances than in the past of divergences between the interests of private firms and what the Japanese government considers to be the national interest can be expected. For example, the purchases by Sony and Matsushita, respectively, of Columbia Pictures and MCA did not please the Japanese government because of the continuing criticism in the United States of Japanese takeovers of U.S. corporations and real estate. It made

sense, however, from a private business perspective for Sony and Matsushita, two global producers of electronic hardware products, to integrate the software end of the business represented by Columbia Pictures and MCA within their world-wide operations. The divergence in interests between large multinational firms and government policies is neither new nor unique to Japan. Many U.S. firms established offshore production facilities during the 1960s and 1970s, against the U.S. government's desire to keep jobs inside the U.S. and/or save foreign exchange (e.g., Ford Motor Company's massive foreign direct investment in the U.K. against President John F. Kennedy's policy).

(8) The Japanese government's present policy regarding Japanese multinational firms, and the possible hollowing out of employment in particular, seems to be a passive one which relies on the notion that excess labour made available will be absorbed in emerging high value-added domestic industries. The present policy also presumes that Japanese multinationals will not shift their production facilities overseas to the extent that U.S. multinationals have done. One reason for the relatively optimistic view about the possible adverse effects of hollowing out is that the Japanese government, in fact, expects some types of labour shortages in the near future (Japan Economic Planning Agency, 1993).

5

# Foreign Trade and Direct Investment

## Introduction

The composition of goods exported to and from Japan has changed considerably in the last two decades. For example, Japanese statistics show that automobiles and auto parts exported from Japan to the U.S. and to Canada increased from US$10.1 and 0.6 billion, respectively, in 1980 to US$23.6 and 2.9 billion in 1991. And office equipment exported from Japan to the U.S. and to Germany increased from US$0.8 and 0.2 billion, respectively, in 1980 to US$10.5 and 2.4 billion in 1991. Increases in exports of automobiles and office equipment were achieved despite an appreciation of the Japanese currency by more than 100% during this period. During the same period steel products exported from Japan to the U.S. and Canada declined from US$2.7 and 0.25 billion, respectively, to US$2.1 and 0.16 billion. Also during the same period Japanese imports of oil declined from US$52.8 to 30.2 billion, imports of textile and steel products increased from US$3.2 and 0.9, respectively, to US$13.7 and 5.5 billion, and office equipment imported from the U.S. increased from US$0.7 to 3.4 billion.

Note that the Japanese government export figures are based on Free-On-Board (FOB) prices including the cost of goods and delivery onto a carrier. Their import figures are based on Cost-Insurance-Freight (CIF) prices including the costs of goods, insurance and freight. This practice of measuring trade figures differs from Canada's, resulting in some discrepancies in the official trade statistics. Another factor which contributes to statistical discrepancies is the substantial amount of goods traded between Canada and Japan which go through U.S. ports (*Globe and Mail*, November 15, 1993).

These changing patterns of Japan's foreign trade reflect shifts in Japan's comparative advantage. These shifts have taken place over time in response to changing labour supply, wage rates and other economic conditions in Japan. To the extent that government policies influence firms' development of stocks of skills (or human capital) in targeted industries and product areas, comparative advantage may be created.

Before summarizing Japan's foreign trade experience, shifts in Japan's comparative advantage will be reviewed. How Japanese firm behaviour and industrial and trade policy may have caused these shifts to occur, and may have contributed to Japan's increased foreign direct investment also will be discussed in this chapter.

One measure of a country's comparative advantage is the ratio between its share in world exports by a particular commodity category and its share in total world merchandise exports. An industry with a value of this comparative advantage measure that is greater than one (less than one) is considered to have a comparative advantage (comparative disadvantage) in the world market. Using this revealed comparative advantage measure, Balassa and Noland (1988), have examined the shifts in Japan's comparative advantage over the period 1967–1986. In 1967, Japan had a comparative advantage in unskilled labour-intensive commodities (e.g., textiles, apparel, rubber and plastic products, leather products, stone, clay and glass products) as well as certain skill-intensive or human capital-intensive products (e.g., general and electrical machinery, transportation equipment, instruments and related products). Japan had a comparative disadvantage in food, beverages, tobacco, agricultural raw materials and non-oil mineral products. It also had a comparative disadvantage, although to a lesser extent, in lumber and wood products, and furniture. By 1983, Japan had gained a substantial comparative advantage in skill-intensive products, with the largest gain in general machinery. During the same period it lost its comparative advantage in the apparel, leather products and unskilled labour-intensive categories. Its comparative disadvantage in natural resource-intensive products (food, beverages, tobacco, agricultural raw materials, lumber and wood products, furniture) increased further.

It is particularly interesting to compare the U.S. with Japan in terms of revealed comparative advantage in high-technology products. (High-technology products are defined in the U.S. to be those goods whose output value at production contains at least 3.5% worth of R&D expenditure.) In 1983, the U.S. had a comparative advantage in the following high-technology products: aircraft, aircraft engines, office machinery, steam engines and turbines. (In 1963 the U.S. had a comparative advantage only in aircraft.) At the same time, Japan had a comparative advantage in photographic equipment and supplies, scientific instruments, calculating and accounting machines, platework and boilers, and medical instruments. During the period of 1967–1983, the U.S. increased its comparative advantage in seven out of 19 high-technology product categories (aircraft, optical instruments, agricultural chemicals, synthetic fibres, cellulose fibres, steam engines, turbines), while Japan increased its comparative advantage in the remaining 12 high-technology product categories.

The pattern of comparative advantage for the U.S. and Japan shows that firms in these two countries have traditionally divided the high-technology area into respective territories. Many explanations have been put forward for this complementary pattern of specialization. For example, strategic trade theory argues that, in internationally oligopolistic markets, existing firms use investment to precommit production, and this then acts as a deterrent to potential entrants. The greater the size of the sunk cost of production, the greater the deterrent effect is believed to be. This explains why U.S. industries have a comparative advantage in industries requiring large sunk costs for product development and production (e.g., aircraft and mainframe computers) in which U.S. firms have been engaged for a much longer period than Japanese firms, while Japan increased its comparative advantage in industries with lower entry costs.

Despite the high cost of entry, however, Japanese mainframe computer manufacturers managed to increase their global market share from a negligible amount in the late 1950s to almost 50% by the later 1980s. One factor that enabled Japanese mainframe computer manufacturers to become competitive players in the world market is the long-term orientation of their business practices and decision processes.

With a long-run planning horizon, business strategies tend to emphasize market share and value-added maximization (Tsurumi and Tsurumi, 1991; Aoki, 1988). The shifts in the composition of Japanese exports in recent years are consistent with this observation. The shifts are also consistent with the shifts in Japan's comparative advantage in foreign trade from the 1960s to the 1980s. These shifts have resulted in a decline in the import share of raw materials for industrial use, and a general increase in the import share of manufactured goods. Since high value-added products use relatively small amounts of raw materials, it is likely that raw material imports (including imports of coal and iron ore from Canada) will continue to decline. Nevertheless, as the Japanese manufacturing sector continues to move to the production of high value-added products, considerable room for low and medium value-added intermediate manufactured imports will open up. Higher income in Japan arising from the production of high value-added products will also stimulate household sector demand, including demand for high value-added consumer imports. These foreign trade patterns and the accompanying trade policies are discussed in the next section.

As the volume of foreign trade increases, firms often find it advantageous to shift production overseas for some of their manufactured export goods. This process is accelerated by import restrictions abroad (e.g., automobile and colour television import restrictions in the U.S. and Canada). Japan has moved considerable amounts of production overseas recently (outward direct investment). Similarly, increasingly large numbers of foreign firms are establishing business operations in Japan (inward direct investment), even though the total amount of inward direct investment is still only a small fraction of outward direct investment.

## Foreign Trade

Substantial growth in Japanese exports of high value-added products took place in the 1980s. Figure 5.1 shows that during the period of 1980–1984 the industries which enjoyed high growth rates in value-added terms were also the ones which experienced high growth rates in exports. These industries include communication/electronics equipment, electrical machinery, automobiles, and precision instruments. In 1985, net foreign trade (exports minus imports) constituted 19% of the total value-added (835 billion yen) of Japanese manufacturing industries. For the U.S. manufacturing industries, net foreign trade contributed only 7% of the total value-added of US$626 billion in 1984. The proportion for Japan declined to 12% by 1991. If the current upward trends in the volume and value of Japanese imports of manufactured goods continue, in the

**Fig. 5.1** Growth in Value Added and Exports, 1980–1984

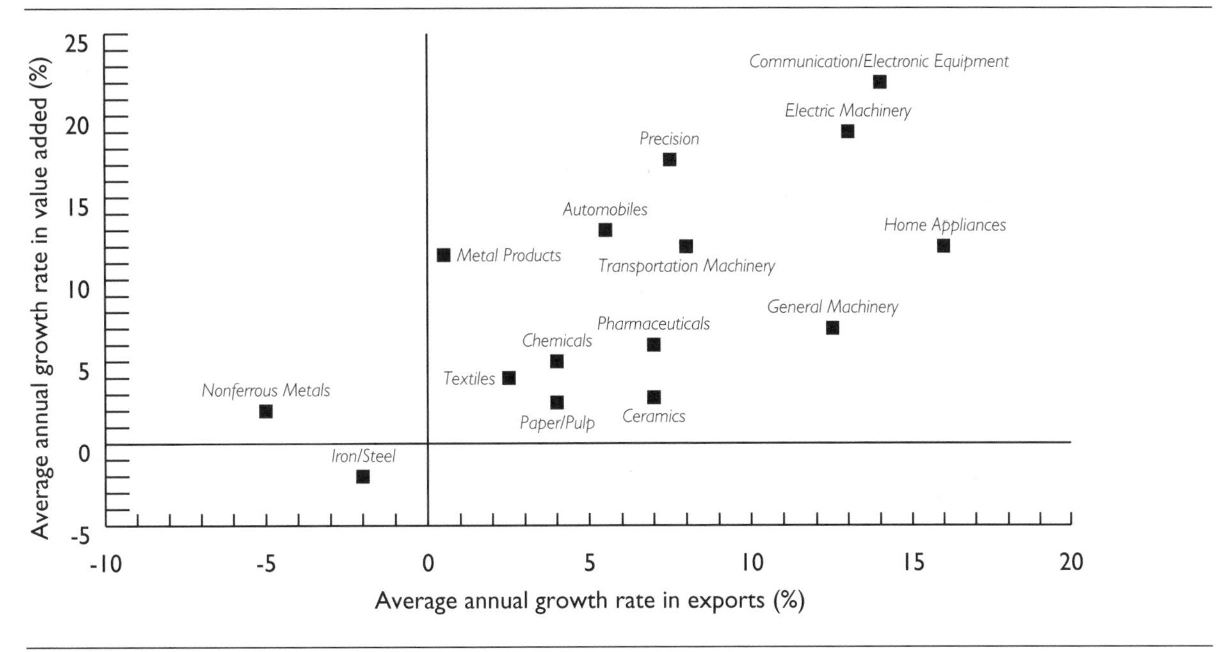


SOURCE: Calculated from Economic Planning Agency, *Summary of Economic Statistics* and *White Paper on the Economy* (various issues).

future the trade contribution of manufacturing value-added may be negative, as is the case for the United States. However, this seems unlikely as Japan would need surpluses in manufacturing to finance imports of natural resources. Manufacturing will likely continue to be the area of Japan's comparative advantage, even though net imports are expected for certain manufactured goods for which Japan has lost its competitiveness in the global market.

Another important factor which affected the patterns of foreign trade and resource allocation among Japanese industries was the 100% upward revaluation of the Japanese currency against the U.S. dollar over the period of 1985–1988. Table 5.1 shows changes in Japanese foreign trade during this period and reveals that the growth in the export quantity index was quite small while the change in the yen-based export price index was generally negative, reflecting the negative impact of the exchange rate adjustments on Japanese exports. The Japanese unit costs of production rose to among the highest in the world (Daly, 1991).

In the 1984–1986 period, when the exchange rate dropped from 251 to 160 yen per U.S. dollar, manufacturing firms managed, on average, to offset about 60% of the exchange losses by price increases, but there was considerable variation among industries. Much larger portions of the exchange losses were passed on to customers for high value-added products (e.g., 75%, 58%, 50% and 44%, respectively, for photocopiers, passenger cars, metal processing machinery and data processing equipment) than for low value-added products (e.g., 38%, 36% and 14%, respectively, for colour TV sets, chemicals and iron/steel products). The stable export performance of high value-added products compared with low value-added products over this period of large and unfavourable exchange rate changes was largely due to the ability of high-value added industries to offset exchange losses by raising prices. High value-added products are mostly sold in highly differentiated markets characterized by less price sensitivity and more stable demand.

Over the period of 1985–1987, the upward revaluation of the Japanese currency resulted in a decline in yen-based import prices and considerable gains in the import of manufactured goods. Table 5.2 shows that the import quantity indexes for food, chemicals, metals, and machinery rose considerably more than those for raw materials during this period when yen-based prices dropped by about 30%. This suggests that Japanese price elasticities of import demand for manufactured goods may be considerably higher than the price elasticities for raw materials.

In the 1980s, the share for oil imports in total Japanese imports declined from 50% in 1980 to 26% in 1987 while the import shares for food and manufactured goods from Europe, North America and Asia increased from 23% in 1980 to 60% in 1987. These manufactured imports included both low and high value-added products. On the high value-added end, highly priced European brand name products were successfully marketed to high-income Japanese households.

The shifts in Japan's comparative advantage in world trade are consistent with the change in the composition of Japanese exports from low to medium value-added to high value-added products. Shifts in Japan's comparative advantage are often attributed to firms' efforts over time to achieve economies of scale, take advantage of learning curves and pursue dynamic innovation. Product life cycle theory (Vernon, 1966; Tsurumi, 1984; Tsu-

**Table 5.1** Exchange Rate and Japanese Exports, 1975–1991

| | All | Textiles | Chemicals | Iron/Steel | Metals | Machinery[a] | Yen/US$[b] |
|---|---|---|---|---|---|---|---|
| | | | *Export Quantity Index (1985 = 100)* | | | | |
| *1975* | 45 | 85 | 74 | – | 77 | 36 | 305 |
| *1980* | 71 | 87 | 80 | 92 | 115 | 65 | 204 |
| *1981* | 78 | 96 | 81 | 91 | 115 | 74 | 220 |
| *1982* | 76 | 91 | 80 | 89 | 117 | 72 | 235 |
| *1983* | 82 | 101 | 90 | 94 | 108 | 78 | 232 |
| *1984* | 96 | 102 | 97 | 101 | 106 | 94 | 251 |
| *1985* | 100 | 100 | 100 | 100 | 100 | 100 | 201 |
| *1986* | 99 | 96 | 108 | 92 | 92 | 100 | 160 |
| *1987* | 100 | 88 | 120 | 84 | 73 | 101 | 122 |
| *1988* | 105 | 78 | 124 | 77 | 67 | 108 | 126 |
| *1989* | 109 | 75 | 132 | 66 | 68 | 114 | 143 |
| *1990* | 115 | 78 | 143 | 58 | 69 | 120 | 135 |
| *1991* | 118 | 80 | 148 | 62 | 66 | 124 | 125 |
| | | | *Export Price Index (1985 = 100, yen-based)* | | | | |
| *1975* | 87 | 87 | 85 | 114 | 84 | 83 | 305 |
| *1980* | 99 | 110 | 105 | 118 | 94 | 95 | 204 |
| *1981* | 102 | 110 | 101 | 124 | 100 | 98 | 220 |
| *1982* | 108 | 113 | 107 | 133 | 110 | 103 | 235 |
| *1983* | 101 | 104 | 100 | 100 | 105 | 100 | 232 |
| *1984* | 100 | 105 | 101 | 100 | 103 | 100 | 251 |
| *1985* | 100 | 100 | 100 | 100 | 100 | 100 | 201 |
| *1986* | 85 | 81 | 80 | 72 | 86 | 87 | 160 |
| *1987* | 80 | 76 | 76 | 67 | 87 | 82 | 122 |
| *1988* | 77 | 76 | 78 | 78 | 99 | 78 | 126 |
| *1989* | 83 | 84 | 83 | 95 | 110 | 82 | 143 |
| *1990* | 86 | 88 | 87 | 95 | 117 | 86 | 135 |
| *1991* | 85 | 89 | 85 | 91 | 127 | 86 | 125 |

SOURCE: Japanese Economic Planning Agency, *Summary of Economic Statistics* (1993).

[a] Includes general, electrical and transportation machinery.
[b] Year-end rate.

**Table 5.2** Exchange Rate and Japanese Imports, 1975–1991

| | RAW MATERIALS | | | | | | | | | | |
|---|---|---|---|---|---|---|---|---|---|---|---|
| | All | Food | Textile | Metal | Oilseeds | Lumber | Oil | Chemicals | Machinery[a] | Metal Products | Yen/US$[b] |
| | *Import Quantity Index (1985 = 100)* | | | | | | | | | | |
| *1975* | 70 | 61 | 92 | 90 | 64 | 106 | – | 29 | 54 | 40 | 305 |
| *1980* | 91 | 79 | 91 | 105 | 86 | 122 | 129 | 69 | 86 | 66 | 204 |
| *1981* | 90 | 83 | 88 | 95 | 84 | 94 | 116 | 72 | 87 | 74 | 220 |
| *1982* | 89 | 87 | 101 | 95 | 87 | 102 | 108 | 78 | 76 | 86 | 235 |
| *1983* | 90 | 90 | 90 | 92 | 97 | 99 | 105 | 86 | 81 | 88 | 232 |
| *1984* | 100 | 96 | 101 | 99 | 92 | 94 | 100 | 98 | 99 | 104 | 251 |
| *1985* | 100 | 100 | 100 | 100 | 100 | 100 | 100 | 100 | 100 | 100 | 201 |
| *1986* | 109 | 112 | 98 | 95 | 98 | 102 | 96 | 110 | 111 | 98 | 160 |
| *1987* | 120 | 128 | 118 | 94 | 101 | 119 | 94 | 123 | 130 | 128 | 122 |
| *1988* | 140 | 143 | 104 | 104 | 100 | 116 | 98 | 136 | 185 | 161 | 126 |
| *1989* | 151 | 148 | 105 | 104 | 96 | 124 | 105 | 149 | 214 | 164 | 143 |
| *1990* | 159 | 154 | 85 | 105 | 104 | 114 | 115 | 155 | 245 | 181 | 135 |
| *1991* | 164 | 166 | 91 | 106 | 99 | 107 | 120 | 164 | 252 | 205 | 125 |
| | *Import Price Index (1985 = 100, yen-based)* | | | | | | | | | | |
| *1975* | 79 | 115 | 94 | 97 | 139 | 83 | 52 | 108 | 79 | 81 | 305 |
| *1980* | 113 | 113 | 115 | 122 | 110 | 146 | 112 | 105 | 87 | 141 | 204 |
| *1981* | 112 | 113 | 114 | 112 | 116 | 117 | 121 | 102 | 86 | 118 | 220 |
| *1982* | 117 | 112 | 109 | 118 | 109 | 125 | 127 | 111 | 100 | 111 | 235 |
| *1983* | 107 | 106 | 104 | 113 | 106 | 105 | 108 | 102 | 102 | 111 | 232 |
| *1984* | 104 | 106 | 111 | 105 | 126 | 110 | 103 | 104 | 97 | 113 | 251 |
| *1985* | 100 | 100 | 100 | 100 | 100 | 100 | 100 | 100 | 100 | 100 | 201 |
| *1986* | 63 | 78 | 62 | 69 | 60 | 75 | 43 | 78 | 75 | 71 | 160 |
| *1987* | 58 | 68 | 64 | 63 | 52 | 85 | 38 | 72 | 72 | 69 | 122 |
| *1988* | 55 | 70 | 78 | 69 | 61 | 86 | 30 | 70 | 62 | 84 | 126 |
| *1989* | 62 | 77 | 83 | 82 | 67 | 98 | 34 | 74 | 70 | 95 | 143 |
| *1990* | 68 | 79 | 86 | 84 | 65 | 102 | 47 | 75 | 80 | 87 | 135 |
| *1991* | 63 | 75 | 70 | 74 | 58 | 95 | 41 | 72 | 76 | 75 | 125 |

SOURCE: Japanese Economic Planning Agency, *Summary of Economic Statistics* (1993).

[a] Includes general, electrical and transportation machinery.
[b] Year-end rate.

**Table 5.3** Ratio of Final Product Imports to Total Imports, 1960–1987 (Percent)

| | JAPAN | U.S. | E.C. |
|---|---|---|---|
| *1960* | 22.1 | 45.9 | 34.5 |
| *1965* | 22.7 | 56.0 | 38.7 |
| *1970* | 30.3 | 68.0 | 46.8 |
| *1975* | 20.3 | 55.8 | 41.2 |
| *1980* | 22.8 | 56.8 | 46.1 |
| *1985* | 31.0 | 76.5 | 51.6 |
| *1987* | 44.1 | 79.6 | 59.3 (1986) |

SOURCE: Japanese Economic Planning Agency.

rumi and Tsurumi, 1993) and, more recently, strategic trade theory (Krugman, 1986; Brander, 1986) particularly emphasize these factors which the traditional static comparative advantage theory does not deal with.

Japanese industrial and technology policy explicitly deals with these issues as related to foreign markets and foreign producers but the government policy does not always work as planned. Krugman (1984) observed that the industries favoured by the Japanese government (e.g., steel and semi-conductors) have not been particularly profitable. Baldwin and Krugman (1986) also note that Japan experienced social losses (i.e., the losses to consumers exceeded the gains to producers) in the case of 16K random access memories (RAMs) while this is not the case for 64K RAMs. If the production process of 16K RAMs is viewed as part of a dynamic learning curve for Japanese producers for producing 64K RAMs (and 128K, 256K and higher capacity RAMs) then the more appropriate measure of social loss (or gain) is the one which aggregates all social losses (gains) over the dynamic product life cycles for the products starting from 16 RAMs and moving to 64K RAMs, to 128K RAMs, to 256K RAMs, and onwards. Calculations for this example have not yet been carried out.

Since 1955, when Japan joined the GATT, the number of import restrictions and tariffs has steadily declined. At present, the only remaining import restrictions are for 22 agricultural commodities and coal. Over this same period, invisible barriers to the sale of foreign goods have also gradually come down, resulting in an increase in the share of final product imports (Table 5.3). This trend has continued into the 1990s. In the reces-

**Table 5.4** Japanese Direct Overseas Investment, 1978–1992 (US$million)

| | 1978 | 1979 | 1980 | 1981 | 1982 | 1983 |
|---|---|---|---|---|---|---|
| North America | 1,264 | 1,438 | 1,596 | 2,322 | 2,905 | 2,701 |
| Latin America | 616 | 1,207 | 588 | 1,181 | 1,503 | 1,878 |
| Asia | 1,340 | 976 | 1,186 | 3,339 | 1,385 | 1,847 |
| Middle East | 492 | 130 | 158 | 96 | 124 | 175 |
| Europe | 323 | 495 | 578 | 798 | 876 | 990 |
| Africa | 225 | 168 | 139 | 573 | 489 | 364 |
| Oceania | 239 | 582 | 448 | 424 | 421 | 191 |
| Total | 4,598 | 4,995 | 4,693 | 8,906 | 7,703 | 8,145 |

SOURCE: Japanese Ministry of Finance.

sionary conditions of 1992, when domestic shipments of all types of goods declined, the market shares in Japan for imported consumer durable and nondurable goods expanded (Japan Economic Planning Agency, 1993).

Nevertheless, observed increases in Japanese imports have not been dramatic in the latter half of the 1980s and the early 1990s. The domestic market share of imported goods and services in Japan is still quite limited except for mineral products. In 1991, the market shares for imports were: oil, coal and other mineral products (77%), precision instruments (17%), textiles (15%), petroleum and coal products (12%), food (10%), chemicals (8%), primary metal products (8%), transportation and communication (5%), electrical machinery (5%), pulp and paper (4%), transportation machinery (4%), ceramics (3%), general machinery (3%), services (3%), metal products (2%), finance and insurance (2%), and retail (1%). Informal barriers to imports and changing Japanese firm behaviour are discussed later in this chapter.

## Direct Investment

### *Outward Direct Investment*

Japanese foreign direct investment (FDI) abroad increased substantially in the latter half of the 1980s. It peaked at US$67.5 billion in 1989, but declined after that to US$34.1 billion in 1992 (Table 5.4). This decline can be partially attributed to a decline in potential opportunities and deteriorating profitability in some regions, as is discussed

| 1984 | 1985 | 1986 | 1987 | 1988 | 1989 | 1990 | 1991 | 1992 |
|---|---|---|---|---|---|---|---|---|
| 3,544 | 5,495 | 10,441 | 15,357 | 22,328 | 33,902 | 27,142 | 18,823 | 14,600 |
| 2,290 | 2,616 | 4,737 | 4,816 | 6,428 | 5,238 | 3,628 | 3,337 | – |
| 1,628 | 1,435 | 2,327 | 4,868 | 5,569 | 8,238 | 7,054 | 5,036 | 6,400 |
| 273 | 45 | 44 | 62 | 259 | 66 | 27 | 90 | – |
| 1,937 | 1,930 | 3,469 | 6,576 | 9,116 | 14,808 | 14,294 | 9,371 | 7,100 |
| 326 | 172 | 309 | 272 | 653 | 671 | 551 | 748 | – |
| 157 | 525 | 992 | 1,413 | 2,669 | 4,618 | 4,166 | 3,278 | – |
| 10,155 | 12,217 | 22,320 | 33,364 | 47,022 | 67,540 | 56,911 | 41,584 | 34,100 |

below. The largest share of Japanese FDI over the period of 1951–1990 was for investments in North America (44%), followed by Europe (19%) and Asia (15%). The shares for Central and South America, Oceania, Africa and the Middle East are, respectively, 13%, 5%, 1.9% and 1.1%. More than 70% of Japanese FDI has been in nonmanufacturing (finance/insurance, real estate, services, commerce, transportation and mining). In particular, Japanese direct investment in distribution networks and sales and other commerce activities for Japanese manufactured goods contributed significantly to increased the exports of these goods to the U.S. (Yamawaki, 1991).

Despite this, it is direct investment in manufacturing industries that has attracted recent attention overseas, due primarily to the implications of these investments for local employment and technology transfer. Japanese FDI in North American manufacturing industries is summarized in Table 5.5.

Some of the factors that contributed to the surge in Japanese FDI in the late 1980s are the following:

(1) The appreciation of the yen after 1984, from 251 yen per (U.S.) dollar to the range of 120–140 yen per dollar, made overseas production competitive relative to domestic Japanese production.

(2) The rising value of the stocks and land owned by Japanese corporations allowed firms to raise sufficient capital to undertake FDI. This factor disappeared to a large extent in 1990 when the bubble, caused by abnormal asset price appreciation, burst.

**Table 5.5** Japanese Direct Investment in North America: Manufacturing, 1978–1991 (US$million)

| | 1978 | 1979 | 1980 | 1981 | 1982 | 1983 |
|---|---|---|---|---|---|---|
| Food | 26 | 76 | 30 | 103 | 54 | 39 |
| Textiles | 37 | 22 | 14 | 26 | 10 | 11 |
| Lumber/Pulp | 10 | 7 | 64 | 34 | 58 | 74 |
| Chemicals | 58 | 60 | 13 | 40 | 101 | 89 |
| Steel/Metals | 13 | 96 | 48 | 24 | 40 | 100 |
| General Machinery | 28 | 52 | 31 | 122 | 75 | 34 |
| Electrical Equipment | 116 | 88 | 167 | 330 | 150 | 368 |
| Trans. Machinery | 3 | 28 | 18 | 276 | 250 | 204 |
| Other | 36 | 18 | 14 | 52 | 79 | 73 |

SOURCE: Japanese Ministry of Finance.

(3) The general relaxation of government regulations allowed firms and financial institutions to expand into new lines of business.

(4) New import restrictions in North America and Europe encouraged firms in the affected manufacturing industries to substitute local production for exports. This seems to be the case, for example, with colour television sets and automobiles (Ries, 1993). Import restrictions played a major role in Japanese manufacturing firms' decisions to set up production facilities to serve local markets in North America and Europe. This is in contrast to Japanese direct investments in Asia. Table 5.6 shows that the output of the production facilities that Japanese firms have established in Asia is exported to Japan and other third countries in larger quantities than is the output from their facilities in North America and Europe. Japanese firms' operations in Asia also purchase somewhat larger fractions of their procurement needs from local sources than from abroad.

As of October, 1992, Japanese-affiliated firms (i.e., those owned at least 10% by Japanese firms) employed 541,245 in the U.S. and 39,490 in Canada, excluding executives sent by Japanese parent firms. Of these, 17,276 workers in the U.S. and 866 in Canada were workers (excluding executives) sent by Japanese parent firms. For manufacturing industries these figures are: 319,164 workers (including 6,273 sent from Japan) for the U.S. and 23,367 workers (including 275 sent from Japan) for Canada. Canada's share of the

| 1984 | 1985 | 1986 | 1987 | 1988 | 1989 | 1990 | 1991 |
|---|---|---|---|---|---|---|---|
| 59 | 43 | 66 | 150 | 210 | 551 | 346 | 379 |
| 15 | 1 | 22 | 132 | 96 | 158 | 108 | 233 |
| 98 | 8 | 45 | 301 | 425 | 470 | 214 | 143 |
| 118 | 78 | 294 | 536 | 812 | 1,270 | 1,243 | 697 |
| 378 | 125 | 223 | 389 | 903 | 1,108 | 527 | 464 |
| 82 | 242 | 460 | 481 | 894 | 667 | 696 | 429 |
| 242 | 403 | 577 | 1,719 | 1,501 | 2,734 | 2,413 | 868 |
| 157 | 241 | 290 | 715 | 809 | 1,423 | 577 | 688 |
| 92 | 81 | 221 | 424 | 3,542 | 1,210 | 669 | 1,975 |

**Table 5.6** Sales and Procurement of Japanese Overseas Production Facilities, by Location of Facility, 1990 (Percent distribution)

| | LOCATION OF FACILITY | | |
|---|---|---|---|
| Location of Output Sales | North America | Asia | Europe |
| Local market | 93.8 | 59.8 | 95.6 |
| Exports to Japan | 4.0 | 13.7 | 1.7 |
| Exports to other countries | 2.2 | 26.5 | |

| | LOCATION OF FACILITY | | | |
|---|---|---|---|---|
| Location of Input Procurement | North America | NIES | ASEAN | Europe |
| Local purchase | 36.9 | 41.9 | 49.6 | 37.2 |
| Imports from Japan | 60.8 | 39.2 | 41.9 | 51.6 |
| Imports from other countries | 2.3 | 18.9 | 8.5 | 11.2 |

SOURCE: Japanese Ministry of Industry and International Trade, *Japanese Firms' Overseas Business Activities* (1990).

Japanese FDI employment is approximately 7% of that for the U.S., but the proportions of Japanese workers (including managers but excluding executives) to total employment for all Canadian industries (2%) and for manufacturing (1%) are lower than the U.S. proportions (3% and 2%). Many of the Japanese personnel in manufacturing industries are sent to train local workers, to transfer technology and to deal with maintenance problems of the production facilities.

The number of workers, including managerial personnel, sent from Japanese parent firms is considerable, and is thought to be large compared with the number sent by parent firms for U.S. firms' overseas operations, particularly after the initial setup for production is completed. Reasons given for why Japanese parent firms assign relatively large numbers of their employees to their overseas operations include: (1) Japanese manufacturing methods such as total quality control and the just-in-time (Toyota) production method are intertwined and require complex steps, involving all levels of personnel, that cannot be entirely delegated to local managers who are not familiar with these methods; (2) because of the complexity discussed in (1), communications within production operations in Japan are often carried out orally without detailed job manuals; (3) many Japanese firms believe transplanting essential steps of their production methods is important for manufacturing quality products; (4) some managerial and engineering positions in Japanese manufacturing facilities require qualifications in technical areas for which local labour supply may be scarce; and (5) Japanese firms use some of the managerial positions at their foreign operations as a part of regular job rotation schemes for their future managers and executives.

White and Trevor (1983) report that 60% of the workers (84% of supervisors and 52% of ordinary workers) at Japanese firms' operations in the U.K. receive on-the-job training from the Japanese workers sent by the parent firms. Only 11% of the workers at other non-Japanese foreign operations receive this sort of training. Higuchi (1991) also reports that more workers at Japanese firms' operations in the U.S. receive on-the-job training than those at indigenous U.S. firms' operations (24.4% for Japan versus 13.5% for the U.S.).

In general, local production workers seem to develop an appreciation for Japanese production methods and for the production-related personnel sent from Japanese parent firms. They see first-hand the fruit, often in

**Fig. 5.2** Ratios of Direct Investment and Exports to GNP, 1978–1988

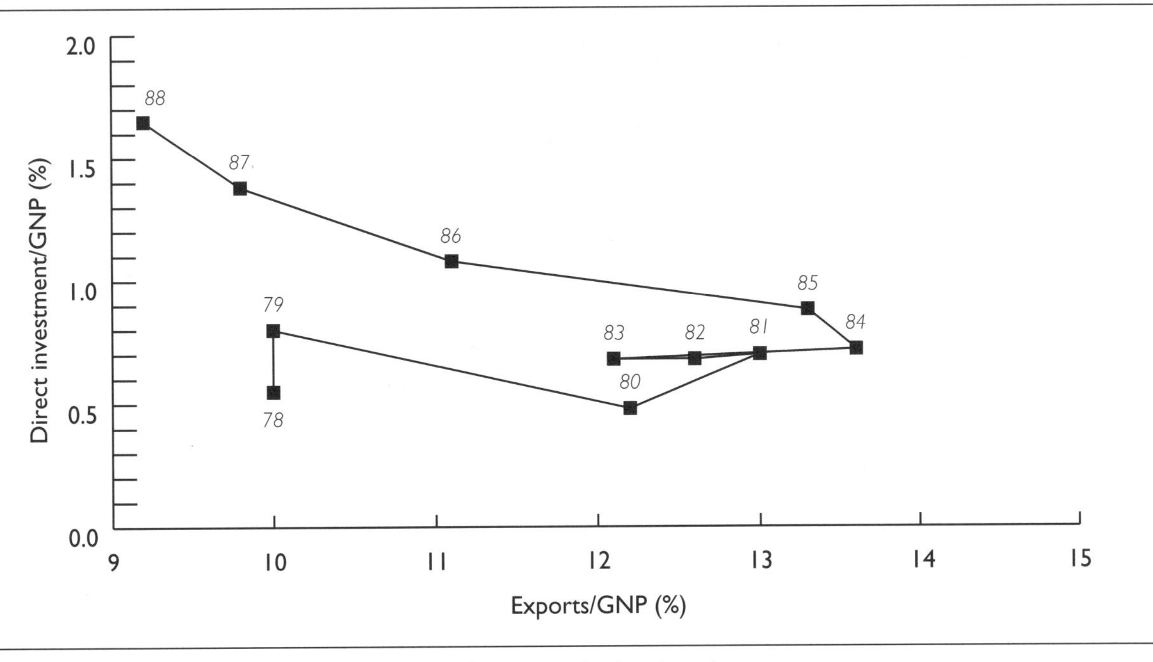


SOURCE: Economic Planning Agency, *White Paper on the Economy* (various issues).

terms of quality products, of the production methods these workers help to institute. But, local office workers have difficulty understanding the value of having Japanese office managers as part of the Japanese parent firms' rotation schemes. This is unlike the usual situation in the operations of many North American and European firms in Japan in which most, if not all, day-to-day responsibilities are delegated to local Japanese managers. The types of difficulty Japanese firms face in North America include discrimination suits involving women, minorities, and the disabled. Delegating more responsibilities to local managers may somewhat lessen the burden of Japanese parent firms, but some cost of relaxing the present industrial relations system may arise (see Nakamura, 1993 for a further discussion on Japanese firms and internationalization).

The move by Japanese manufacturing industries over the period of 1978–1988 to substitute local (overseas) production for exports is shown in Figure 5.2. After reaching a peak of over 13% in 1984, the exports-to-GNP ratio declined to close to 9%. At the same time, the direct investment-to-GNP ratio increased from 0.8% in 1984 to 1.65% in 1988. Many of these direct ventures in Asia, and some of the recent ones established in North America, export their products back to their Japanese parent firms. For the foreseeable future, imports via intra-firm transfers by Japanese firms are expected to increase and are seen as part of the long-term, profit maximizing global strategies of these firms (Nakamura, 1991a).

The size of the Asian economy and its growth opportunities are reflected in the substantial FDI in this region. In 1991 (1990), NIES countries (South Korea, Taiwan, Hong Kong and Singapore) invested 8.8 (2.0), 2.0 (2.6), 0.7 (3.0) and 1.6 (8.8) billion dollars U.S., respectively, in China, Indonesia, Malaysia and Thailand. Japan's FDI in these countries in 1991 (1990) was: 0.8 (0.5), 0.9 (2.2), 0.2 (1.6) and 1.8 (2.7) billion dollars U.S. In comparision, U.S. FDI in these countries was: 0.5 (0.5), 0.3 (0.1), 0.2 (0.2) and 1.1 (1.1) billion dollars U.S.

Globalization provides Japanese firms the considerable benefits of diversification. Nevertheless, their overseas operations have only limited success in producing profit. For example, the profitability (ordinary profits divided by sales) of Japanese firms' manufacturing operations in 1990 (1989) in North America, Asia and Europe were, respectively, –0.96 (0.29), 1.46 (0.91) and 2.16 (1.31). For transportation machinery including automobiles, these figures for North America, Asia and Europe were, respectively, –2.52 (–2.32), 4.64 (2.25) and 3.45 (3.01). By 1992, the profitability of Japanese operations in both North America and Europe was, on average, negative and only their operations in Asia continued to be profitable according to standard accounting measures. This is consistent with the findings of a U.S. government study (Landefeld, Lawson and Weinberg, 1992) that the operations of non-U.S. firms in the U.S. are considerably less profitable than those of U.S. firms. It is unknown if the generally poor performance of Japanese manufacturers in North America and Europe is a temporary phenomenon or is based on more fundamental structural problems (e.g., the difficulty of implementing Japanese production and industrial relations practices). It is possible that these profitability considerations will mean that further Japanese direct investment will take place primarily in the Asian region.

Considerable amounts of technology transfer will occur as a result of

Japanese direct investments overseas. Tables 4.5 and 4.6 show that, in 1991, Japan exported manufacturing technologies worth 370 billion yen. Most of these exports were to Asia (170 billion yen), North America (117 billion yen) and Europe (67 billion yen). Substantial portions of these technology exports are from Japanese parent firms to their foreign affiliates and subsidiaries in these regions. Technology exports to Asia are concentrated in the electric machinery, auto, steel and chemical industries (Tsurumi, 1984, discusses in detail the forms of technology transfer that take place as part of Japanese foreign direct investments.)

*Inward Direct Investment*

Foreign firms' direct investments in Japan have also increased significantly in recent years (Table 5.7). Inward direct investment increased from US$749 million in 1982 to US$940 million in 1986 to US$4,340 million in 1991. Nevertheless, inward FDI is still relatively small compared to outward FDI—the ratio between inward and outward FDI for 1990 was 10% for manufacturing industries and less than 10% for all industries combined.

In contrast to outward FDI, inward FDI comes mostly from North America and Europe. Of the total inward FDI outstanding over the period 1950–1991 (US$22.8 billion) the shares for the U.S., the Netherlands, Switzerland, Germany, the U.K., Canada and Hong Kong were, respectively, 43%, 8%, 6%, 5%, 5%, 5% and 2%.

Foreign firms' subsidiaries in Japan are large relative to domestic Japanese firms. About one third of foreign firms' subsidiaries are capitalized at more than 100 million yen, while 99% of all domestic Japanese firms are capitalized at less than 100 million yen. Also, foreign firms' operations in Japan include large operations from a global perspective. For example, U.S. firms' subsidiaries in Japan are large relative to U.S. foreign affiliates in other countries. The mean sales for U.S. foreign affiliates in 47 countries were US$21 million in 1977 and US$49 million in 1982. The mean sales per U.S. foreign affiliate in Japan were $60 million in 1977 and $122 million in 1982. In both years, these numbers were the highest country-specific mean sales per U.S. foreign affiliate (U.S. Department of Commerce, 1980, 1985).

OWNERSHIP AND PROFITABILITY OF FOREIGN OPERATIONS Government policies from the late 1940s to the early 1970s discouraged FDI in

**Table 5.7** Foreign Direct Investment in Japan by Industry, 1950–1991

| | 1989 | | 1990 | | 1991 | | 1950–1991 | TOTAL |
|---|---|---|---|---|---|---|---|---|
| Industry | C[a] | $[b] | C | $ | C | $ | C | $ |
| *Manufacturing* | | | | | | | | |
| Machinery | 1,093 | 808 | 886 | 806 | 581 | 439 | 10,855 | 6,616 |
| Chemicals | 194 | 203 | 234 | 438 | 120 | 902 | 2,571 | 4,061 |
| Petroleum | 24 | 8 | 59 | 30 | 45 | 173 | 569 | 895 |
| Metals | 187 | 40 | 125 | 151 | 211 | 79 | 1,203 | 727 |
| Food | 126 | 17 | 74 | 29 | 150 | 124 | 1,354 | 436 |
| Glass/Ceramics | 8 | 6 | 73 | 6 | 132 | 5 | 580 | 152 |
| Rubber/Leather | 34 | 29 | 7 | 1 | 6 | 56 | 133 | 132 |
| Textile | 13 | 0 | 26 | 18 | 4 | 9 | 201 | 78 |
| Other | 387 | 61 | 546 | 92 | 417 | 109 | 2,984 | 568 |
| Total | 2,066 | 1,172 | 2,030 | 1,570 | 1,666 | 1,896 | 20,450 | 13,666 |
| *Non-Manufacturing* | | | | | | | | |
| Commerce | 1,710 | 544 | 2,057 | 730 | 1,315 | 783 | 14,193 | 3,727 |
| Service | 972 | 138 | 1,098 | 263 | 685 | 545 | 7,304 | 1,606 |
| Finance/Insurance | 40 | 180 | 64 | 109 | 27 | 890 | 338 | 1,571 |
| Real Estate | 121 | 647 | 114 | 24 | 33 | 69 | 521 | 887 |
| Communication | 14 | 23 | 13 | 21 | 46 | 99 | 159 | 247 |
| Transportation | 149 | 47 | 63 | 12 | 63 | 26 | 545 | 165 |
| Construction | 419 | 9 | 366 | 9 | 313 | 23 | 1,849 | 113 |
| Other | 197 | 100 | 134 | 40 | 64 | 8 | 1,988 | 788 |
| Total | 3,622 | 1,688 | 3,909 | 1,208 | 2,546 | 2,444 | 26,897 | 9,104 |

SOURCE: Japanese Ministry of Finance.

[a] Number of cases.
[b] Figures in US$million.

Japan by technology-based foreign firms and are thought to be the main reason for the imbalance, at least up to the early 1980s, between inward and outward FDI. These policies encouraged Japanese firms to purchase technical licensing agreements. Foreign exchange allocations were provided to make these purchases possible. See Mason (1992) for a detailed discussion of the establishment of some of the major U.S. firms in Japan and their interactions with the Japanese business and government sectors and the U.S. government.

The ownership patterns of foreign firms' subsidiaries were under strict government supervision until 1950. The 1950 Law Concerning Foreign Investment permitted foreign firms to acquire ownership of up to 49% of a Japanese firm. This law was changed in 1973 to permit foreign firms to obtain full ownership, subject to certain exceptions. Most of the remaining government restrictions on FDI have been removed in recent years. Starting in 1980, most FDI proposals received automatic approval.

In 1977, 7% of U.S. firms' subsidiaries reported they were required to limit their U.S. parent firms' equity. In 1982 the fraction decreased to 3%. This compares with 1982 fractions of, for example, 1% for France and for West Germany, 2% for Italy and 3% for Australia (Contractor, 1990). Thus it appears that the shares of foreign ownership in Japan could be, and were, adjusted relatively frequently in recent years in response to changing government and company policies.

In 1991, the approval requirement was replaced by a prior notice requirement, which was further lessened to an ex post notice requirement in 1992. Thus, these days a foreign firm need only notify the Japanese government of its establishment of direct investment in Japan. Furthermore, this notification is not required if the direct investment involves acquisitions of less than 10% of the stock of an unlisted firm. The only exceptions to these liberalized rules are investments in agriculture, forestry and fishing, mining, petroleum, leather, and industries viewed as directly related to national security.

Foreign operations in Japan, when successful, tend to be highly profitable compared to similar Japanese domestic businesses. Part of the competitive advantage and profitability of the foreign operations is believed to be attributable to their imports of large amounts of intermediate goods from foreign parent firms (Nakamura, 1991b). About 45% of their procurement (raw materials, intermediate goods and other purchases of goods) is imported, and 27% of their procurement is from foreign parent firms (i.e., intra-firm transfer). Intra-firm transfers account for more than 60% of all purchases in the precision instruments, textile, and printing industries. Successful foreign operations have also been able to capitalize on the high growth of the

Japanese market, on technical and other intangible skills available in Japan, and on the exposure to Japanese competitors' production technologies. For example, it is generally believed that substantial formal and informal acquisition of production technology from its successful Japanese joint venture (Fuji Xerox Company) has enabled Xerox Corporation to stay competitive in the global market for photocopiers. Similar technology feedback from subsidiary firms in Japan to the U.S. parent firms has also helped boost productivity and profits at IBM, General Electric, Ford Motor and Caterpillar.

In addition to local profit and growth opportunities, Japan offers foreign parent firms a foothold for possible expansion into the growing Asia-Pacific market, as seen for Canadian subsidiaries. However, only 9% of the total sales of foreign firms' subsidiaries come from exports—most of their sales come from the Japanese market.

Japan also offers substantial R&D opportunities to foreign firms. Northern Telecom, for example, is reported to be planning to spend $100 million over the next five years on R&D activities in Japan. Many major U.S. and European high technology firms already have R&D operations in Japan. It is also the case that many major Japanese firms in high technology industries have R&D activities in the U.S. and Europe. In this sense, R&D activities in the U.S., Europe and Japan appear to play complementary roles in the context of the global strategies of large multinational firms.

Japan provides differentiated markets which could be very profitable for foreign firms' direct investments. Successful foreign operations in Japan typically operate on long-run planning horizons; form long-term business relationships with their distributors, suppliers, customers and banks; and adopt many aspects of Japanese management practices including the bonus payment system.

INDUSTRIAL RELATIONS PRACTICES OF FOREIGN OPERATIONS Japanese firms' overseas subsidiaries tend to have more workers and managers sent from their parent firms compared to U.S. and European firms' foreign operations, and that the reason for this may be the types of production and industrial relations practices many Japanese firms use at home. It is of interest to look at how foreign firms' subsidiaries in Japan operate in this regard.

The fraction of local (Japanese) company board directors (who are usually also company executives) for foreign affiliated firms in Japan is about 80%, and the fraction of local managers is about 98%. Thus the delegation of managerial responsibilities to local personnel is quite extensive. While foreign parent firms retain their interest in the decisions related mostly to board appointments, transfer pricing, basic research, and some head office functions, most other managerial responsibilities in personnel, production, marketing and finance are delegated to Japanese workers.

Many characteristics of indigenous Japanese firms are also found in foreign firms' subsidiaries. This is particularly true in larger, more established firms. For example, established foreign firms are able to hire new university graduates for whom long-term employment is implicitly promised. They also provide Japanese-like bonus payments.

There are, however, certain practices which seem to distinguish foreign firms' operations from indigenous Japanese firms. These practices include: the existence of job-specific manuals, 5-day a week operation and shorter hours of work, hiring of many mid-career job changers (even for firms which hire new graduates) and women, later mandatory retirement ages (often past 60 years of age), fewer job rotations, performance-based managerial compensation and the use of incentive bonus systems, line-based (rather than personnel department-based) personnel management, and the use of partitioned (or individual) office space rather than a large, common office space.

Well-established foreign firms that could attract as many new graduates as needed still hire many mid-career job changers to satisfy their personnel needs (Table 5.8). This persistent reliance on mid-career workers from outside is not observed for large Japanese firms and suggests that industrial relations practices at these foreign firms' subsidiaries are a hybrid between Japanese and North American practices. The fact that foreign-affiliated firms in Japan provide unique employment opportunities to Japanese women and mid-career job seekers led Mauer (1989), for instance, to recommend that U.S. firms should take advantage of female and other skilled workers bumped out of the Japanese system. There is considerable anecdotal evidence that this is in fact happening.

### *Research and Development, Foreign Researchers and Direct Investment*

Starting in the 1980s many Japanese firms began to employ foreign researchers in their R&D facilities in Japan. In 1991, the total number of such foreign researchers was estimated to be about 750 (Japan Science and Technology Agency, 1991). The largest number came from Asia (397), many of whom graduated from Japanese universities. There were also 189 researchers from the U.S., 125 from Western Europe and 40 from other regions. Firms differ in the numbers of foreign researchers they expect to employ in their R&D facilities, but many expect to employ at least some since the supply of Japanese scientists and engineers is forecast to become limited in the near future (Japan Science and Technology Agency, 1991).

More than 60% of the researchers working for foreign firms' operations in Japan are Japanese nationals. These foreign firms report that the most important reason for maintaining their R&D operations in Japan is to develop or design products suitable for the Japanese market. Like indigenous Japanese firms, these foreign firms operating in Japan also suffer from difficulties in attracting qualified researchers (Japan Science and Technology Agency, 1991).

The majority of large Japanese firms are already operating, or are interested in locating, some R&D facilities at foreign sites. These overseas R&D facilities are set up, for example, to adapt certain Japanese technologies to local needs and for developing independent R&D capabilities, particularly at some North American R&D facilities. Some of these facilities are also used for testing whether or not newly developed drugs satisfy U.S. Federal Drug Administration requirements or whether new automobiles satisfy Environmental Protection Agency pollution requirements. Japanese firms' R&D expenditures in the U.S. are estimated to be about 10% of total corporate R&D expenditures in the U.S., according to the Japan Development Bank. Japanese firms have some concerns with their R&D facilities abroad. They report fears of losing their corporate trade secrets to competitors due to researchers moving to other firms, and they also fear potential legal difficulties associated with transferring new technologies developed in their European or U.S. laboratories to their overseas facilities, including those in Japan.

## Trade Policy, and Formal and Informal Barriers to Japanese Imports and Inward Direct Investments

Foreign trade has been an integral part of Japan's strategy for economic growth. Various forms of industrial policy were used to help develop infant industries into internationally competitive ones. For example, Yamawaki (1988) argues that the policy-based supply of funds, tax reductions and importation of important tech-

**Table 5.8** Newly-Hired Workers at U.S. and Canadian Firms' Operations in Japan, 1990

| Foreign Firms' Operations | NEW GRADUATES | | |
|---|---|---|---|
| (year established; % foreign ownership; no. of employees) | Men | Women | Mid-Career |
| IBM Japan[1] (1937; 100; 23,019) | 1,000 | 300 | 400 |
| Nippon Roussell (1959; 80; 260) | 554 | 190 | 45 |
| Nihon Unisys (1958; 33.3; 4,656) | 386 | 111 | 60 |
| Fuji Xerox (1962; 50; 13,353) | 315 | 80 | 0 |
| McDonald's (Japan) (1971; 50; 2,970) | 151 | 17 | 206 |
| Nihon Digital Equipment (1982; 100; 3,100) | 350 | 0 | 0 |
| Nippon Glaxo (1953; 50, 1,370) | 76 | 46 | 21 |
| NCR Japan (1920; 70; 4,254) | 82 | 40 | 23 |
| American Family Life Insurance (1974; 100; 1,200) | 44 | 83 | 50 |
| Berlitz School of Languages (Japan) (1980; 100; 1,000) | 0 | 2 | 250 |
| American Express (– ; 100; 730) | 100 | 0 | 200 |
| Kirin-Seagram (1972; 50; 527) | 25 | 0 | 20 |
| Toppan Moore (1965; 45; 2,858) | 21 | 13 | 102 |
| MacMillan Bloedel (1963; 100; 43) | 0 | 0 | 6 |

SOURCE: Toyo Keizai, *Foreign-Affiliated Firms in Japan* (various years).

1 These figures are for 1989.

nologies, and the exclusion of foreign competition, were among the factors responsible for the success of the steel industry. Similarly, Mutoh (1988) argues that the automobile industry benefitted from the MITI guidelines which provided protection of the domestic market from direct investments by, and imports from, foreign competitors, and from measures to allow domestic firms to import foreign technologies at favourable terms and with government financial assistance. Shinohara (1982) claims that these measures permitted the steel and automobile industries to acquire a leading world position. There is controversy about the effectiveness of the particular policies MITI and other government agencies undertook, since there seems to be no empirical research which relates the success of certain Japanese industries directly to government policy tools. Evidence for the effectiveness of these policies is mostly anecdotal (Chapters 3 and 4). Nevertheless policy measures for the protection of infant industries that the Japanese government regarded as strategically important were actively taken up to the 1970s. Some targeted industries turned out to be unprofitable (Krugman, 1984; Baldwin and Krugman, 1986). In fact, some targeted industries and recent Research Association projects are considered to be near-failures (e.g., aluminum, aircraft, chemicals, pharmaceuticals and computer software). Another important factor associated with industrial policy is that, even though MITI did not use foreign producers to increase domestic competition, there were multiple domestic producers in every targeted industry and this may have helped to insure significant competition in the domestic market. Competition among bank-based corporate groups, for example, was sometimes responsible for the presence of multiple producers.

As government policies shifted in the late 1970s and 1980s towards those which are more consistent with market forces, tariffs and nontariff barriers designed to protect strategically identified infant industries declined in importance in Japan's trade policy. On the whole, Japan's tariff rates on nonagricultural products are similar to those found in the U.S. and the European Community. But, Japanese tariffs on raw and processed agricultural, fishery and forestry products are higher than the rates found in the E.C. and the U.S.

Nontariff barriers (border measures which limit imports directly or indirectly) typically involve agricultural commodities (e.g., beef, pork, lamb, chicken, rice, oranges, fish, silk products). Japan has 22 quotas on agricultural and fishery products, the U.S. has 1, Belgium has 2, France has 19, Germany has 3, Italy has 3 and the U.K. has 1. As a reflection of Japan's inefficient agriculture, many of these nontariff barriers are responsible for high consumer prices of various foodstuffs, among other commodities. It is generally believed that the conflict of interest among Japanese government agencies (e.g., MITI encourages rice imports while the Ministry of Agriculture opposes rice imports), combined with their conflicting constituencies (corporations for MITI versus farmers for Agriculture), makes it difficult for the government to formulate a more consumer-oriented agricultural policy.

### INFORMAL BARRIERS TO IMPORTS AND INWARD DIRECT INVESTMENT

In addition to formal barriers (tariffs and nontariff measures) Japan has informal barriers to imports and inward FDI. These informal barriers take different forms: administrative guidance (informal suggestions given by a government ministry), customs procedures, standards, requirements for testing and certification, procurement practices, industrial policy, and distribution channels. Some of these barriers (e.g., distribution channels) are directly tied to Japanese business practices and do act to effectively exclude newcomers. Others are tied to intentional or unintentional government policies to exclude foreign (or new domestic) producers. For example, many government public construction projects require potential general contractors to be on a government-approved recommended vendor list before they can make a bid on a project. These industrial policies designed to promote domestic industries or to protect depressed domestic industries also work as informal barriers to imports. (A detailed discussion of informal barriers to U.S. exports to Japan by the U.S. Trade Representative's office is summarized in Balassa and Noland (1988). See also Schmitz (1989) and Saxonhouse and Stern (1989) for examples of formal and informal trade barriers in Canada and the U.S. as well as in Japan.)

The presence of informal barriers to imports is often considered responsible for Japan's small import shares of manufactured goods compared to the European Community or the U.S. This view is not always shared, however; see, for example, Saxonhouse (1985). This issue is particularly interesting from an academic point of view since Japan's current account surplus has increased considerably in the last five years at a time when no major changes in informal (and other) trade barriers have occurred.

While formal barriers for imports and inward direct investments are being eliminated, the informal barriers based on Japanese business practices and customs seem to remain in certain industries. For example, long-term business relationships found among Japanese firms mean that newcomers (both Japanese and foreign) have difficulty in achieving access to the market—many wholesalers and retailers in Japan are integrated into established distribution networks which are not inclined to deal with products from newcomers. Ito (1992) and Marvel (1993) point out the economic efficiency bases for the Japanese distribution system. As another example, the thin labour market for mid-career workers hinders the establishment of foreign firms since they must depend on being able to attract experienced personnel from other (possibly competing) firms, at least in the beginning. As a final example, the lack of a market for corporate control means it is not usually feasible to start a business in Japan by buying into existing firms through either a friendly or a hostile takeover.

Another informal barrier is the high price level in Japan as measured in dollars. This depends, of course, on the foreign exchange rate, which in turn depends on foreign trade involving Japan. Informal barriers may explain in part why Japanese imports are relatively low compared to exports and why foreign firms' direct investments in Japan are limited compared to Japanese direct investments overseas. Such informal barriers, combined with certain government practices, appear to be contributing to the marginal status of foreign banks' operations in Japan. This is so despite the recent measures taken by the Japanese government to liberalize the Japanese banking sector (Sarnet, Thibault, Ursacki and Vertinsky, 1992; Ursacki and Vertinsky, 1992).

The Japanese government has put forward policy initiatives to encourage inward direct investment. These include: subsidized financing from the Japan Development Bank for investment projects of the subsidiaries of foreign firms; inclusion of foreign firms' subsidiaries in some Research Associations; and the establishment in 1993 of a firm to provide foreign firms' subsidiaries with consulting services, and assistance in worker training programs. (These initiatives are to be funded 50–50 by the Japanese government and Japanese private firms). These policies do not appear to be directly aimed at lowering informal barriers caused by certain Japanese business practices, but they may be helpful in acquainting foreign firms with Japanese business practices and they may also, in some cases, help foreign firms to enter into long-term business relationships. Many foreign firms of different sizes which have established successful operations in Japan have managed to develop long-term relationships with Japanese firms, distributors and/or customers. Some of these relationships take the form of corporate groups. The lesson of these successful operations may be "if we can't beat them, let's join them." The successful operations of foreign firms in Japan can take different forms of ownership structure: fully owned, or jointly owned subsidiaries. There are several corporate groups involving foreign firms' subsidiaries that are either fully owned by foreign parent firms or jointly owned by both foreign and Japanese parent firms.

While removal of barriers created by certain business practices and of other formal and informal trade impediments may facilitate imports to Japan, the trade imbalance between the U.S. and the rest of the world including Japan, which is sometimes associated with these impediments, will not disappear necessarily. Since the U.S. trade deficit is simply total U.S. gross domestic product minus U.S. domestic expenditure, which in turn is equal to total (private and government) savings minus total investment, the deficit will not vanish so long as domestic expenditure exceeds domestic production, or equivalently, total investment exceeds total savings (Samuelson, Nordhaus and McCallum, 1988). Removal of Japanese impediments to imports can, however, change the amount and composition of goods imported into the U.S. and also the countries from which these goods are imported (Komiya, 1988; Sazanami, 1989). Savings and other macroeconomic behaviour for Canada, Japan and the U.S. are analyzed in detail in Helliwell (1989).

# Part II

## Canada and Japan

6

# The Determinants of Japan's Competitive Position

## Implications for Canada

### Introduction

The fundamental factors that explain Japan's economic growth, provide comparisons to the performance of other industrial countries and attempt to distill some lessons from Japan's experience and phenomenal economic success must be examined. Since the data base of this study is limited and the number of confounding variables large, this analysis cannot serve to properly test the validity of alternative economic growth models. Indeed, alternative models were used to provide a normative basis for interpreting the association identified between policies, actions, institutional arrangements and socio-economic conditions and performance. This exercise can also serve to indicate whether the predictions of some growth models are less universal than their proponents claim (e.g., finding examples where policies that do not correspond to those derived from the models have been, nevertheless, successful). Clearly, any study based only on associations between variables cannot avoid the danger of interpreting spurious correlations as causal relationships.

International comparisons to assess the role of government in Japan and its success in providing a stable macro-economic policy environment that enhances competitiveness were used in this analysis. The role of government in intervening to correct market failures is then examined. Considered next is Japan's experience in adopting "industrial policies," i.e., the attempt of Japanese governments to create comparative advantage rather than let market forces alone allocate resources in accordance with the existing underlying patterns of comparative advantage. The success of these policies is examined and the conditions that prevented "government failures" and the means that were used to increase the probability that governments would support winners, not buttress losers, are identified.

The institutional structures underlying Japan's economic system then are analyzed and those characteristics that ensure synergistic relationships between the different elements of the economic system and enhance international competitiveness and economic growth are identified. Finally, the question of whether Japanese government policies and institutional approaches are appropriate for Canada is explored. In particular, the preconditions for successful government intervention that existed in Japan are identified and then contrasted with the Canadian situation.

## Japan: A Comparative Record of Success

In the three decades that began in 1960 Japan grew at an average annual rate of about 6.4% a year. Since 1965, the "little tigers" of Taiwan, Korea, and Singapore have grown at an average rate of over 8%, while Hong Kong's average growth has exceeded 7%. The United States and the European Community have grown at just over 3%. During the period 1961–1973, the average real growth rate in Japan was 9.6%, while the second highest average real growth rate among the G7 countries, achieved by Canada, amounted to only 5.5%. During the period 1974–1990 the average real growth rate in Japan declined to 3.9%, but was still significantly higher than all other G7 countries (see Table 6.1).

The long-term sustainability and quality of growth depends to a large degree on the ability of a country to improve the productivity of its resources. Table 6.2 provides a comparison of total factor productivity growth in major industrialized countries during the three periods 1961–1973, 1974–1979 and 1980–1991. Total factor productivity is a measure of the quality of a nation's capital and labour resources and the efficiency of their use. During the 1961–1973 period, the average annual growth rate of total factor productivity in Japan was 5.8% (about 80% more than the G7 average). During the 1974–1979 period, total factor productivity in Japan grew annually by only 1.3%, below that of France, Germany and Italy. How-

**Table 6.1** Real GDP Growth Performance, G7 Countries, 1961–1992 (Average annual growth rate)

| | 1961–1973 | 1974–1990 | 1991 | 1992 |
|---|---|---|---|---|
| Canada | 5.5 | 3.3 | –1.7 | 0.9 |
| France | 5.4 | 2.5 | 0.7 | 1.3 |
| Germany[a] | 4.3 | 2.2 | 3.7 | 2.0 |
| Italy | 5.2 | 2.8 | 1.3 | 0.9 |
| Japan | 9.6 | 3.9 | 4.0 | 1.3 |
| United Kingdom | 3.2 | 2.0 | –2.2 | –0.6 |
| U.S. | 4.0 | 2.4 | –1.2 | 2.1 |
| Unweighted average | 5.3 | 2.7 | 0.7 | 1.1 |

SOURCE: OECD, *Economic Outlook*, (June 1993) and OECD, *Economic Outlook Historical Statistics 1960–1990* (1992).

[a] Western Germany until 1992. Includes the former German Democratic Republic in 1992.

**Table 6.2** Business Sector Total Factor Productivity Growth, G7 Countries, 1961–1991 (Average annual growth rate)

| | 1961–1973 | 1974–1979 | 1980–1991 |
|---|---|---|---|
| Canada | 2.0 | 0.8 | –0.1 |
| France | 4.0 | 1.7 | 1.4 |
| Germany[a] | 2.7 | 1.8 | 0.8[b] |
| Italy | 4.4 | 2.1 | 1.2 |
| Japan | 5.8 | 1.3 | 1.9[c] |
| United Kingdom | 2.3 | 0.6 | 1.3 |
| U.S. | 1.6 | –0.4 | 0.2[b] |
| Unweighted average | 3.3 | 1.1 | 1.0 |

SOURCE: OECD, *Economic Outlook* (June 1993).

[a] Western Germany.
[b] 1980–1992.
[c] 1980–1990.

**Table 6.3** Consumer Price Inflation Performance, G7 Countries, 1961–1992 (Average annual growth rate)

| | 1961–1973 | 1974–1990 | 1991 | 1992 |
|---|---|---|---|---|
| Canada | 3.2 | 7.3 | 5.0 | 1.5 |
| France | 4.6 | 8.2 | 3.2 | 2.4 |
| Germany[a] | 3.4 | 3.5 | 3.5 | 4.0 |
| Italy | 4.7 | 12.5 | 6.5 | 5.3 |
| Japan | 6.2 | 5.2 | 3.3 | 1.7 |
| United Kingdom | 5.1 | 10.4 | 5.9 | 3.7 |
| U.S. | 3.2 | 6.6 | 4.2 | 3.0 |
| Unweighted average | 4.3 | 7.7 | 4.6 | 3.1 |

SOURCE: OECD, *Economic Outlook* (June 1993) and OECD, *Economic Outlook Historical Statistics 1960–1990* (1992).

[a] Western Germany.

ever, in the 1980–1991 period, Japan again achieved much faster growth—an average annual growth rate of 1.9% (almost double the average for the G7 countries).

## Macro-Economic Environment

The conservative neoclassical view of the proper role for government in facilitating growth recognizes the importance of maintaining macro-economic stability and emphasizes the need for constraints on government activity to ensure that the private sector can grow and expand. It also prescribes that the level and structure of taxes must not impede the ability of a country to compete internationally, lead to distortion of the domestic price system, or reduce incentives for increasing productivity of the resources deployed in the economy. In the past two decades Japan satisfied some of these basic prescriptions better than other G7 governments.

### *Price Stability*

Price stability is an important indicator that macro-economic policy is conducive to the maintenance of growth. Inflation may undermine productivity and growth in several ways. Perhaps the highest risk of inflation is one that stems from the destabilization of labour-management relations result-

**Table 6.4** Trends in Interest Rates[1], Japan and the U.S., 1980–1993 (Percent)

| | JAPAN | | | U.S. | | |
|---|---|---|---|---|---|---|
| | Lending Rate[2] | Money Market Rate[3] | Government Bond Yield[4] | Lending (Prime) Rate[2] | Federal Funds Rate[3] | Government Bond Yield[4] |
| *1980* | 8.35 | 10.93 | 9.22 | 15.27 | 13.36 | 11.46 |
| *1981* | 7.86 | 7.43 | 8.66 | 18.87 | 16.38 | 13.91 |
| *1982* | 7.31 | 6.94 | 8.06 | 14.86 | 12.26 | 13.00 |
| *1983* | 7.13 | 6.39 | 7.42 | 10.79 | 9.09 | 11.11 |
| *1984* | 6.75 | 6.10 | 6.81 | 12.04 | 10.23 | 12.52 |
| *1985* | 6.60 | 6.46 | 6.34 | 9.93 | 8.10 | 10.62 |
| *1986* | 6.02 | 4.79 | 4.94 | 8.35 | 6.81 | 7.68 |
| *1987* | 5.21 | 3.51 | 4.21 | 8.21 | 6.66 | 8.38 |
| *1988* | 5.03 | 3.62 | 4.27 | 9.32 | 7.61 | 8.85 |
| *1989* | 5.29 | 4.87 | 5.05 | 10.92 | 9.22 | 8.50 |
| *1990* | 6.95 | 7.24 | 7.36 | 10.01 | 8.10 | 8.55 |
| *1991* | 7.53 | 7.46 | 6.53 | 8.46 | 5.70 | 7.86 |
| *1992* | 6.15 | 4.58 | 4.94 | 6.25 | 3.52 | 7.01 |
| *1993 (Mar.)* | 5.56 (Jan.) | 3.24 | 4.17 | 6.00 | 3.07 | 5.98 |

SOURCE: IMF, *International Financial Statistics Yearbook, 1992* (1993) and *International Financial Statistics* (June 1993).

1 Rates are means of monthly unweighted averages of daily rates except as noted.
2 Japan: rate charged by all banks on short and long term loans, weighted average.
U.S.: rate charged by large banks to best customers on short-term loans.
3 Japan: lending rate for collateral and overnight loans in Tokyo call money market.
U.S.: borrowing rate in interbank market.
4 Japan: yield of bonds with 7 years to maturity, based on end-of-month data.
U.S.: yield of bonds with 10 years to maturity.

ing in higher rates of strikes and reduced incentives for improving productivity. Inflation may erode the economy's competitive position, destabilize exchange rates and increase the risk premia in the economy, thus raising the cost of capital. It may interact with the tax system to create severe distortions in the allocation of resources throughout the economy. Table 6.3 shows that Japan's record in the post-1974 period has been second only to Germany's among the G7 countries, despite Japan's high energy dependency and the impact of two oil price crises on inflation rates during the period (as outlined in Chapter 1).

Lower inflation rates mean lower risk premia on borrowing. Table 6.4 provides a comparison of interest rates in Japan and the United States show-

**Table 6.5** Size of Government: General Government[a] Total Outlays, G7 Countries, 1960–1992 (Percent of GDP)

| | 1960–1973 | 1974–1990 | 1991 | 1992 |
|---|---|---|---|---|
| Canada | 31.6 | 41.5 | 48.8 | 49.7 |
| France | 38.0 | 47.7 | 50.6 | 52.0 |
| Germany[b] | 37.5 | 47.0 | 48.7 | 49.4 |
| Italy | 33.7 | 46.0 | 53.6 | 53.2 |
| Japan | 19.5 | 30.7 | 31.4 | 32.3 |
| United Kingdom | 36.8 | 42.4 | 40.8 | 44.1 |
| U.S. | 29.5 | 32.5 | 34.2 | 35.4 |
| Unweighted average | 32.4 | 41.1 | 44.0 | 45.2 |

SOURCES: OECD, *Economic Outlook* (June 1993) and *Economic Outlook Historical Statistics 1960–1990* (1992).

[a] Includes federal, provincial or state and municipal governments and the Canada and Quebec pension plans. Based on data in current prices.
[b] Western Germany.

ing significantly lower costs of borrowing in Japan throughout the 1980s, although the differences had narrowed considerably by the early 1990s. These lower interest rates provided domestic entrepreneurs in Japan with the advantage of a lower cost of capital compared to their U.S. rivals, thus facilitating investment.

### *The Size of Government and the Quality of Its Expenditures*

The size (although not the influence) of government in Japan as measured by total government outlays as a percentage of GDP has been consistently the lowest among the G7 countries. Table 6.5 shows, however, that average total Japanese government outlays grew from 19.5% of GDP in the period 1960–1973 to 32.3% in 1992—a growth of about 65% compared to an increase in the G7 average from 32.4% during 1961–1973 to 45.2% in 1992, a growth of about 30%.

Not only the size but also the purpose of government expenditures is important in determining government's role in enhancing growth. An important indicator of the "quality" of government spending, and a long-

**Table 6.6** Government Investment[a], G7 Countries, 1970–1992
(Percent of GDP)

| | 1970–1979 | 1980–1990 | 1991 | 1992 |
|---|---|---|---|---|
| Canada | 3.3 | 2.5 | 2.4 | 2.4 |
| France | 3.4 | 3.1 | 3.4 | 3.4 |
| Germany[b] | 3.8 | 2.6 | 2.3 | 2.4 |
| Italy | 3.1 | 3.5 | 3.3 | – |
| Japan | 5.4 | 5.3 | 5.1 | – |
| United Kingdom | 4.1 | 1.9 | 1.7 | 1.7 |
| U.S. | 2.0 | 1.5[c] | – | – |

SOURCE: OECD, *Quarterly National Accounts 1993* (1993) and *Economic Outlook*, statistics on microcomputer diskette, December 1992.

[a] Based on data in current prices.
[b] Western Germany.
[c] 1980–1988.

term indicator of prudence in managing public financial affairs, is government net public debt relative to nominal GNP. Japan's debt to GNP ratio has generally been well below the G7 average, falling to under 20% of the average in 1991. The lower ratio of government debt to GNP and lower interest rates in Japan mean that government debt has been less of a drag on the economy than has been the case elsewhere.

While generally there is a consensus among neoclassical economists that the role of government in the economy should be minimal, some concede that government can have a role in attempting to correct market failures. In particular, governments may be called upon to supply physical infrastructure, "especially that which has high fixed costs in relation to variable costs, such as harbours, railways, irrigation canals, and sewers" (Wade, 1990). Government should also supply "public goods" including education and basic research. Japan, despite a lower share of government in the economy, topped the G7 countries in the share of government investment in infrastructure as a percentage of GDP. Government investment in Japan averaged more than 5.0% of GDP during the two decades starting in 1970, well above the rate for the other G7 countries (see Table 6.6).

**Table 6.7** R&D Expenditures, G7 Countries, 1986 and 1991

| | R&D EXPENDITURES[a] (US$MILLION) | | PERCENT OF GDP | | PERCENT FINANCED BY PUBLIC FUNDS | |
|---|---|---|---|---|---|---|
| | 1986 | 1991 | 1986 | 1991 | 1986 | 1991 |
| Canada | 5,732 | 7,568 | 1.47 | 1.46 | 46.3 | 44.6 |
| France | 16,609 | 25,196 | 2.23 | 2.42 | 52.5 | 48.8 |
| Germany[b] | 23,661 | 34,813 | 2.73 | 2.58 | 35.3 | 37.2 |
| Italy | 7,921 | 13,446 | 1.13 | 1.38 | 55.3 | 52.0 |
| Japan | 42,080 | 71,994 | 2.75 | 3.04 | 21.3 | 18.5 |
| United Kingdom[c] | 16,199 | 20,178 | 2.33 | 2.22 | 41.5 | 35.8 |
| U.S. | 121,629 | 154,348 | 2.91 | 2.78 | 48.1 | 46.8 |

SOURCE: OECD, *Main Science and Technology Indicators 1993(1)* (1993).

[a] Based on purchasing power parity exchange rates.
[b] Western Germany.
[c] 1990.

In support of research and development (R&D), the government in Japan spent 0.59% of GDP in 1986 and 0.56% in 1991 (see Table 6.7). The U.S. government, in comparison, spent about 1.40% of GDP in 1986 and 1.30% in 1991. Thus while the share of publicly financed R&D of total R&D expenditures in Japan was 21.3%, and 18.5% in the years 1986 and 1991 respectively, it reached 48.1% and 46.8%, respectively, in the U.S. during the corresponding years. The share of government financing of R&D in other major industrialized countries was also generally much higher than that of Japan (e.g., 37.2% in West Germany, 48.8% in France, 44.6% in Canada in 1991). In absolute terms, however, the Japanese government spent more in 1991 than the governments of the other G7 countries with the exception of the U.S.

Japan's record in public spending on education is not outstanding. Indeed, when one considers total educational expenditures as a percent of GDP in 1987, Japan spent only 6.38% compared to 6.44% for the U.S. and over 7% for some other countries (see Table 6.8). Private sector expenditures on training and education were generally higher in Japan during the 1980s than in the U.S., France and Canada, but significantly lower than in West Germany.

**Table 6.8** Total Educational Expenditure[a], Selected OECD Countries, 1987 (Percent of GDP)

| | |
|---|---|
| Canada | 7.12 |
| Denmark | 7.57 |
| France[b] | 6.59 |
| Germany[c] | 4.41 |
| Japan[b] | 6.38 |
| Netherlands | 7.33 |
| U.S.[b] | 6.44 |

SOURCE: OECD, *Education in OECD Countries, 1987–1988* (1990).

[a] Includes both public and private expenditures on education. Based on data in current prices.
[b] 1986.
[c] Western Germany.

*The Tax System*

The level and structure of taxes play an important role in the promotion of efficient markets. The tax system affects private decisions with respect to consumption, investment and saving. Taxes may also distort the pricing system. Table 6.9 shows that in 1980 personal income taxes and social security taxes as a percentage of GDP in Japan were the lowest in the G7. Indeed, combined personal income taxes and social security taxes as a percentage of GDP were roughly 25% lower than the average in the G7 (only France had slightly lower personal taxes). The total rate of taxation in Japan was among the lowest in the industrialized countries (22.2% of GDP in 1990 excluding social security taxes and 31.3% including social security taxes)—see Table 6.10.

The structure of taxes in Japan (in 1990) showed a relatively low reliance on sales taxes and a relatively high corporate income tax share compared to the other G7 countries (see Table 6.11). The tax system contains relatively fewer incentives for R&D and other types of investments. Warda (1990) provides a comparison of R&D incentives in the G7 countries. He uses the B index which represents a minimum benefit-cost ratio at which an R&D investment becomes profitable in a country (i.e., the higher the B index the lower are the incentives). Japan was ranked as having relatively lower incentives (higher B index) than Canada, France, the U.S. and the U.K., but better

**Table 6.9** Personal Income Taxes (PIT) and Social Security Taxes (SST), G7 Countries, 1980 and 1990 (Percent of GDP[a])

| | PIT (%) | | EMPLOYEE SST (%) | | COMBINED PIT AND EMPLOYEE SST (%) | |
|---|---|---|---|---|---|---|
| | 1980 | 1990 | 1980 | 1990 | 1980 | 1990 |
| Canada | 10.8 | 15.2 | 1.2 | 1.6 | 12.0 | 16.8 |
| France | 5.4 | 5.2 | 4.6 | 5.8 | 10.0 | 11.0 |
| Germany[a] | 11.3 | 10.3 | 5.8 | 6.0 | 17.1 | 16.3 |
| Italy | 7.0 | 10.3 | 2.1 | 2.5 | 9.1 | 12.8 |
| Japan | 6.2 | 8.4 | 2.6 | 3.4 | 8.8 | 11.8 |
| United Kingdom | 10.5 | 10.4 | 2.4 | 2.4 | 12.9 | 12.8 |
| U.S. | 10.9 | 10.7 | 2.9 | 3.5 | 13.8 | 14.2 |
| Unweighted average | 8.9 | 10.1 | 3.1 | 3.6 | 12.0 | 13.7 |

SOURCE: OECD, *Revenue Statistics of OECD Member Countries, 1965–1991* (1992).

[a] Based on data in current prices.
[b] Western Germany.

**Table 6.10** Total Taxation Revenues[a], G7 Countries and Sweden, 1980 and 1990 (Percent of GDP)

| | TAX REVENUE EXCLUDING SOCIAL SECURITY | | SOCIAL SECURITY | | TOTAL TAX REVENUE | |
|---|---|---|---|---|---|---|
| | 1980 | 1990 | 1980 | 1990 | 1980 | 1990 |
| Canada | 28.3 | 31.9 | 3.3 | 5.2 | 31.6 | 37.1 |
| France | 23.9 | 24.4 | 17.8 | 19.3 | 41.7 | 43.7 |
| Germany[b] | 25.1 | 23.8 | 13.1 | 13.9 | 38.2 | 37.7 |
| Italy | 18.7 | 26.3 | 11.5 | 12.8 | 30.2 | 39.1 |
| Japan | 18.0 | 22.2 | 7.4 | 9.1 | 25.4 | 31.3 |
| United Kingdom | 29.5 | 30.3 | 5.8 | 6.4 | 35.3 | 36.7 |
| U.S. | 21.8 | 21.1 | 7.7 | 8.8 | 29.5 | 29.9 |
| Sweden | 34.9 | 41.2 | 14.2 | 15.7 | 49.1 | 56.9 |

SOURCE: OECD, *Revenue Statistics of OECD Member Countries, 1965–1991* (1992).

[a] Based on data in current prices.
[b] 1990 includes the former German Democratic Republic for the second half of the year.

**Table 6.11** Sources of Tax Revenue by Type of Tax, G7 Countries, 1990 (Percent of total tax revenue)

| | PERSONAL | CORPORATE | SALES | SOCIAL SECURITY | OTHER[a] | TOTAL |
|---|---|---|---|---|---|---|
| Canada | 40.8 | 6.8 | 27.4 | 14.2 | 10.8 | 100.0 |
| France | 11.8 | 7.3 | 16.5 | 29.5 | 10.9 | 100.0 |
| Germany[b] | 27.4 | 4.7 | 27.4 | 36.8 | 3.7 | 100.0 |
| Italy | 26.3 | 10.0 | 28.0 | 32.9 | 2.8 | 100.0 |
| Japan | 26.8 | 21.5 | 13.2 | 29.2 | 9.3 | 100.0 |
| United Kingdom | 28.4 | 11.0 | 30.4 | 17.5 | 12.7 | 100.0 |
| U.S. | 35.8 | 7.3 | 16.5 | 29.5 | 10.9 | 100.0 |

SOURCES: OECD, *Revenue Statistics of OECD Member Countries, 1965–1991* (1992).

[a] Other includes payroll and property taxes.
[b] Western Germany.

incentives (lower B index) than Germany and Italy. Thus while the level of taxes in the economy corresponds in relative terms to the neoclassical prescriptions of lower tax levels, the structure of taxes with their higher emphasis on corporate taxes appears to be inconsistent with the accepted belief among economists as to what constitutes a fiscal policy that promotes international competitiveness (i.e., lower corporate taxes and an economy-wide added value tax).

When one examines the patterns of investment in the economy, however, it is obvious that in Japan, perhaps despite the tax system, the private sector has aggressively invested in machinery and equipment and in R&D, exceeding significantly the levels of private investment in the other G7 countries (see Table 6.12). For example, during the period of 1968–1973, investment in machinery and equipment in Japan was 14.4% of GDP, and 11.1% in 1974–1990. In contrast, in the U.S. only 7.0% of GDP was invested in machinery and equipment in 1960–1973 and 7.7% in 1974–1990. Similarly, examination of Table 6.7 reveals that in 1991 Japan spent 3.04% of its GDP on R&D compared to 2.78% in the U.S. and lower relative outlays in the other G7 countries.

The conclusion that can be distilled from the comparative examination of Japan's macro-economic policies is that in terms of actual spending the Japanese government left ample breathing space for the private sector. In relative terms, Japan's government was (and is) a small government. Its macro-economic policies, while ensuring relative stability, did not outperform significantly the policies of other countries. Yet despite the relative low size of government there is ample evidence to indicate that the Japanese government exercised a large measure of control on its economy; control which appears to be inconsistent with neoclassical prescriptions of how a country can exploit its comparative advantages to improve the value of its output.

## Trade, Investment and Industrial Policies: A Departure from the Neoclassical Prescription

The neoclassical theory indicates that every nation will be better off if free markets prevail domestically and internationally. Each nation will focus on those activities in which its costs are relatively cheapest. Wade (1990, p. 14) observed, however, that "the theory of comparative advantage covers the effects of once-and-for-all changes in trade restrictions. It does not specify a causal mechanism linking realization of comparative advantage to higher growth." Indeed, while it is possible that market forces will ensure the allocation of resources in an efficient manner given the prevailing pattern of resources in the economy, there is no assurance that the growth path they will lead to is one of high growth. A radical change in the quality and/or quantity of resources available may create new types of comparative advantage that assure higher growth paths.

Governments may act to change comparative advantage by focusing on resource creation or enhancement. This, in a way, is an extension to the role prescribed by some neoclassical economists in correcting market failures. High public investment in education or measures aimed to create capital, if not targeted to specific sectors, may change the comparative advantage in the economy, while still leaving market forces to determine the optimal resource allocation in the economy. Governments may also attempt to affect the price system if they perceive distortions in the existing operations of markets (i.e., they may attempt to bring about, by intervention, the price patterns that competitive market forces would have produced had they prevailed).

The record of Japan in the past three decades is clearly one of strong intervention in markets and relatively tight control on its international economic relationships. There are those who argue that the interventionist past

**Table 6.12** Machinery and Equipment Investment[a], G7 Countries, 1960–1992 (Percent of GDP)

| | 1960–1973 | 1974–1990 | 1991 | 1992 |
|---|---|---|---|---|
| Canada | 7.2 | 7.5 | 7.4 | 7.4 |
| France | 9.0 | 8.7 | 9.4 | 8.7 |
| Germany[b] | 9.1 | 8.3 | 10.0 | 9.3 |
| Italy | 9.5 | 10.2 | 9.4 | 9.0 |
| Japan | 14.3[c] | 11.1 | – | – |
| United Kingdom | 8.6 | 8.4 | 7.4 | 7.3 |
| U.S. | 7.0 | 7.7 | 6.4 | 6.4 |

SOURCE: OECD, *Quarterly National Accounts, 1993(1)* (1993) and *Economic Outlook Historical Statistics, 1960–1990* (1992).

[a] Based on data in current prices.
[b] Western Germany.
[c] 1968–1973.

merely reflected attempts by the Japanese government to correct for market failures. Saxonhouse (1983, 1985), for example, saw the role of MITI's industrial policies as providing information which, in countries with developed capital markets, are provided by those markets. Patrick (1977) viewed the Japanese economy as one where private individuals and enterprises respond to "quite free" market forces.

The evidence presented in Chapters 3, 4, and 5, however, indicates that government actions in Japan were and continue to be more than just attempts to correct for market failures. Indeed, it is argued that the "Japanese were the first to recognize that international competitive advantage could be deliberately created by government not just to nurture a few infant industries to supply the domestic market but to push broad sets of industries towards areas of growth and technological change in the world economy" (Wade, 1990, p. 25).

As pointed out in Chapter 3, MITI has consistently engaged in picking industrial sectors as targets for special promotion while facilitating the retrenchment of declining sectors. Sectors with high income elasticity where technological progress is rapid and labour productivity rises quickly were targeted as strategic sectors offering Japan the maximum potential for achieving full employment of its dense population, with the prospect of a rising standard of living.

While there are those who attributed Japanese economic success to government leadership, in particular to the guidance and control exercised by MITI, the more "tenable formulation is a synergistic connection between a public system and a mostly private market system, the outputs of each becoming inputs for the other, with the government setting rules and influencing decision-making in the private sector in line with its view of an appropriate industrial and trade profile for the economy" (Wade, 1990, p. 5). This mechanism provides for the imposition of market discipline (through competition) and an efficient means of information processing and risk spreading (through multiple experiments and decentralization) on a long-term vision. At the same time, the vision is insulated to a degree from the instabilities and randomness to which market processes are susceptible.

To steer the economy towards its long-term vision, Japan, far from liberalizing its trade and investment regulations, engaged in strict control and active discouragement of foreign direct investment and adopted a combination of trade policies, restricting and protecting some domestic industries, while promoting exports (see Chapter 5). The Japanese have closed domestic markets to imports in industries they chose to encourage, so domestic producers could expand from a stable demand base, gain the benefits of climbing the learning curve, obtain economies of scale and achieve international competitiveness.

Export competitiveness was not achieved by opening the domestic market to foreign competitors. It was achieved by removing constraints on imports of raw materials to be used for export production. Constraints were imposed even on intermediate inputs to the export industry. Exports were promoted by direct provision of export tax credits and export-import links. The competitiveness of the export industry, however, was also maintained by the strong rivalry among Japanese producers in the domestic market. The protection and incentives offered in domestic market by the government allowed them to price exports below their average costs in order to gain market shares and enjoy future benefits of economies of scale.

Shinohara (1982) points out the early debates between the economists in the Bank of Japan and the Ministry of Finance who subscribed to the neoclassical notions, and MITI's position of deliberately creating new comparative advantage by promoting and funding investment in the heavy and chemical industries as well as the automobile industry. MITI won the debate. "From that time on MITI saw one of its key functions to encourage the introduction of new technologies through new investment" (Wade, 1990, p. 298).

The implementation route of this policy, however, involved a major role for the private sector (see Chapter 3). As evidence presented earlier shows, public funds have not been spent in any sizable amounts compared to the total requirements (see also Trezise, 1983). Wade (1990, p. 329) observes that "at issue, however, is not the absolute amounts of public funds but whether they had an important signalling effect on private bank lending or on company management. The close correlation between the sector composition of industrial loans from public financial institutions and the same for private financial institutions suggests a strong signalling effect."

MITI's choice of strategic sectors for promotion, however, was not entirely divorced from attending to market signals. MITI conducted studies of demand elasticities for various goods in major world markets. It studied trends in technological change in related industries. It examined income elasticities of these products. It then focused on products with high income elasticity and rapid technological change, examining whether the share of these products in Japanese exports was comparable to the share of these products in world trade. Thus the target of MITI was to ensure Japanese participation in promising growth industries where rapid technological change offered the prospect of increasing productivity. Targeting some sectors for promotion by government did not mean, however, that private initiatives in other sectors were stifled. As indicated in Chapter 3, many firms in sectors that were not targeted for government assistance managed to grow and compete successfully in global markets.

Other factors that ensured that bureaucratic decisions were sensitive to market signals were the tight linkages and special power balance between the bureaucracy and industry. Krasner (1978) has suggested that government can achieve one of three qualitatively different levels of control over economic behaviour. The most forceful government can change the behaviour of private economic agents as well as the structure of the economy itself. On the contrary, a weaker government can resist private demands but is unable to transform the behaviour of private economic agents. Japan, however, appears to defy this hierarchy of intervention capabilities. Samuels (1983, p. 49), on analyzing Japan's post-war energy policy, observes that:

> transwar Japanese energy policy seems neither a story of a dominant state nor one of a state captive to private interests. Nor even does it seem one of an impartial "broker" state. It is one of an activist state, a "player" with comprehensive visions and a role, but with capabilities that do not seem consistent with general characterizations that posit Japan should necessarily resemble France more than the United States.

Johnson (1983) observed that, even during the war, the zaibatsu (pre-war business groups) managed to resist attempts by the government to achieve full control of production and distribution. Samuels (1983, p. 49) concludes, on the basis of his and Johnson's studies, that:

> It is hard to come away from these studies with any impression about state autonomy short of its very existence. State and private interests clashed often and with such widespread effects that any imputation of the Japanese state as a passive institution "sans" autonomous (even if often uncoordinated and hopelessly unachievable) goals and visions for the nation is inconceivable. The state seems an autonomous player, but its role is clearly limited by historically determined configurations of the negotiated market economy. Secondly, these studies suggest it is at least debatable whether or not the transwar Japanese state enjoyed a capacity to see these visions through to their attainment. While the Japanese state may have a strategic position in these negotiations, one is struck as much by the constraints upon the Japanese state as by its unfettered prerogatives.

The checks imposed by private interests (who are concerned with market realities) on the long-term vision expressed in public policies ensures an optimal policy formulation where "short-termism" dictated by markets does not rule but long-term visions are scrutinized by those close to the market. The history of the auto industry in Japan provides an excellent illustration of this interplay between government policies and market forces.

> In 1952, the government did succeed in curbing automobile imports under a strict quota system. Those import controls, which continued until October 1965, did help Japan's automobile industry stand on its own feet. But when MITI tried in 1955 to shape the development of the auto industry directly with a plan to build a national car it went too far. The plan sought to have a single company mass produce an ultra small popular car that was both inexpensive and exportable. MITI proposed to grant the manufacturer of such a car financial aid and legal protection in a bid to increase employment, improve technical know-how, and lay the groundwork for an automobile export industry. However by the time MITI introduced this grand scheme, consumer choices were already influencing corporate strategy. The forces of the marketplace ultimately led Japan's auto makers into a growth pattern totally different from what MITI had in mind (Tsuruta, 1983, p. 45).

A system of business-government advisory committees, an intricate signalling system and an informal communication network buttressed by permanent career patterns ensure a continuous flow of information between the government and the private sector (see Samuels, 1981; Johnson, 1978 and 1982; Nemetz, Vertinsky and Vertinsky, 1985).

Wade (1990) observed that the government of Japan had not so much picked winners as made them. The targeting of specific industries was only part of creating a larger environment conducive to viability of new industries and the promotion of productivity and competitiveness. Such an environment must encourage productive investment while discouraging unproductive investment. The creation of such an environment by a bureaucracy requires it not only to have the ability to generate and evaluate creative options but also to be single-minded in its pursuit of economic growth. Such a bureaucracy must be insulated from the interference of interest groups or politicians (see e.g., Johnson, 1982 and 1984).

MITI's strategies were more successful at the industry level than when it attempted to intervene at the firm level (see Chapter 3). Governments may be able to create comparative advantage as long as they do not try to choose winners among firms, but rather allow competitive processes to choose winners and losers.

While the government played a significant role in developing the social capabilities of the nation to grow, it relied on a vigorous and disciplined private sector. The unique features of Japanese industrial organization and business practices and the role they played in ensuring economic growth are reviewed in Chapter 2. The system of industrial relations, for example, created on environment conducive to (1) innovation, (2) increases in productivity, and (3) enhancement of and investment in human capital, and (4) maintenance of stability. It is a system that facilitates growth but is somewhat dysfunctional in times of retrenchment.

The industrial organization, in particular the role corporate groups play, facilitated cooperation while maintaining the benefits of a competitive environment, provided opportunities for risk sharing, information diffusion and the development of network economies. It also provided an institutional infrastructure through which government-industry communication could flow effectively. Finally, the concentration of power in large business groups created the necessary counter balance to an activist government. The nature of corporate control which encourages a long-term perspective in business decisions also contributes to an alignment between the collective interest espoused by the government and the specific interest of the firm.

## Lessons for Canada from the Japanese Experience

Are there lessons from the Japanese experience for Canada? There can be serious dangers in drawing conclusions from the experience of one country and applying them to another. It is possible that a given mix of policies appropriate in a particular international economic environment and a specific domestic economic and institutional environment may fail in other circumstances. It is also possible that the particular policy mix employed in the same country at different times may fail to yield the results it obtained in a different international environment. It is important to remember that the analysis in this book has not dealt with an important variable that may condition social capabilities for growth—the national culture. It is possible that for the Japanese type of business-government relationship to emerge, for the industrial relations system to operate efficiently and for industrial organization to function as it does, a culture which is collectivistic rather than individualistic is necessary. The extent to which the relationships discovered in the Japanese economic experience are culture bound is not clear, thus any generalization is uncertain. Canada can learn some lessons from Japan if we keep these caveats in mind.

An important lesson Canada can learn is that comparative advantage can be *created,* and the fact that Canada enjoys a comparative advantage in natural resource products need not confine it to a path which dooms it to continuous erosion of its terms of trade. Policies to create a change in comparative advantage (i.e., industrial policies) are less risky in Japan, since a large competitive domestic market can be used to "create winners" by offering them a secure demand base as they climb the learning curve and obtain economies to scale. Canada's small domestic market does not provide as many options for the government to use protection of the domestic market as a launch-pad for internationally competitive firms. Protection of small and uncompetitive markets rarely creates the appropriate incentives that ensure the growth of productivity and innovation. It is more likely that Canada's industrial policies will end up perpetually shoring up losers rather than creating winners.

The size and intensity of competition in the domestic market are only two of the preconditions for the implementation of a successful industrial policy (they are not even necessary conditions, as the Korean experience suggests). For the bureaucracy to be able to "pick winners," it needs to be insulated from the influence of other interests outside those directly relevant to efficiency and economic growth. Canada's federal structure and the preoccupation of the political system with questions of distribution of income (e.g., concerns for inter-regional equity and the use of the economic system to solve social problems) probably would generate industrial policies that are unlikely to be attuned to achieving success in world markets. Indeed, in the long run it is a political system that creates pressures on the bureaucracy to save losers and ignore winners.

A more economically centralized country, a higher commitment to economic growth and a bureaucracy insulated from the influence of interest groups are important preconditions that may increase the probability that industrial policies could achieve a higher growth path than would free market forces (market forces at least ensure allocative efficiency and reduce the intensity of rent seeking behaviours).

One also must consider the limits on the arsenal of policy tools available to a government. Canada's federal structure, its international commitments and its relatively high dependence on foreign capital impose severe constraints on the options of the government to intervene selectively in the economy.

Perhaps the most important lesson for Canada from Japan's experience is that government influence and a strong vision do not require a large government as measured in expenditure terms. The smaller size of government in Japan leaves room (and incentives) for the private sector to grow and implement effectively the government's long-term vision of economic growth without stifling the creative private search for opportunities. Implementation left to the private sector also allows an economic system the flexibility necessary to adapt to new environmental conditions. Synergistic linkages of the private and the public sectors in Japan ensure that the vision espoused by government is not divorced from market realities and that multiple independent voices (e.g., the variety of independent advisory boards) contribute to the vision and help disseminate it.

Finally, Japan's experience shows that a stable macro-economic policy environment is desirable, but temporary small sacrifices of stability are necessary to support long-term restructuring. The use of induced crises has often facilitated the acceptance of sometimes painful means by the private sector and the public.

7

# Canada and Japan

## Bilateral Economic Relations

### Introduction

Japan is Canada's largest single overseas market and constitutes the world's second largest free-market economy. It enjoys a growing share of world trade and continues to be one of the fastest growing major economies in the world. Japan is also on the leading edge of technological developments, and its current account surpluses make it the world's largest exporter of capital. These qualities and the promise of growing access to the Japanese market (due to the gradual removal of structural and regulatory impediments to trade) provide a focus for Canadian policy development with respect to bilateral economic relations with Japan.

In this chapter, the pattern of the bilateral economic relationship are analyzed and the policy objectives and impacts of Canada's responses to threats and opportunities in three complementary areas—trade, investment, and technology development and transfer—are analyzed

## Macro-Patterns of Canada-Japan Trade*

Exported goods and services consist of commodities and differentiated goods and services. Commodity suppliers largely compete in terms of prices. Thus, low-cost producers obtain larger market shares, driving rivals with higher costs of production out of the market. Increases in productivity or the lowering of the relative exchange rate for "home" currencies are often the key variables explaining increases in market share of firms from a specific country in a particular foreign market (provided free access to that market exists). Competition among producers of differentiated goods is less sensitive to cost advantages and is reflected in the attempts of producers to match the demands of customers for specific product attributes (e.g., quality, custom tailoring to the needs of particular customers). Increases in market shares of differentiated products reflect the ability of producers to respond to changes in market demand or their ability to influence demand through product and service innovations and the employment of effective marketing strategies.

Canada's comparative advantage rests largely in the production of natural resource-based commodities, with only a few examples of comparative advantage manifested in sectors producing differentiated goods and services. In contrast, Japan possesses few natural resources, and its economic growth in the past three decades has been based on comparative advantages created by investment, production management skills and technological innovation as described in Chapter 5. In this section, how the countries'

* Two sources of data are used in this discussion of Canada-Japan trade relations. The primary source is Statistics Canada's World Trade Database on CD-ROM which contains information for 1980–1991. Ideally, trade data as reported by one country should match data reported by other countries. For example, data on imports from Japan as reported by Statistics Canada should match data on exports to Canada as reported by the Japanese authorities, since the same trade transactions are covered. In practice, large discrepancies are observed. In the introduction to Chapter 5, we noted the different conventions used in Canadian and Japanese trade statistics. The unique feature of the World Trade Database is the presentation of bilateral trade flow data for over 100 countries and 600 commodities with complete internal consistency—thus the data for imports by country A from country B always match the data for exports of country B to country A. The second source of data used here is the regularly published international trade data of Statistics Canada. These data include 1992, but use a different commodity classification scheme than that used in the World Trade Database. They provide useful information on trade volumes for recent years, from which unit values can be derived.

**Fig. 7.1** Canadian Trade with Japan

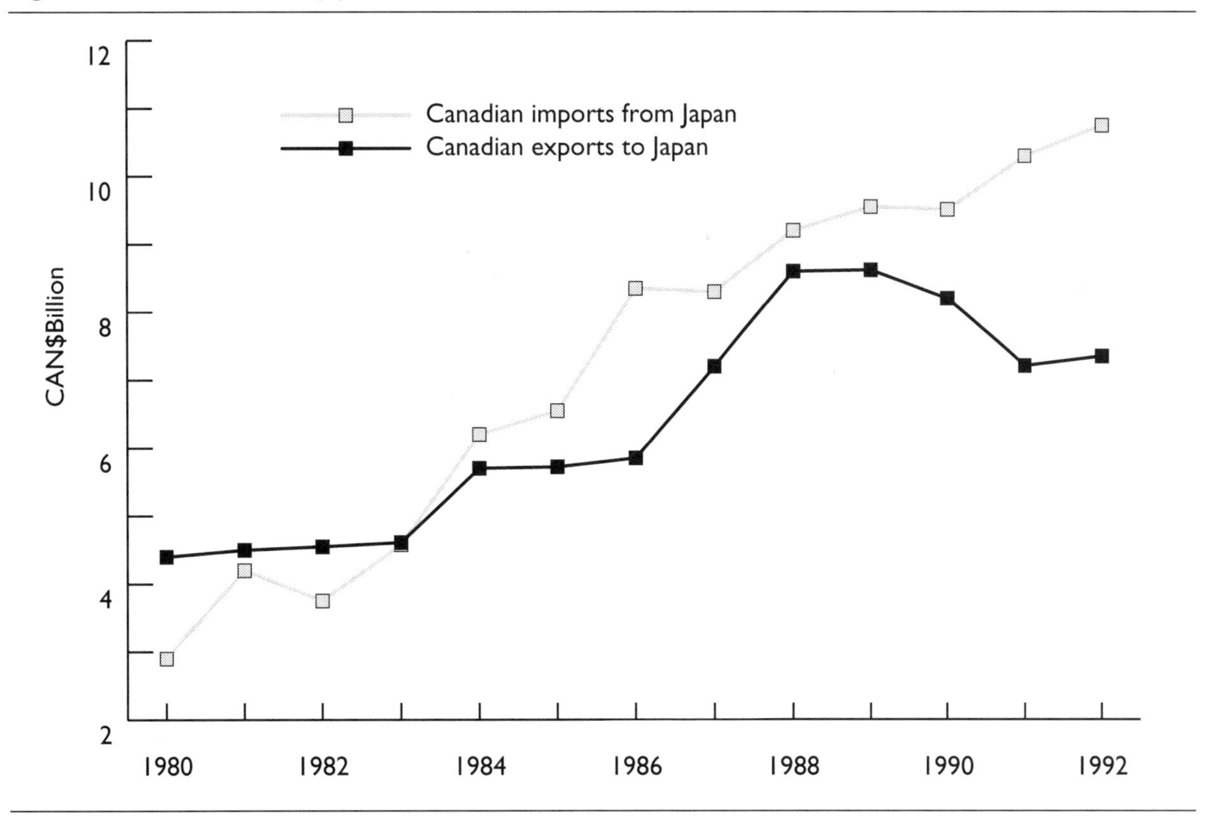


SOURCE: Statistics Canada, Catalogues 65–002 and 65–203 (various years).

respective specializations have effected the structure and trends in their trading relationship is examined.

In 1992, Canada exported CAN$7,485 million worth of goods to Japan, up 71% from the 1980 level of CAN$4,373 million, but below the 1989 peak of CAN$8,844 million (see Figure 7.1). This peak was created at least in part by the 1985 Plaza Accord which resulted in a significant appreciation of the yen vis-à-vis the Canadian dollar in 1985–1988 (a 68% appreciation). Imports did not suffer a corresponding fall despite the appreciation, although import growth did level off somewhat. Overall, however, imports rose from CAN$2,904 million in 1980 to CAN$10,762 million in 1992, a 271% increase. This could partially reflect a willingness on the part of

Japanese exporters to absorb the impact of price increases and exchange rate appreciations by reducing profit margins, in an effort to maintain market share. Thus, although a substantial drop in Canada's trade deficit with Japan occurred in 1986–1987, the deficit quickly increased back to a record high of CAN$3,277 million in 1992.

The United States dominates Canada's international trade as the destination for 75% of exports and the source of 70% of imports in 1991. Japan is Canada's second most important export market, taking 5.1% of Canadian exports in 1991 (about one-fifth of all exports to destinations other than the United States). On the import side, Japan also ranks second with 6.4% of total Canadian imports.

Canada is less important for Japan, both as an import source and as an export destination. On the import side, the United States accounted for 22.3% of total Japanese imports in 1991, followed by South Korea, Australia and Indonesia each with 5–6%. Canada ranked tenth with about 3% of the Japanese import market. On the export side, the United States accounted for 29.3% of total Japanese exports in 1991, followed by the Federal Republic of Germany and fast-growing South Korea, Taiwan and Hong Kong, all with shares of over 5% in 1991. Canada ranked tenth, holding a share of 2.6%.

## *Canadian Exports to Japan*

Table 7.1 summarizes the Canada-Japan trading relationship for the years 1980, 1985 and 1991. The first three columns of data in Table 7.1 show the structure of Canadian exports to Japan using two-digit Standard Industrial Trade Classification (SITC) categories. Only categories that account for over CAN$100 million in exports in 1991 are included, and the categories are presented in order from largest to smallest 1991 share in total exports to Japan. The table also presents a disaggregation of total Canadian exports to Japan into major product groupings.* Columns four to six show the impor-

* The aggregate groupings are defined as follows: food, beverages and tobacco, SITC 00–12; crude resources excluding fuel, SITC 21–29, 41–43; fuels, SITC 32, 33, 34; resource based manufactures, 61–69; chemicals, SITC 51–59; machinery and equipment, SITC 71–79, 87; and consumer and other manufactured goods, SITC 81–85, 88–89. SITC category 9, commodities and transactions not classified, is not included in these broad groupings.

tance of Canadian firms as suppliers of Japanese import demand for each category. The next three columns indicate the importance of Japan as a market for Canadian exporters of each product category. Finally, the last two columns show the average annual growth rate of Canadian exports to Japan and of total Japanese import demand.

In 1991, Canada's principal exports to Japan were coal (17.8% of Canadian exports to Japan), wood (17.3%), metal ores (10.2%), cereals (7.5%), oil seeds (7.4%) and pulp (7.1%). All of the 12 commodity categories shown in Table 7.1 are resource-based, with varying degrees of manufacturing involved—overall, crude materials and resource-based manufactures excluding fuels and foods accounted for over 50% of Canadian exports to Japan. Fuels (almost entirely coal) and foods products (primarily fish and shellfish, cereals and meat) accounted for another 36% of exports. Higher valued added machinery and equipment and light manufacturing consumer goods accounted for less than 5% of Canadian exports. Over the decade of the 1980s, there was little change in the predominance of resource products in Canadian exports to Japan although there were important shifts in the mix of resource product exports (in value terms).

Canada accounted for 3% of Japanese imports in 1991 and thus is not a major supplier to the Japanese import market. However, Canadian firms hold a significant market share in Japan in some commodity categories (see Table 7.1). In 1991, 30% of Japanese pulp imports, 28% of oil seed imports (98% of canola imports), 22% of coal imports and between 10–20% of paper, wood and cereal imports were provided by Canadian sources. Canadian firms were also important suppliers of some products which account for a relatively small share of Canadian exports to Japan, but which nevertheless hold a large market share in Japan (animal fats and oils at 25%, manufactured fertilizers at 16%). Over the 1980s and into the early years of the current decade Canada has maintained its market share in food, fuels and resource products but its share of machinery and equipment and consumer and other manufactured goods remained low and fell slightly.

The implications of these broad characteristics of Canada's position in the Japanese import market can be placed in perspective by examining the evolution of Japanese import demand (see Table 7.1). Total imports grew at an average annual rate of 4.8% in 1981–1991 (slightly higher than the average annual growth of imports from Canada of 4.6%). This aggregate figure

**Table 7.1** Principal Canadian Exports To Japan by 2-Digit SITC Categories, 1980, 1985 and 1991 (Percent)

| SITC Code | Product Category | Product share in total Canadian exports to Japan | | | Canadian share in Japanese imports by product | | |
|---|---|---|---|---|---|---|---|
| | | 1980 | 1985 | 1991 | 1980 | 1985 | 1991 |
| 32 | Coal | 13.1 | 24.9 | 17.8 | 14.5 | 23.8 | 21.6 |
| 24 | Wood | 13.2 | 9.6 | 17.3 | 8.9 | 13.0 | 16.2 |
| 28 | Metal ores and scrap | 18.2 | 10.9 | 10.2 | 10.8 | 9.3 | 8.9 |
| 04 | Cereals | 10.2 | 8.6 | 7.5 | 10.1 | 10.5 | 12.8 |
| 22 | Oil seeds | 7.9 | 9.8 | 7.4 | 18.5 | 24.8 | 27.7 |
| 25 | Pulp | 10.5 | 7.0 | 7.1 | 41.7 | 36.2 | 30.0 |
| 03 | Fish and shellfish | 2.5 | 5.6 | 6.0 | 3.6 | 5.8 | 3.7 |
| 68 | Nonferrous metals | 5.5 | 4.6 | 4.8 | 6.0 | 5.0 | 3.5 |
| 51 | Organic chemicals | 1.5 | 3.3 | 3.2 | 4.1 | 6.8 | 4.9 |
| 64 | Paper and paperboard | 1.0 | 1.3 | 2.1 | 8.9 | 11.0 | 12.4 |
| 01 | Meat | 3.2 | 2.2 | 1.9 | 9.3 | 5.3 | 2.5 |
| 08 | Feed for animals | 1.0 | 1.1 | 1.4 | 8.3 | 12.6 | 7.3 |
| | Subtotal | 87.8 | 88.9 | 86.7 | 10.6 | 12.1 | 9.7 |
| | Food, beverages and tobacco | 17.4 | 18.1 | 17.8 | 5.3 | 5.7 | 3.8 |
| | Crude resources excluding fuels | 52.3 | 39.1 | 43.9 | 10.4 | 11.0 | 11.8 |
| | Fuels | 14.6 | 25.4 | 18.0 | 0.9 | 2.5 | 2.4 |
| | Resource-based manufactures | 7.9 | 6.7 | 8.4 | 3.7 | 2.8 | 1.9 |
| | Chemicals | 4.0 | 5.9 | 5.4 | 3.1 | 3.7 | 2.5 |
| | Machinery and equipment | 3.3 | 2.2 | 3.9 | 1.6 | 0.8 | 0.6 |
| | Consumer and other manufactured goods | 0.4 | 0.3 | 0.8 | 0.4 | 0.2 | 0.2 |
| | Total | 100.0 | 100.0 | 100.0 | 3.2 | 4.0 | 3.0 |

SOURCE: Based on data from Statistics Canada, *World Trade Database on CD-ROM.*

[a] Growth rates are based on values in Canadian dollars.

gives a somewhat misleading picture because of Japan's dependence on fuel imports—the share of fuels in the total value of Japanese imports was 52.1% in 1980, compared to 23.3% in 1991. Excluding fuels, Japanese import demand has risen at an average rate of over 9% a year since 1980. Figure 7.2 shows that import growth has been strongest in the categories of

| JAPANESE SHARE IN CANADIAN EXPORTS BY PRODUCT | | | AVERAGE ANNUAL GROWTH IN VALUE[a], 1981–1991 | |
|---|---|---|---|---|
| 1980 | 1985 | 1991 | Canadian Exports to Japan | Total Japanese Imports |
| 67.8 | 68.7 | 59.3 | 8.3 | 3.7 |
| 16.8 | 11.0 | 22.3 | 8.8 | 2.6 |
| 19.8 | 18.2 | 19.3 | –0.2 | 1.1 |
| 9.7 | 10.9 | 12.8 | 2.7 | 0.1 |
| 56.5 | 67.5 | 73.1 | 5.1 | 0.4 |
| 12.3 | 11.7 | 10.5 | 3.3 | 5.4 |
| 9.1 | 17.6 | 18.1 | 15.4 | 13.4 |
| 6.0 | 6.2 | 5.8 | 5.1 | 9.8 |
| 7.5 | 14.4 | 15.0 | 15.3 | 10.4 |
| 1.0 | 1.1 | 1.7 | 14.5 | 8.4 |
| 28.1 | 15.5 | 15.1 | 1.4 | 12.6 |
| 17.7 | 29.1 | 25.7 | 9.7 | 10.8 |
| 13.5 | 14.8 | 14.9 | 4.4 | 5.1 |
| 9.7 | 10.9 | 10.9 | 5.2 | 7.9 |
| 16.3 | 13.9 | 18.2 | 3.4 | 1.8 |
| 6.6 | 9.7 | 8.8 | 7.1 | –1.0 |
| 2.7 | 2.2 | 2.6 | 5.5 | 12.0 |
| 4.5 | 6.2 | 5.3 | 8.1 | 9.6 |
| 0.8 | 0.3 | 0.5 | 9.7 | 14.8 |
| 1.3 | 0.6 | 1.3 | 14.3 | 17.2 |
| 6.1 | 4.9 | 5.1 | 4.6 | 4.8 |

consumer and other manufactured goods, and in machinery and equipment. In the 1980–1991 period, total Japanese imports of consumer goods grew at an average rate of over 17% per year, while machinery and equipment imports grew at an average of almost 15% per year (see Table 7.1). Some categories of high valued added imports have risen at over 20% per

**Fig. 7.2** Japanese Total Imports

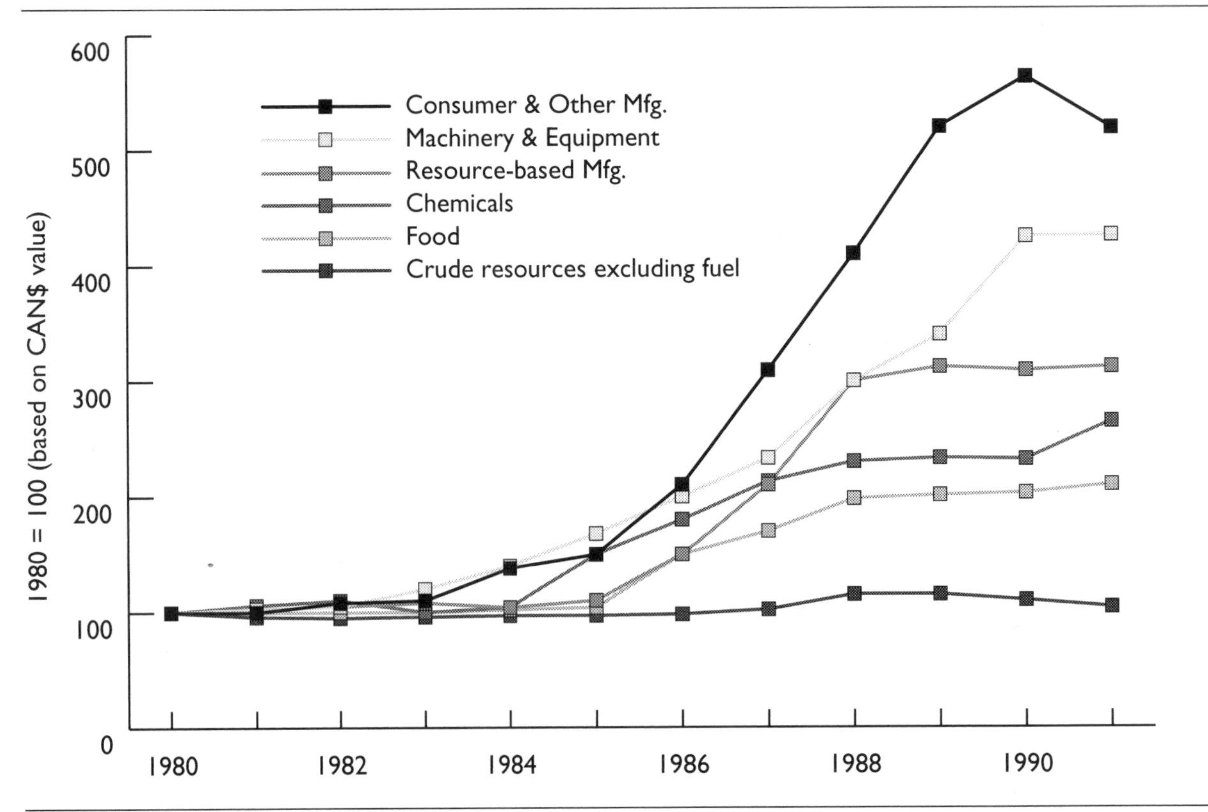


SOURCE: Statistics Canada, *World Trade Database on CD-ROM.*

year—for example, telecommunications equipment, road vehicles and parts, building fixtures, travel goods and furniture. In contrast, Canada's role in the Japanese market is concentrated in areas that are declining in importance. While resource-based manufactures grew at an average of 12% per year, crude resources excluding fuels, the segment which accounts for a substantial portion of imports from Canada, grew at an average of only 1.8% per year. The value of fuel imports declined in absolute terms although coal imports managed to grow slowly.

Another interesting perspective on Canadian exports is the importance of the Japanese market for Canadian exporters. Although the United States clearly dominates Canadian exports, Japan is a major market for Canadian firms in a number of product categories. These include oil seeds (73% of exports go to Japan—99% of canola exports go to Japan), coal (59%), wood (22%) and fish and shellfish (18%).

Changes in the structure (in value terms) of Canadian exports to Japan may result from either changes in the volume or price of Canadian exports. Table 7.2 provides some insights into these changes by examining the top 25 six-digit Harmonized System (HS) categories of Canadian exports to Japan in 1992. The table shows average annual growth rates for value, volume and unit value over the 1989–1992 period. The products listed accounted for 71% of export value in 1988, and by 1992 accounted for 77%. Note that all of these products are crude resources or resource-based manufactured products.

Over the 1988–1992 period, prices fell for half of the 24 products for which unit value figures could be calculated. The export value of ten of the 24 products declined. In five cases, both volume and price fell (coal, copper, unalloyed aluminum, chemical softwood pulp and fish livers and roe). In two cases, price increases were not enough to overcome volume declines while price decreases outweighed volume increases in three cases. Of the remaining 14 products for which export value grew, in eight cases both volume and price increased. In two cases, the price increase outweighed volume decline, while the reverse was true in four cases.

The price movements associated with many of these exports are representative of some of the problems that a specialization in commodities can entail. In many cases, exporters are subject to extremely volatile price fluctuations resulting from world market conditions. For example, the price of the three pulp commodities appearing in Table 7.2 fell by between 20% and 40% in 1989–1991. As another example, the prices of the fish and shellfish products shown experienced annual price changes ranging from –30% to 120%. In some cases, prices fell in every year over the 1988–1992 period. This was the case with rape seed (a total fall of 19%) and alloyed and unalloyed unwrought aluminum (falls of about 40% each).

In summary, many of Canada's major exports to Japan have faced declining and/or volatile prices and relatively low growth in demand. Structural changes in Japan's economy—particularly divestment or shifts to foreign production in many resource-consuming and resource-processing sectors and increased investments in high technology—have led to reduced demand

**Table 7.2** 25 Major Canadian Exports To Japan: Value, Volume and Price, 1988 and 1992 (Unit value)

| | | VALUE (CAN$MILLION) | | VOLUME[a] | |
|---|---|---|---|---|---|
| HS Code | Product Description | 1988 | 1992 | 1988 | 1992 |
| 4407.10 | Softwood lumber, thickness > 6mm | 859.9 | 1,325.5 | 3,429,963 | 4,732,800 |
| 2701.12 | Bituminous coal, not agglomerated | 1,409.6 | 1,006.7 | 19,260,400 | 14,119,700 |
| 2603.00 | Copper ores and concentrates | 680.5 | 541.5 | 252,383 | 237,504 |
| 1205.00 | Rape or colza seeds | 541.2 | 482.0 | 1,546,532 | 1,702,820 |
| 4703.21 | Bleached chemical softwood pulp n.e.s. | 695.9 | 374.9 | 859,243 | 635,741 |
| 1001.90 | Wheat n.e.s. and meslin | 266.5 | 272.0 | 1,186,100 | 1,267,000 |
| 4801.00 | Newsprint | 96.5 | 183.8 | 131,032 | 221,153 |
| 7601.20 | Aluminum, unwrought, alloyed | 154.9 | 164.9 | 58,553 | 108,473 |
| 0203.29 | Frozen swine cuts n.e.s. | 111.3 | 143.5 | 19,952 | 29,886 |
| 4403.20 | Softwood logs and poles n.e.s. | 220.6 | 125.6 | – | – |
| 0305.20 | Fish livers and roes except fresh | 167.2 | 121.9 | 7,202 | 5,596 |
| 1003.00 | Barley | 97.9 | 120.2 | 817,200 | 860,400 |
| 4703.29 | Bleached chemical hardwood pulp | 135.1 | 111.8 | 173,092 | 193,023 |
| 0303.10 | Frozen pacific salmon except livers and roes | 96.6 | 97.4 | 9,807 | 12,922 |
| 4401.21 | Softwood chips | 50.1 | 85.5 | 581,400 | 618,800 |
| 0306.14 | Frozen crabs | 70.7 | 77.4 | 5,784 | 9,040 |
| 1107.10 | Unroasted malt | 41.9 | 73.7 | 127,829 | 216,217 |
| 3104.20 | Potassium chloride, packages > 10 kg | 77.3 | 70.6 | 657,570 | 513,000 |
| 2608.00 | Zinc ores and concentrates | 61.8 | 65.2 | 100,266 | 73,439 |
| 2710.00 | Petroleum oils except crude | 31.6 | 65.0 | 1,985,609 | 3,939,262 |
| 1214.10 | Alfalfa meal and pellets | 40.6 | 62.3 | 304,705 | 447,987 |
| 7601.10 | Aluminum, unwrought, not alloyed | 149.3 | 50.8 | 66,739 | 37,586 |
| 4701.00 | Mechanical wood pulp | 54.1 | 45.9 | 116,546 | 111,827 |
| 2524.00 | Asbestos | 46.9 | 47.3 | 101,198 | 95,366 |
| 0303.79 | Frozen fish n.e.s. except livers & roes | 69.2 | 40.1 | 36,556 | 14,274 |
| | Subtotal | 6,227 | 5,756 | | |
| | Total exports to Japan | 8,813 | 7,485 | | |

SOURCE: Statistics Canada, *Catalogue 65–202: Exports Merchandise Trade* (various issues).

[a] All volume data are tonnes, except softwood lumber ($m^3$), pulp (air dried tonnes) and petroleum oils (hectolitres).
[b] All prices are $/tonne except softwood lumber ($/$m^3$), pulp ($/air dried tonne) and petroleum oils ($/hectolitre)

n.e.s. —not elsewhere specified.

| PRICE[b] | | AVERAGE ANNUAL GROWTH RATE 1989–1992 | | |
| --- | --- | --- | --- | --- |
| 1988 | 1992 | Value | Volume | Price |
| 251 | 280 | 12.0 | 11.4 | 4.4 |
| 73 | 71 | –7.6 | –6.9 | –0.6 |
| 2,696 | 2,280 | –5.0 | –1.0 | –3.3 |
| 350 | 283 | –2.4 | 2.8 | –5.1 |
| 810 | 590 | –11.6 | –5.6 | –6.5 |
| 225 | 215 | 2.3 | 2.1 | 0.2 |
| 736 | 831 | 33.1 | 28.0 | 3.8 |
| 2,645 | 1,520 | 1.9 | 17.3 | –12.3 |
| 5,577 | 4,802 | 9.7 | 14.1 | –3.4 |
| – | – | –5.2 | – | – |
| 23,215 | 21,783 | –7.2 | –5.3 | –0.4 |
| 120 | 140 | 5.4 | 1.5 | 4.4 |
| 780 | 579 | –2.5 | 4.3 | –5.6 |
| 9,851 | 7,537 | 2.9 | 14.0 | –5.0 |
| 86 | 138 | 25.4 | 6.3 | 13.5 |
| 12,231 | 8,562 | 10.7 | 16.6 | –7.5 |
| 328 | 341 | 19.1 | 15.2 | 1.9 |
| 118 | 138 | –2.0 | –5.6 | 4.1 |
| 617 | 888 | 11.5 | –4.9 | 15.9 |
| 15.92 | 16.49 | 112.1 | 156.2 | 3.0 |
| 133 | 139 | 11.8 | 11.0 | 1.9 |
| 2,238 | 1,353 | –19.2 | –9.1 | –11.6 |
| 464 | 410 | –0.6 | 1.1 | –2.6 |
| 464 | 496 | 0.7 | –0.9 | 2.0 |
| 1,893 | 2,808 | –12.0 | –17.4 | 20.6 |
| | | –1.7 | | |
| | | –3.8 | | |

for natural resources. Similarly, the gradual shift to a consumer society in Japan, while opening new opportunities for exports to Japan, had a neutral or somewhat negative impact upon resource imports, with the exception of increasing softwood lumber sales in the late 1980s (reflecting an increase in housing construction in Japan since 1986).

The Plaza Accord and its effect on the value of the yen stimulated growth in the value of world exports to Japan, and this will likely continue. The composition of these imports by Japan, however, will leave Canadian exporters at a disadvantage unless new types of comparative advantages are created in Canada—comparative advantages that can ensure penetration of the Japanese market in those segments that will grow relatively quickly. Clearly, firms must be able to translate the comparative advantage of their sector to an absolute competitive advantage. Furthermore, free market access must be ensured. Indeed, some role for government intervention can be justified if structural impediments in Japan or Canada prevent market penetration by Canadian producers, when such entry is warranted on the basis of fundamental, long-term economic prospects. The question of restructuring and creating competitive advantages (shifting comparative advantages through industrial polices and ensuring translation of comparative advantages to absolute competitive advantages through appropriate macro-economic relations) was discussed briefly in the previous chapter.

### *Japanese Exports to Canada*

Table 7.3 lists all the two-digit SITC categories that accounted for over $100 million in Japanese exports to Canada in 1991. The 14 product categories shown accounted for almost 95% of Canada's imports from Japan in 1991, up from about 88% in 1980. The contrast with the principal categories of products that Canada ships to Japan as shown in Table 7.1 is dramatic. Nine of the 14 categories, and all of the top five, are machinery and equipment. Road vehicles and parts dominate (44.1% of total Japanese exports to Canada), followed by office machinery and ADP equipment (10.3%) and telecommunications and recording equipment (10.1%). Of the five categories that are not machinery and equipment, three are resource-based manufactures (iron and steel, rubber manufactures n.e.s. and metal manufactures n.e.s.). The remaining two categories, miscellaneous manufactures n.e.s. (primarily musical instruments and sound recordings) and photographic and optical goods, are high value-added manufactured products.

The summary of Japanese exports by major product grouping shown in Table 7.3 clearly reveals the changing structure of Japanese exports to Canada. The share of resource-based manufactures fell from 19.7% in 1980 to 7.6% in 1991, in large part due to relatively slow growth in iron and steel exports. The share of consumer and other manufacturing goods fell from 12% to 6.7%. The share of machinery and equipment rose substantially to offset these reductions—from 62.3% in 1980 to 83.2% in 1991. Crude resources, fuels and food products combined accounted for less than 1% of exports to Canada in 1991.

Given the predominant role played by the United States in Canada's trade, it is not surprising to observe that Japan's share of the Canadian import market was just 6.4% in 1991, even though Japan is Canada's second most important trading partner. However, this share rose steadily over the course of the 1980s from 4.3% in 1980, and there have been significant changes across product categories in the importance of Japanese suppliers (see Table 7.3). Over 20% of Canadian imports of telecommunications and recording equipment, and photographic and optical goods, were imported from Japan in 1991, down from earlier years. Japanese firms also lost significant import market share in 1980–1991 in rubber and iron and steel, both resource-based manufactures. At the same time, Japanese firms achieved large increases in import market share in road vehicles, office machinery and ADP equipment, and power generating and metalworking machinery. Thus, by 1991, Japan's share of Canadian machinery and equipment imports had almost doubled to 10% from 5.7% in 1980. This reflects the very high average growth of 15.7% per year in imports of machinery and equipment from Japan, a rate well above the growth in total Canadian import demand for machinery and equipment. Japan lost market share in all the other major product groupings.

Canadian import demand grew at an average annual rate of 7.7% in 1981–1991, with growth in the various broad categories of manufacturing products all in the 8% to 11% range. Growth was highest in the chemicals and consumer and light manufacturing groups, but machinery and equipment accounts for over 50% of total Canadian imports. Thus Japan's con-

**Table 7.3** Principal Japanese Exports To Canada by 2-Digit SITC Categories, 1980, 1985 and 1991 (Percent)

| SITC Code | Product Category | Product Share in Total Japanese Exports to Canada | | | Japanese Share in Canadian Imports by Product | | |
|---|---|---|---|---|---|---|---|
| | | 1980 | 1985 | 1991 | 1980 | 1985 | 1991 |
| 78 | Road vehicles and parts | 32.5 | 35.8 | 44.1 | 8.0 | 8.0 | 14.5 |
| 75 | Office machinery and ADP equipment | 2.5 | 3.5 | 10.3 | 4.3 | 4.9 | 12.7 |
| 76 | Telecommunications & recording equipment | 12.2 | 15.3 | 10.1 | 24.8 | 35.9 | 22.9 |
| 71 | Power generating machinery | 2.0 | 5.2 | 5.4 | 1.9 | 6.2 | 7.6 |
| 77 | Electrical machinery & appliances | 3.2 | 4.3 | 4.5 | 3.9 | 6.0 | 3.6 |
| 88 | Photographic & optical goods | 8.8 | 5.8 | 3.8 | 25.8 | 28.3 | 21.8 |
| 74 | General industrial machinery and parts | 3.0 | 2.6 | 2.9 | 3.0 | 4.4 | 4.0 |
| 72 | Specialized industrial machinery | 3.7 | 4.5 | 2.5 | 2.2 | 5.4 | 4.5 |
| 89 | Miscellaneous manufactures n.e.s. | 2.7 | 2.9 | 2.4 | 3.3 | 5.4 | 3.2 |
| 62 | Rubber manufactures n.e.s. | 2.8 | 1.9 | 2.0 | 18.4 | 15.3 | 11.5 |
| 67 | Iron and steel | 8.7 | 4.1 | 2.0 | 17.9 | 14.2 | 6.9 |
| 87 | Professional & scientific equipment | 1.1 | 1.2 | 1.9 | 2.4 | 3.5 | 5.8 |
| 73 | Metalworking machinery | 1.4 | 1.0 | 1.3 | 5.0 | 8.1 | 16.3 |
| 69 | Manufactures of metal n.e.s. | 3.2 | 1.7 | 1.3 | 5.2 | 5.4 | 3.3 |
| | Subtotal | 87.8 | 89.8 | 94.5 | 6.8 | 8.5 | 9.7 |
| | Food, beverages and tobacco | 1.8 | 1.1 | 0.5 | 1.1 | 1.4 | 0.5 |
| | Crude resources excluding fuels | 1.6 | 1.1 | 0.3 | 1.4 | 1.9 | 0.7 |
| | Fuels | 0.0 | 0.0 | 0.0 | 0.0 | 0.0 | 0.0 |
| | Resource-based manufactures | 19.7 | 11.8 | 7.6 | 7.2 | 6.7 | 3.9 |
| | Chemicals | 2.4 | 2.6 | 1.3 | 1.9 | 3.0 | 1.3 |
| | Machinery and equipment | 62.3 | 73.9 | 83.2 | 5.7 | 7.8 | 10.0 |
| | Consumer & other manufactured goods | 12.0 | 9.3 | 6.7 | 6.9 | 7.5 | 4.3 |
| | Total | 100.0 | 100.0 | 100.0 | 4.3 | 6.0 | 6.4 |

SOURCE: Based on data from Statistics Canada, *World Trade Database on CD-ROM.*

[a] Growth rates are based on values in Canadian dollars.

n.e.s. —not elsewhere specified.

| CANADIAN SHARE IN JAPANESE EXPORTS BY PRODUCT | | | AVERAGE ANNUAL GROWTH IN VALUE[a], 1981–1991 | |
|---|---|---|---|---|
| 1980 | 1985 | 1991 | Japanese Exports to Canada | Total Canadian Imports |
| 2.6 | 3.6 | 5.0 | 15.8 | 9.4 |
| 2.4 | 1.8 | 3.5 | 29.6 | 15.5 |
| 2.3 | 3.1 | 2.5 | 11.6 | 10.9 |
| | | | | |
| 1.3 | 4.5 | 4.0 | 26.2 | 7.9 |
| 0.8 | 1.3 | 1.0 | 19.6 | 16.3 |
| 3.4 | 3.0 | 2.4 | 4.5 | 5.0 |
| 1.1 | 1.4 | 1.3 | 15.2 | 8.7 |
| 1.6 | 2.5 | 1.2 | 13.0 | 1.7 |
| 1.8 | 2.3 | 2.2 | 12.8 | 10.8 |
| 3.9 | 4.3 | 4.4 | 9.7 | 14.5 |
| 1.3 | 1.3 | 1.2 | 4.2 | 10.5 |
| 1.5 | 1.6 | 2.0 | 19.3 | 8.9 |
| 1.8 | 1.5 | 2.2 | 36.5 | 4.2 |
| 1.8 | 2.1 | 2.0 | 3.6 | 7.6 |
| 2.0 | 2.6 | 2.9 | 13.4 | 9.1 |
| | | | | |
| 2.6 | 3.6 | 2.1 | –0.1 | 6.7 |
| 2.4 | 3.2 | 1.3 | –0.8 | 3.0 |
| 0.0 | 0.0 | 0.0 | 0.0 | –1.7 |
| 1.5 | 1.8 | 1.6 | 4.2 | 8.7 |
| 0.8 | 1.5 | 0.6 | 6.3 | 9.4 |
| 1.9 | 2.6 | 2.9 | 15.6 | 9.0 |
| 2.7 | 2.7 | 2.3 | 7.0 | 10.5 |
| 1.8 | 2.4 | 2.6 | 12.5 | 7.7 |

centration in this area has allowed it to take advantage of both a large and a fairly rapidly growing segment of Canadian import demand.

In general, Japanese exporters do not rely on the Canadian market to nearly the same extent as described above with respect to some Canadian exports. Canada is not a highly significant market for any of the export categories shown in Table 7.3—the most important Canadian markets are for road vehicles and parts (5.0% of Japanese exports go to Canada), rubber manufactures n.e.s. (4.4%) and power generating machinery (4.0%). Even at a greater level of product disaggregation, there are few products for which Canada accounts for more than 5% of Japanese exports. Nevertheless, in aggregate the importance of Canadian import demand has increased, from 1.8% of Japanese exports in 1980 to 2.6% in 1991.

One of the reasons for the large growth rate of Japanese exports to Canada (an average annual rate of 12.5% in the 1981–1991 period) has been Japanese specialization in areas of relatively fast growing import demand. Further light on this rapid growth rate is shed by Table 7.4, which is similar to Table 7.2, and which shows the top 25 products (in value terms) that Japan shipped to Canada in 1992. Volume and unit value data are available for 16 of the 25 products. Half of the 16 products experienced both price and volume increases. Two others experienced volume declines but price increases. The remaining six experienced price declines but five of these six underwent a volume increase sufficient to offset the price fall. On an average annual basis, the greatest price decline was 8.5% for television cameras and 5% for bus and truck tires. The four other products all had average annual price declines of under 3%.

In summary, Japanese exports to Canada have been less susceptible to price decreases and price volatility than has been the case with Canadian exports. In addition, the structure of Japanese trade with Canada has exhibited a fair degree of dynamism as Japanese exporters have increasingly concentrated on machinery and equipment and moved away from resource-based manufactures and consumer and other manufactured goods.

## Micro-Patterns of Canada-Japan Trade

Our analysis of bilateral trade patterns has revealed that, while the overall profile of Japanese imports has changed significantly, the composition of the competitive goods and services

Canada has available for export to Japan has not changed much, causing Canada to miss some opportunities to profit from the surge in Japanese imports after the 1985 Plaza Accord. In this section, a more detailed analysis of the performance and prospects of specific commodity categories (related to those shown in Table 7.2 and Table 7.4) including a description of changing market shares and the impact of price changes are provided. As in the previous section, the analysis here uses value data for 1980–1991 based primarily on the SITC system, and supplements these data with volume and price data for 1988–1992 based on the Harmonized System. Recall that these classification schemes are not identical.

### *Coal*

Coal continues to be one of the dominant components of Canada's exports to Japan. Expansion of Canadian production capacity, stimulated by Japanese investments and long-term contracts, led to a steady increase in Canada's share in the imports of coal to Japan in the early 1980s. Between 1984 and 1990, Canada's market share remained fairly constant at about 24%—it fell to 22% in 1991. Japan is Canada's largest coal export market, accounting for an average of about 70% of the value of coal exports in most years in the 1980–1991 period. The share of Japan reached a low of 63% in 1991 and other countries, especially South Korea, have grown in importance as markets for Canadian coal exporters.

Canada's major competitor in the Japanese coal market is Australia which in 1991 accounted for 50% of Japanese coal imports, a share which has improved somewhat over the 1980s. Further increases in the market share of Australian coal suppliers may be limited by the desire of Japanese importers to diversify sources of supply. At the start of the past decade the United States rivalled Australia as a major Japanese supplier, far ahead of Canada, but it steadily lost market share to the point that in 1991 it accounted for only 10% of the total Japanese market (compared to 37% in 1980). The major disadvantage of the U.S. producers is their tendency to shift from export to domestic markets during boom periods, reducing their reliability for Japanese importers. The major threat to Canadian coal producers now appears to be new producers from South Africa and the less developed countries, especially Indonesia.

World prices of coal have generally declined since the early 1980s but the

**Table 7.4** 25 Major Canadian Imports From Japan: Value, Volume and Price, 1988 and 1992 (Unit value)

| HS Code | Product Description | VALUE (CAN$MILLION) 1988 | VALUE (CAN$MILLION) 1992 | VOLUME 1988 | VOLUME 1992 |
|---|---|---|---|---|---|
| 8703.23 | Autos, engine > 1500–3000 cc | 1,772.1 | 2,358.3 | 162,035 | 171,137 |
| 8703.22 | Autos, engine > 1000–1500 cc | 406.1 | 537.1 | 54,474 | 62,434 |
| 8407.34 | Engines, spark-ignition, > 1000 cc | 196.9 | 405.2 | 155,853 | 334,951 |
| 8471.92 | Input or output units | 200.3 | 383.0 | 563,752 | 821,424 |
| 8473.30 | Parts & accessories of ADP machines | 69.8 | 309.8 | – | – |
| 8542.11 | Digital monolithic integrated circuits | 152.7 | 251.3 | 20,304,183 | 29,867,737 |
| 8704.31 | Gas-powered trucks < 5 tonnes | 256.8 | 237.6 | 31,073 | 24,331 |
| 8471.93 | Storage units | 115.6 | 208.4 | 838,489 | 1,078,485 |
| 8525.30 | Television cameras | 155.6 | 185.2 | 168,502 | 292,010 |
| 8703.21 | Autos, engine 1000 cc or less | 255.1 | 182.8 | 51,352 | 36,250 |
| 8708.99 | Motor vehicle parts n.e.s. | 106.0 | 176.0 | – | – |
| 8708.40 | Motor vehicle transmissions | 42.6 | 174.4 | – | – |
| 8708.29 | Motor vehicle body parts n.e.s. | 63.5 | 163.2 | – | – |
| 8521.10 | Video recording equipment | 191.9 | 158.2 | 562,288 | 515,859 |
| 8703.24 | Autos, engine > 3000 cc | 8.1 | 138.3 | 543 | 4,450 |
| 9009.12 | Photocopiers, indirect process type | 71.8 | 113.5 | 41,752 | 55,492 |
| 9009.90 | Photocopier parts | 65.8 | 100.6 | – | – |
| 8517.82 | Telegraphic apparatus n.e.s. | 157.5 | 91.5 | – | 124,063 |
| 8519.99 | Sound reproducers without recorder n.e.s. | 46.8 | 87.5 | 283,456 | 554,540 |
| 8429.52 | Excavators with revolving superstructure | 76.5 | 83.7 | 799 | 957 |
| 8471.91 | Digital processing units | 64.1 | 83.2 | – | 15,146 |
| 8407.33 | Engines, spark-ignition, > 250–1000 cc | 0.4 | 65.3 | 1,131 | 87,642 |
| 4011.20 | Rubber tires for buses and lorries | 78.7 | 59.5 | 508,841 | 475,536 |
| 8409.91 | Parts for spark-ignition engines n.e.s. | 39.5 | 51.9 | – | – |
| 9013.80 | Optical devices, appliances, instruments n.e.s. | 3.8 | 48.6 | – | – |
| | Subtotal | 4,598.1 | 6,653.9 | | |
| | Total imports from Japan | 9,267.0 | 10,762.0 | | |

SOURCE: Statistics Canada, *Catalogue 65–202: Exports Merchandise Trade* (various issues).

n.e.s. —not elsewhere specified.

| PRICE | | AVERAGE ANNUAL GROWTH RATE 1989–1992 | | |
|---|---|---|---|---|
| 1988 | 1992 | Value | Volume | Price |
| 10,936 | 13,780 | 7.5 | 1.6 | 6.0 |
| 7,455 | 8,603 | 9.6 | 5.4 | 3.8 |
| 1,264 | 1,210 | 22.4 | 24.1 | –0.4 |
| 355 | 466 | 17.8 | 10.5 | 7.3 |
| – | – | 46.9 | – | – |
| 7.52 | 8.41 | 24.9 | 16.1 | 5.5 |
| 8,264 | 9,764 | –1.4 | –5.6 | 4.6 |
| 138 | 193 | 16.0 | 8.7 | 10.1 |
| 923 | 634 | 6.4 | 18.4 | –8.5 |
| 4,968 | 5,044 | –3.9 | –6.2 | 1.0 |
| – | – | 18.7 | – | – |
| – | – | 49.2 | – | – |
| – | – | 29.2 | – | – |
| 341 | 307 | –2.5 | 0.5 | –2.4 |
| 14,978 | 31,068 | 234.1 | 160.1 | 23.2 |
| 1,719 | 2,045 | 13.0 | 7.9 | 4.5 |
| – | – | 14.1 | – | – |
| – | 738 | –11.5 | – | – |
| 165 | 158 | 17.2 | 18.8 | –0.9 |
| 95,804 | 87,439 | 13.0 | 14.2 | –1.8 |
| – | 5,493 | 19.4 | – | – |
| 397 | 745 | 1942.7 | 1901.3 | 23.5 |
| 155 | 125 | –6.6 | 1.4 | –5.0 |
| – | – | 11.1 | – | – |
| – | – | 111.1 | – | – |
| | | 9.7 | | |
| | | 3.9 | | |

prices that Canadian exporters have received held fairly constant in the 1988–1992 period. At the same time, shipments of coal to Japan from Canada rose during the 1980s to reach 20 million tonnes in 1989. In 1992, however, the volume purchased by Japan plummeted to 14 million tonnes, resulting in a substantial fall in export value.

*Metal Ores and Concentrates*

Copper ore and concentrate is by far the most important raw metallic mineral exported from Canada to Japan. It accounted for 83% of the exports of metal ores in 1991, a share that has risen steadily since 1980 when copper represented 53% and iron ore was a fairly important export. Canadian firms continue to export iron, lead, zinc and molybdenum ores, among others, but the firms are rather unimportant players in the shrinking or stagnant markets in Japan for these metals.

Canada is the largest supplier of copper to Japan, holding roughly one-quarter of the market, and Japan is Canada's principle foreign customer (over the 1980–1991 period about 70–75% of Canada's foreign copper sales were to Japan). Japan displays a highly cyclical demand for copper and Japanese importers have changed their supply sources quite considerably over the last decade. Major suppliers at the beginning of the decade, like the Philippines and Papua New Guinea, have lost significant market share, although they remain important. Chile and Indonesia are now Canada's two major competitors.

Copper prices rose steadily in the early and mid 1980s but declined steadily between 1989 and 1992. Canadian export volume to Japan fell between 1990 and 1992 so that a significant decline in export value has occurred. In 1991, for example, a 14% decrease in price compared to 1990 and a 6% fall in Canada's export volume led to a 19% decline in export value at a time when the quantity of copper imported to Japan from all sources went up by 19%.

*Metals*

Aluminum is the only nonprecious metal that Canada exports to Japan in any great quantity. Other metals exported to Japan include iron and steel, nickel and zinc but the export volumes are relatively small and their growth potential is rather limited. Canada has been one of the world's most competitive aluminum producers and was the third most important supplier of aluminum to Japan in the early 1980s, after the United States and Venezuela, with a 13% share of Japanese import demand in 1980. However, Canada's share fell fairly steadily to 1987 and has remained in the 6% range since then. Venezuela has also lost significant ground as Australia and Brazil have rapidly grown to rank as the second and third most important suppliers after the United States.

The United States is the most important market for Canadian aluminum exports (taking 69% of the value of Canadian exports in 1991). Japan is the second largest export market with a share of 9.4% although its importance appears to be declining. Korea, and more recently Germany, have risen in importance as markets for Canadian aluminum but their shares still remain small.

Canadian aluminum exporters faced rapidly falling prices in 1988–1992 (a total fall of 40%) yet the value of exports to Japan did not fall until 1991 because of large volume increases. There has been a distinct shift in Japanese import demand for Canadian aluminum towards higher priced alloyed aluminum and away from the unalloyed product. Despite equal price declines for the two commodities, the export value of the former has risen as the volume exported to Japan almost doubled between 1988 and 1992.

*Lumber*

In 1992, lumber displaced coal for the first time as Canada's single most important export to Japan. The value of Canada's lumber exports to Japan almost tripled in the second half of the 1980s—in part this was the result of the Japanese construction boom of the late 1980s which caused Japanese total lumber imports to more than triple between 1985 and 1989. Softwood lumber now accounts for around 70% of Japanese demand for imported lumber, down from over 80% in the early 1980s. While softwood lumber export value has grown considerably the most impressive growth has occurred in the value of hardwood lumber exports.

Canada is Japan's most important foreign lumber supplier, holding 41% of the market in 1991, the same as the average 1980–1991 share. All but 1% or 2% of Canada's lumber exports to Japan are softwood and Canada's only important competition is the United States. Canada has held a fairly constant market share in softwood lumber in the 50–55% range over the

1980–1991 period. The United States, while it has maintained its share in the softwood lumber market, has also become increasingly important in Japan's hardwood lumber market.

Japan's importance as a market for Canadian softwood lumber has grown steadily since 1984 (when it accounted for 8.3% of Canadian exports). By 1991, Japan purchased 21% of the Canadian softwood lumber sold abroad. The growing importance of Japan as an export market has meant that the share of the United States in Canadian softwood exports has fallen from a high of 83% in 1985 to 61% in 1991 (the same share as in 1980). The United Kingdom is the only other market of any great significance for Canadian suppliers, and Japan thus provides an important opportunity for Canadian firms to diversify their market. The prospects for Canadian lumber in Japan depend to a large extent on the success of Canadian efforts to change building codes in Japan so as to accommodate effective use of Canadian lumber in construction, and efforts to demonstrate to Japanese builders the use of building techniques appropriate for Canadian lumber.

*Pulp* Canada is a major world exporter of pulp but its preeminence is threatened by several factors. The traditional preference for softwood pulp and the premium it has commanded have disappeared as new technologies have permitted the production of high quality pulps from hardwoods. Environmental concerns associated with the bleaching processes used in Canada and the increasing costs of production have eroded the competitive position of the industry in recent years.

The share of the Japanese market held by Canadian pulp declined from a high of 43% in 1981 to a low of 32 per cent in 1991 (it declined steadily from 42 per cent in 1987). Canada sells primarily bleached softwood pulp to Japan, although the share of bleached hardwood pulp seems to be rising. In 1989, over 15% of Canadian pulp was shipped to Japan, the highest percentage in the 1980–1991 period, but this fell to 10.5% by 1991. Germany is now on par with Japan as an export market for Canadian producers. Although the United States continues to be the major importer of Canadian pulp, accounting for about 45% of the value, the share has fallen from 50% and above in the first half of the 1980s. Traditionally, the United States has been Canada's major competition in Japan. Its share of the Japanese import market was 44% in 1991, a share that has risen steadily as Canada's share has fallen. Other newer competitive sources of fibre supply such as Chile have emerged and also threaten Canada's traditional pulp markets.

Market pulp is a highly volatile commodity in terms of price and demand. Pulp prices fell quite dramatically at the end of the 1980s and into the 1990s but some modest recovery was experienced in 1992. The volume of exports to Japan also fell quite significantly in 1990 and then started to rise again. The result has been a quite significant decline in the value of exports to Japan and, as noted, a significant fall in market share. Higher fibre costs may further reduce the competitive position of Canadian producers in the Japanese market.

*Newsprint*

Canada's share of Japanese import demand for newsprint fluctuated considerably in the 1980–1991 period from a low of 6% in 1982 to 36% in 1986, 16% in 1989 and 34% in 1991. Nevertheless, on average, Canadian suppliers do appear to have gained some ground compared to the United States, the dominant supplier of the Japanese market. Together the United States and Canada account for 95% of the Japanese newsprint import market. Sweden has made some inroads but remains a relatively minor supplier.

Although Canada is a major Japanese source of newsprint supply, Japan is of fairly minor importance for Canadian exporters. Japan accounted for only 1.9% of total Canadian newsprint in 1991. The United States remains the major export destination with an average of 82% of foreign sales over the 1980–1991 period. The United Kingdom and Germany are more important markets than Japan.

The prices that Canadian exporters of newsprint to Japan have received fell substantially between 1988 and 1990 but then rose even more significantly over the following two years. At the same time, significant volume increases meant that the value of Canadian newsprint exports to Japan more than quadrupled between 1989 and 1992, resulting in a large market share increase.

*Meat*

The value of Japanese meat imports from the world increased by about 250% between 1980 and 1991—almost all the growth in imports occurred in the four years after the 1985 Plaza Accord increased the openness of the Japanese market. Canada did not gain from this growth: in fact, its market share fell from a high of 12% in 1982 (the third most important supplier of meat to Japan) to a low 2.5% in 1991.

Pork accounted for about three-quarters of total Canadian meat sales to Japan in 1991. In the early 1980s, pork accounted for up to 90% of meat exports to Japan but the share of beef exports has increased recently. The Japanese market has become increasingly less important for Canadian meat exporters who have shifted their attention to the United States market. This is especially true of pork exporters who shipped 52% of their foreign sales to Japan in 1981, but only 21% in 1991.

The major competitors for Canadian pork in the Japanese market are Taiwan, Denmark and the United States. These countries all enjoy significantly larger shares of the pork market although in the early 1980s Canada held a market share roughly similar to those of Denmark and the United States. Taiwan's dominance occurred only over the course of the 1980s—in 1991 it supplied 51% of Japanese demand for imported pork, compared to 11% in 1981. Thailand is a rising competitor in meat products other than pork.

There are few opportunities for further growth in meat exports to Japan. Fierce competition from established U.S. suppliers, and the emergence of Taiwan in the pork market, limits the opportunities for Canadian exporters to regain their market shares. A marketing effort focusing on higher quality and the introduction of new types of meat may offer some opportunities for meat export growth to Japan.

### *Fish and Shellfish*

The share of Canadian exports in the Japanese seafood import market ranged during 1980–1991 from a low of 3.6% in 1980 to a high of 5.8% in 1985 (with a share of 3.7% in 1991). About 40% of the Canadian exports to Japan of seafood is frozen fish while another third is prepared or preserved fish. Shellfish accounts for most of the rest although a small amount of fresh and chilled fish is exported to Japan. Preserved fish livers and roes, frozen Pacific salmon and frozen crabs are the major export products.

The United States is the largest market for Canadian fish and shellfish with an average 1980–1991 share of Canadian sales abroad of 57%. Japan has grown in importance as an export destination with a peak share of exports of 23% in 1988. Since then its share has fallen to 18%. European countries account for much of the remainder of Canada's fish and shellfish exports. Japan is the major foreign buyer of Canadian seafood in the category of preserved and prepared fish.

No single country holds a dominant position in the Japanese import market for fish and shellfish, likely a reflection of the degree of product diversification across countries. The United States and Taiwan are the largest suppliers but South Korea, Thailand, Vietnam, Indonesia and China are also important. Taiwan is the major supplier of preserved and prepared fish products in aggregate but Canada is the major supplier of preserved livers and roe. The United States is Canada's prime competitor in this product area although the average quality of United States exports has been somewhat lower. In the frozen fish segment the United States is the major supplier, having supplanted South Korea, and it dominates the Japanese market for imported frozen salmon.

*Canola*

Canadian rapeseed has excellent attributes and is identified by the trade name canola. It is crushed to produce oil used in cooking and for preparation of mayonnaise. Canola is the single most important Canadian agricultural commodity exported to Japan and Canadian exporters dominate the Japanese market. In 1991, 98% of Japanese canola imports came from Canada, up from 89% in 1980. Over 99% of Canada's foreign canola sales were to Japan in 1991, the highest proportion in the 1980–1991 period (the lowest was 75% in 1980). Thus Canada has no competition in the Japanese market, but in turn is completely dependent upon Japanese import demand.

Despite its special attributes, the price of canola is highly cyclical, reflecting changes in the prices of other oilseeds (especially soybeans which command a large share of Japanese imports of oilseeds). The price that Canadian exporters received declined steadily between 1988 and 1992, but volume increases meant that the value declines were not as severe.

*Wheat and Barley*

The United States, Canada and Australia supply virtually all of Japan's import demand for these grains. Canada currently dominates the Japanese barley import market with a 67% share in 1991. However, Japanese importers have continually shifted their supply between the three sources so that market shares have been highly variable. In contrast, the shares in Japanese wheat imports have been relatively stable, although Canada does seem to have picked up some ground at the expense of the United States. In 1991 Canada held a 32% share, up from 26% in 1980.

The importance of Japan as a market for Canadian barley producers has been variable in the same way that Canada's share in the Japanese market has varied. In general, however, Japan usually ranks as one of the top two markets. As a market for wheat, Japan is fairly important (taking 7.8% of Canada exports in 1991), ranking behind the two major markets of China and the former Soviet Union.

Prices in international grain markets were driven substantially downward in 1989–1991 as a result of increasing supply induced by favourable growing conditions and intensified competition based on export subsidies. Wheat has been more affected by these conditions than has barley. Canadian grain farmers receive relatively lower subsidies than some of their competitors in the United States and the European Community. They have endured significant losses and require government help to stay solvent. Attempts to reach international agreement on the reduction of subsidies have met with modest success. It will likely take several years before Canadian grain farmers feel any positive effects.

## The Need for Adjustment in the Canadian Export Portfolio

Analysis of the micro-patterns of Canadian exports to Japan reveals a structural vulnerability. Canada's exports are concentrated in sectors which generally experienced a secular decline in prices. In many of these sectors Canada's competitive advantage as a low cost producer has been eroded leading to market share declines. Canada's ability to supply the market competitively in areas of opportunities for exports that were opened after the Plaza Accord was confined to only a few niches.

For example, the value of Canadian exports to Japan of machinery and equipment grew at an annual average rate of 10.3% in 1981–1991. The share of Canadian exports in the total value of Japanese imports remained relatively low, however (dropping from 1.6% in 1980 to 0.6% in 1991, see Table 7.1). A more significant shift in the structure of Canadian exports from resource intensive commodity products to differentiated products is needed. This requires increased market knowledge and effective communications between producers and consumers. Lack of market knowledge and difficulties of communication between Japanese customers and Canadian producers are important causes of "market failure" that inhibit a shift in the composition of Canadian exports. The use of intermediaries provides one opportunity to remedy this problem and the Japanese trading houses may be the intermediaries which can most productively bridge the knowledge and information gaps.

Japanese trading houses serve two functions. They explore different markets to fill orders from their headquarters (or occasionally from "third country" regional headquarters). They also look for opportunities to export Japanese products to Canada. The focus, however, in each market segment is usually either mostly on imports or mostly on exports, depending on the perceived competitive position of Canadian and Japanese firms. Thus, in markets for natural resources and processed natural resources, the trading houses specialize in identifying and developing Canadian supply sources. In other market segments (e.g., manufacturing) the emphasis is usually on the export of Japanese products to Canada. The "traders" assigned to these markets typically have expertise in product lines where Japan has a superior competitive advantage. The attention of traders, naturally, is focused on familiar product lines (i.e., those which they export to Canada and the related product lines which complement them, occasionally including market segments where the competitiveness of the Canadian industry may be high and exports to Japan a possibility). Approaches by Canadian entrepreneurs with proposals outside the domain of expertise of the trader are likely to be screened out. The "traders" in these market segments where Canada is a potential exporter to Japan (e.g., forest products) serve an important function in informing producers about desirable product attributes and the standards that must be met when exporting to Japan, and serve as intermediaries that prevent "market failures" that may arise from high transaction costs associated with foreign sales, especially for smaller producers.

The trading houses also serve an important function in developing trade opportunities through direct investment. Direct investment serves the interests of trading houses in several ways: it ensures stability of supply, it provides the trading house with a "window" overlooking the producing sector that permits quick strategic adjustments to changing market conditions, and it permits preemption of other traders in specific market niches. Participation in joint ventures also preserves the ability of trading houses to profit from trade flows from which they might otherwise be excluded as Japanese resource-using industries replace arm's-length imports with overseas production.

Intracompany trade is also a means for trade creation where markets fail. Intracorporate trade accounts for a significant proportion of world trade—perhaps as much as one-third of world trade in manufactured goods. This proportion is likely to increase in the future as companies rationalize the geographic distribution of their activities. Services also are increasingly being traded and they now account for about one-quarter of world trade. With the increase in foreign direct investment from Japan, it is possible that the Japanese transplants in Canada will serve not only as sources for Japanese importers to Canada but also as exporters to Japan or to Japanese transplants in other countries (e.g., the U.S.). (See the introduction of Chapter 6 for more discussion of this issue.) Clearly, a growing role for intracompany trade may prevent domestic firms outside a multinational network from exporting or even competing effectively in the domestic market (this is particularly the case in sectors with economies of scale).

## Long-Term Impediments to Trade

In Chapter 5, a wide array of barriers to trade that importers to Japan face were identified. Under international pressure Japan continues its efforts to liberalize its trade policies. Trade liberalization processes usually are reflected in the removal of tariffs and removal of some of the more obvious nontariff barriers (e.g., removal of quotas). The process of removing the more subtle nontariff barriers is slow since it can be difficult to determine the demarcation between the exercise of genuine sovereign rights and duties to protect the population and promote noneconomic goals and the use of these goals as excuses to impede trade. Furthermore, structural and behavioural impediments often are not related to specific government policies or interventions.

In Japan, traditional buying habits, a structure of corporate inter-linkages, and a traditional retail distribution system all present barriers to the exporter. Barriers are also buttressed by a costly economic environment and a unique system of buying habits which reflects the impact of culture and the specific environmental and social conditions of Japanese society. Marketing strategies sensitive to the culture, and products specifically designed and produced to serve the Japanese market (and specific Japanese preferences), are perhaps the most effective immediate means of penetrating the market. The costs of learning and the risks involved, however, may prohibit many firms from attempting to enter the Japanese market unless aided by Japanese intermediaries (e.g., the trading companies). The use of intermediaries (or joint ventures) may also assist in the penetration of the Japanese distribution system. The problem here is that trading companies generally are interested in marketing high-volume goods and services, thus excluding smaller exporters. Other types of (smaller) intermediaries are less accessible since they do not have international networks of offices as the trading companies do. Joint-ventures are also a means through which Canadian producers may combine their production capabilities with the marketing capabilities of a Japanese firm. Strategies aimed at changing the preferences of Japanese buyers are costly. Moreover, such strategies often have the character of a "public good" since the change in preferences may open the market to rival exporters. Thus, projects directed at changing buying habits through demonstration and advertisement can often take place only when supported by government subsidies. For example, the demonstration projects to induce Japanese builders to build residential houses using Canadian building technologies and materials were only possible because a significant share of the investment was borne by the Canadian government.

Japanese industrial structure constitutes an important impediment to trade. The linkages that exist between groups of manufacturing firms, banks and trading companies facilitate information flows within the groups to the exclusion of outsiders, thus presenting competitive advantages to group members over outsiders. While trade relationships are not exclusive to members of the group, they enhance intra-group trade.

Finally, the Japanese business culture, the way in which business relationships are established and maintained, can itself be an obstacle. For example, physical presence is an important ingredient in trade development in many Asian Pacific Rim countries where interpersonal relationships are an important element in developing business relationships. Prohibitively expensive real estate prices and high transaction costs in Japan present significant economic barriers to all but the largest foreign companies. In addition, the informal regulatory system based on administrative guidance rather than formal unambiguous written regulations pose a barrier to those outside the system who may miss its tacit signals. A difficult language, lack of cultural awareness, and lack of knowledge of the system are general impediments that intensify the specific barriers outlined above. Clearly, development of Canadian linguistic and cultural skills requires a long-term sustained investment in education.

## Long-Term Prospects for Canadian Exports

Analysis by the Canadian Embassy in Tokyo (1991) provides the following prognosis:

(1) The volume of imports to Japan increased between 1985–1990 by 60% due mainly to the increase in the exchange rate of the yen to the U.S. dollar. According to some estimates, only about one-fifth of the exchange savings has been passed to consumers. Most of the savings were absorbed in higher corporate profit margins and distributor margins. Competitive forces, which are slow in having an effect on the rigidly constrained retail markets of Japan, are likely to continue to push the growth of imports above the rate of growth of the economy. These forces and continued consumer and foreign pressures for improvement in the Japanese distribution network and removal of trade barriers are likely to ensure sustained growth of imports of consumer products. (Note, however, that the current recession in the aftermath of the burst of the bubble economy is inhibiting, in the short run, the growth of imports to Japan.)

(2) The structural shift in the Japanese economy brought about by labour shortages will continue once the economy rebounds from its recession and will offer more opportunities for importation of higher value-added products and higher technology products. Indeed, the shift may continue to dampen the prospects for imports of unprocessed raw materials, while offering better prospects for exports with higher levels of processing at the source.

(3) The Canadian profile of exports to Japan (with its continuing predominance of resource-based exports) does not match the profile of import growth in Japan. Perhaps more importantly, the profile of resource exports from Canada is not set to take advantage of growth opportunities within the resource sector.

Thus, without a shift in the profile of exports to Japan, Canada may enjoy only modest growth in its exports (failing also to capture its share in the new import opportunities that are likely to be generated in Japan during the next decade). The major opportunities within the resource sector are the export of lumber to take advantage of an expected expansion in housing starts (once the tight monetary policy in Japan is relaxed) and opportunities related to a shift to the export of more intensely processed resources.

A potentially important influence on the long-term prospects for Canadian exports is the impact of U.S-Japanese negotiations aimed at correcting bilateral trade imbalances. Indeed, attempts by the Japanese to safeguard their market interest in the U.S. may very well come at Canada's expense.

## Investment

There are two types of investment flows with distinctly different attributes in terms of motives, patterns and impacts:

(1) *Portfolio investments* are flows of capital in search of the highest risk-adjusted returns. These investments are typically made by buying debt instruments or securities without acquiring control. The majority share of such investments is liquid and responds sensitively to changes in yield expectations and perceived risks.

(2) *Direct investments* involve acquisition of control of the investment opportunity. They often represent the transfer of bundles of capital, technology, information and a variety of other tangible and intangible resources from a parent firm to a subsidiary or an affiliate. The major motive of direct investment is to exploit ownership and location advantages in situations where, due to some type of market failure, internalization of business activities is more beneficial to the firm than arm's-length transactions. Goals for direct investment may typically involve one or several of the following:

(a) the objective of securing resource flows (vertical integration);
(b) the objective of seeking and securing market access;
(c) objectives derived from competitive considerations in oligopolistic global markets (e.g., preemption of rivals); and
(d) objectives derived from optimization of global production (e.g., exploitation of lower foreign resource costs, available local externalities, or special capabilities).

Foreign portfolio investment flows are generated when there is a current account deficit, for example, a country (including its government) consumes and invests more than it produces. Clearly, the more abundant the availability of foreign savings to finance the deficit, the higher is the welfare of the country with a current account deficit that must be financed. (As the supply of foreign savings declines the cost of borrowing increases and the intertemporal possibility curve for the borrowing economy moves downwards.)

In the long run, the economies of borrowing countries such as Canada can be affected significantly by changes in saving patterns and investment preferences in countries which are major suppliers of capital, such as Japan. Such impacts generally are reflected in macro changes in the global supply of capital and its costs. In the short run, the particular composition of portfolio investment in a country and the particular (perhaps idiosyncratic) responses of its investors to changes in its environment can significantly affect the stability of its macro-economic policies. Thus, for example, the practices and standard operating procedures of Japanese insurance companies, which hold significant amounts of Canadian government bonds, determine in the short run the ease and flexibility with which the monetary authorities can implement their exchange rate policies.

The impact of foreign direct investment on the recipient country involves two distinct levels: (1) the flow of capital, and (2) the flow of other tangible and intangible resources including technology and managerial know-how. The cross-border flow of capital which may be involved in foreign direct investment (FDI) has direct macro-economic effects similar to the effect of portfolio investment. However, large cross-border flows of capital are not necessarily involved in all foreign direct investments, since the investing firm may borrow in the capital markets of the host country to finance its investments. It is the micro-economic impact of FDI that is of special importance. The flow of tangible (other than capital) and intangible resources from the parent to its affiliate in the host country may result not only in direct benefits or costs from the operations of the affiliate but also from the externalities it may create for other firms in the host country. Important benefit dimensions often attributed to (but not always substantiated as being due to) foreign direct investment include: (1) technology transfer, (2) management innovation, and (3) export creation. Important costs often attributed include: (1) rent capturing (buying at fire sale prices),

(2) balance of payments impacts as dividends and royalty payments leave the country, (3) increases in imports, and (4) inhibition of domestic R&D and the transfer abroad of domestic technologies.

Comprehensive assessments of the impacts of both portfolio and direct investment from Japan to Canada are not addressed in this book. However, some potential cost and benefit areas that may have implications with respect to Canadian policies that focus upon the bilateral relationship with Japan are briefly explored and the existing evidence regarding some of the commonly held assumptions with respect to these impacts is commented on.

## Portfolio Investment Flows from Japan to Canada*

Persistent large current account surpluses in recent years have made Japan one of the most important suppliers of capital to the world. The growth of Japanese portfolio investment in Canada was propelled by a strong demand created by steadily increasing government debt over the past decade, combined with the search of Japanese investors with large amounts of savings for relatively liquid debt investments with high yields and low perceived political risks. Japanese portfolio investment in Canada grew from less than CAN$10 billion on March 31, 1984 to more than $48 billion on March 31, 1993.

The importance of the Japanese portfolio investors is clear. At the end of 1992, Japanese investors held over 20% of foreign-owned Canadian bonds. They held 40% of all Government of Canada bonds held by nonresidents and 13% of total provincial bonds held by nonresidents. Japanese bondholding increased dramatically until 1990, levelled in 1990 and 1991 and increased again significantly in 1992 (this despite the drop in the Canadian dollar against the yen and the narrowing of interest rate differentials between Canada and the U.S.).

Japanese portfolio investment in Canada has grown substantially since 1984. The estimated total Canadian portfolio of securities and loans held by Japanese investors on March 31, 1993 was CAN$54 billion, accounting for

* All data presented in this section are derived from the annual surveys of Japanese portfolio investment conducted by the Canadian Embassy in Tokyo. The analysis of the motives of portfolio investors is largely based on these surveys and on discussions with B. Smith who directed some of the surveys.

**Table 7.5** Japanese Portfolio Investment in Canada by Type of Investor and Type of Investment, March 31, 1993 (Percent distribution and CAN$million)

| Type of Investor | GOV'T OF CANADA BONDS (%) | FEDERAL GOV'T ENTERPRISES BONDS (%) | PROVINCIAL GOV'T BONDS (%) | PROVINCIAL GOV'T ENTERPRISES BONDS (%) | MUNICIPAL GOV'T BONDS (%) | CORPORATE PRIVATE BONDS (%) |
|---|---|---|---|---|---|---|
| Life Insurance Companies | 31.5 | 0.0 | 3.4 | 1.6 | 0.0 | 1.1 |
| Trust & Banking Corporations | 2.2 | 0.1 | 1.5 | 0.6 | 0.0 | 0.8 |
| Government & Other Financial Organizations | 10.0 | 0.8 | 8.8 | 5.8 | 0.4 | 1.3 |
| Investment Trust/Management Companies | 1.5 | 0.0 | 1.5 | 0.1 | 0.0 | 0.1 |
| Marine & Fire Insurance Companies | 4.6 | 0.0 | 0.6 | 1.4 | 0.0 | 0.1 |
| All Banks | 1.4 | 0.0 | 0.8 | 0.3 | 0.0 | 0.5 |
| Leasing Companies | 0.0 | 0.0 | 0.0 | 0.0 | 0.0 | 0.4 |
| Total % | 51.2 | 1.0 | 16.5 | 9.6 | 0.6 | 4.2 |
| CAN$million | 25,344 | 488 | 8,173 | 4,774 | 279 | 2,081 |

SOURCE: Canadian Embassy, Tokyo.

more than one-fifth of Canada's net deficit in portfolio investment. About 70% of the portfolio was denominated in Canadian funds, about 18% in U.S. dollars, and about 12% in yen. Table 7.5 provides information about the composition (as of March 31, 1993) of the Japanese portfolio of Canadian securities and loans held by the institutional investors who participated in the 1993 Survey of the Canadian Embassy in Tokyo (estimated to be about 91% of the total Japanese portfolio). Life insurance companies held about 44% of the total (down from a share of 54.5% in 1991), followed by government and other financial organizations (mainly the postal savings system) with 27.6% (up from a share of 16.4% in 1991). Banks held about 9.4% (down from a share of 13.7%), while investment trust and management companies' share was 3.3% (down from 3.9%), and marine and fire insurance companies' share was 7.8% (up from a share of 5.5%).

In terms of the composition of the portfolios, government of Canada bonds have constituted the main holdings (more than half) in recent years (51% in 1991 and 1993). Equity investments were a marginal part of the

| TBS | BONDS TOTAL | STOCKS | LOANS | GRAND TOTAL | |
|---|---|---|---|---|---|
| (%) | (%) | (%) | (%) | (%) | CAN$million |
| 0.0 | 37.6 | 0.4 | 6.1 | 44.1 | 21,849 |
| 0.0 | 5.2 | 0.2 | 1.2 | 6.6 | 3,266 |
| 0.0 | 27.1 | 0.0 | 0.5 | 27.6 | 13,646 |
| 0.0 | 3.2 | 0.0 | 0.1 | 3.3 | 1,650 |
| 0.0 | 6.8 | 0.0 | 1.0 | 7.8 | 3,877 |
| 0.0 | 2.9 | 0.2 | 6.3 | 9.4 | 4,677 |
| 0.0 | 0.4 | 0.1 | 0.6 | 1.1 | 538 |
| 0.1 | 83.2 | 1.0 | 15.8 | 100 | |
| 57 | 41,198 | 495 | 7,811 | | 49,503 |

portfolio (about 1% of the total in March 31, 1993, rising from a share of 0.8% in 1991). Provincial government and provincial Crown corporation bonds, which offer marginally higher yields but trade in somewhat less liquid markets, constituted an important part of the core holding. These assets comprised 26% of the portfolio of the surveyed investors. This share has increased significantly in recent years (from 18.5% in 1991), perhaps reflecting the growing debt of provincial governments. The share of corporate bonds in the portfolio has decreased to 4.2% (from 9.8% in 1991). Private corporate bonds have been a significant component of the Canadian portfolio held by banks, but they sold 78% of their private bond portfolio in the year prior to the survey. Loans also constitute an important component of the Japanese portfolio (15.8%, down from 17.3% in 1991). Life insurance companies and banks were the major holders of loans. Because of strategic considerations, life insurance companies generally have a strong preference for high interest instruments and less concern for the prospect of capital gains. Life insurance companies in Japan can transfer interest earnings but not capital gains to their customers as dividends. Competition in dividend levels is an important means of gaining market share and growth, a prime objective for most Japanese companies. In the past, the standard operating procedure for most of the life insurance companies has been to make portfolio adjustments when bonds mature, rather than to actively manage their portfolios. However, the Embassy surveys over the past few years have revealed a growing tendency of the life insurance companies to manage their Canadian portfolios more actively.

An important fact that must be considered in assessing the potential impact of life insurance companies on Canadian macro-economic policies is the concentration of Canadian portfolio holdings. In March 1991, ten life insurance companies held more than CAN$1 billion of Canadian bonds each; three additional life insurance companies had more than half a billion dollars each in their Canadian portfolios. Thus, a decision to restructure the portfolio significantly by one large Japanese insurance company may have a significant effect on the short-run stability of the Canadian dollar and the cost of government debt financing.

The investment pattern of the government financial organizations (i.e., the postal life insurance and savings bureaus) shows little preoccupation with changes in yields. Generally, their pattern of investment has been one of gradual increase in their Canadian portfolio, holding bonds to maturity. Lower preoccupation with liquidity has led these organizations to hold a considerably larger share of their portfolio holdings in provincial bonds and bonds of provincial Crown corporations (about 52% of their total holding in March 1993) in contrast to the life insurance companies (with only 11% of their total portfolio invested in provincial bonds and bonds of provincial Crown corporations).

Banks, which through their branches in Canada can monitor loans relatively inexpensively, hold most of their portfolio in loans. Their monitoring abilities also confer upon them advantages in investing in corporate bonds. Some such investments are motivated by a general global strategy of "following customers" and pre-empting Japanese rivals from dominance in key foreign markets. Recently, the Japanese banks have sold most of their Canadian corporate bond holdings, perhaps because of increased exchange risks, the need to meet the more stringent Bank of International Settlements (BIS) capital adequacy guidelines, and restructuring of their securities portfolios during the prolonged recession.

Portfolio investment in equity constitutes an insignificant proportion of the total Canadian portfolio held by the Japanese. Life insurance companies hold the largest share in equity portfolio holdings—about 40% of all Canadian equity portfolio holdings of Japanese investors. Banks and trust companies each hold about 20% of the equity portfolio. Investment trust and management companies, the holdings of which are frequently traded, have divested most of their Canadian stock holdings in 1993 and 1994.

Individual investors have only a small share of the total portfolio investment in Canada. They typically invest through securities companies (mutual funds), and the most significant type of investment is investment in short-term Canadian treasury bills. These investors, or the mutual funds that manage their assets, shift funds between U.S., Canadian, and yen denominated short-term notes so as to maximize yields while maintaining liquid positions. Some mutual funds had small but significant holdings of Canadian securities, but these are usually held for speculative purposes and not typically as a significant part of the core holdings of the funds (as the recent sell-off of Canadian securities by the mutual funds has demonstrated).

## Japanese Direct Investment in Canada

The Japanese Ministry of Finance reported that the flow of Japanese direct overseas investment totalled US$56.9 billion in the fiscal year that ended March, 1991. This was the first drop (a drop of 15.7% from the preceding year) in eight years. Almost two-thirds of this decline was in the flows to North America. While Japanese direct investment in the U.S. dropped 19.7% from US$32.5 billion in the fiscal year 1989 to US$26.1 billion in the fiscal year 1990, Japanese direct investment in Canada dropped 22% to US$1.06 billion. The cumulative foreign direct investment in the U.S. and Canada accounted for about 44% of all Japanese foreign direct investment, with the U.S. commanding the lion's share of US$130.5 billion and a cumulative value for Canada of US$5.66 billion.

The slowdown of the flow of FDI to North America in the 1990s reflects a variety of temporary economic conditions (e.g., recession in Japan, economic recession followed by a slow recovery in the U.S., a tightening of monetary policies worldwide, the significant rise in Japanese long-term interest rates and increases in earning-price ratios in the Japanese equity markets). The slowdown reflects the reduced need for direct investment abroad on the part of Japanese companies after an extended period of aggressive capital spending to set up manufacturing bases and establish financial institutions in North America.

Historically, Japanese foreign direct investment was a means for ensuring physical and economic access to natural resources, maintaining access to foreign markets and adjusting to changes in the nature of the country's comparative advantage as its economy grew and was restructured. The period after the Plaza Accord marked a shift from defensive FDI to an active move by Japanese firms to globalize, taking advantage of a large domestic surplus of capital and high exchange values for the yen. Japan Ministry of Finance reports on across-the-border FDI flows (based on notification by investors) indicate that 73% of Japan's global FDI flows in 1951–1991 occurred in the fiscal years 1986–1991. Of the total Japanese direct investment flows received in 1951–1991 by the United States and Canada, 81% and 70%, respectively, was received after 1985.

The stock of Japanese investment in Canada is relatively insignificant (about 4.0% of all the stock of FDI in Canada in 1991) compared to U.S. direct investment (63.5%) and U.K. investment (12.9%). Rugman (1990) has observed, however, that Canada is not attracting its proportional "share" of FDI from Japan as compared to the United States. As Canada is about one-tenth the economic size of the United States, it might be expected, all else being equal, that it should at least have one-tenth of the Japanese FDI in the United States. Instead, it has less than half as much as this. This apparent lack of Japanese FDI in Canada, especially in manufacturing and value-added resource-based industries, is of major concern to some Canadian policy makers. Perhaps of more concern is the nature of Japanese investment in Canada compared to Japanese investment in the U.S.

The differences between the U.S. and Canada as recipients of Japanese direct investment flows reflect an important distinction in the niche that Canada occupies in the global investment decisions of Japanese firms. The motives to invest in Canada have been related largely to resource and market seeking. According to a survey taken in 1987, the three most important reasons for Japanese FDI in Canada are, in order of importance: (1) sales expansion in the Canadian market, which may also provide a base for exporting to Third World countries; (2) securing raw materials; and (3) information collection. The wood, pulp and mining sectors attracted 32.7% of the cross-border direct investment flows to Canada from Japan in 1951–1991. Real estate (at 11.5%), finance and insurance (at 10.4%) and transportation (at 8.3%) were also sectors with significant investments. The pattern of recent investment flows to the U.S., while showing a similar emphasis on real estate and services, also shows significant investment in commercial and trade services, compared to the emphasis in Canada on resource-based industries (pulp) and financial and insurance services. The U.S. also has been targeted by Japanese firms as a source of new technologies and R&D capabilities, as evidenced by the recent establishment of Japanese owned R&D labs.

## Future Prospects for FDI from Japan

It is difficult to project volumes of FDI flows to Canada since they are determined by decisions made with respect to a few very large projects. These decisions are affected by both general environmental conditions and specific idiosyncratic circumstances associated with the specific available prospects for investment and the strategic concerns of the Japanese investors.

As an example, consider Japanese investment in the Canadian pulp sector. Ursacki (1992) observed that there are two types of Japanese foreign investors in Canada's forest products sector: trading companies *(Sogo-Shosha)* and pulp and paper companies. Most Japanese investments in the forest products sector in Canada are joint ventures between these two types of companies. Five of the eight largest companies in the pulp and paper industry in Japan have investments in Canada, along with three of the five largest *Sogo-Shosha.* Demand for paper and cardboard has grown in Japan over the past decade faster than the growth in income. In response, Japanese production of both paper and cardboard has increased rapidly. Despite impressive increases in the use of recycled paper, which now constitutes about half of the industry's raw material, the need for virgin pulp has increased steadily. Imports supply the bulk of the increased use of raw materials. When Alberta's northern forests were put up for lease, the Japanese paper industry was running up against fibre and capacity constraints. In particular, there was a perceived need for increased production of appropriate pulp for high quality paper used in books, magazines, computer printouts and fax paper. The opening of a new source of fibre at a time of fibre shortage was an important reason for Japanese interest in investing in Canada. This location's specific advantage was magnified by an important ownership advantage. Japanese firms enjoyed technological superiority in the use of aspen, which comprised 45% of the Alberta forests offered. A high yen to Canadian dollar exchange rate and relatively low capital costs (interest rates in Japan were in the range of 3–4%) provided Japanese investors with a facilitating macro-economic environment. Political risk is another aspect of special concern to Japanese investors. Canada was perceived as a stable supplier of raw materials, compared to alternative suppliers in the Third World such as Brazil. Perhaps the most important factor, however, was the pricing of the resource by the Alberta government. Royalties were indexed to changes in the price of pulp and were set initially at what the Alberta government called competitive levels (others noted that the royalties charged were among the lowest in North America). The Alberta government facilitated the investment decision process by lax enforcement of environmental regulations (e.g., waiving requirements for public hearings).

Ursacki (1992) notes that company-specific strategic concerns also played an important role in the decision of the Japanese investors to take advantage of the attractive opportunities offered them by the Alberta government (e.g., Daishowa's attempt to gamble on ambitious expansion through FDI to overtake Oji paper and become the number one paper producer in Japan).

The combination of special circumstances and opportunities for investment in the pulp sector from 1987–1989 explained more than 30% of the direct investment flows from Japan to Canada in that period. In 1990, as many of these projects were completed, investment flows fell sharply, affecting significantly the total volume of the FDI flow from Japan to Canada (Canadian Embassy reports suggest that 69% of the observed decrease in Japanese FDI flows to Canada between fiscal year 1989 and 1990 can be attributed to the completion of pulp projects). Similar impacts were associated with major investments by automotive plants (Toyota, Honda and CAMI investments.) It is difficult to predict investment flows in the short run since the realization of a particular large project depends on a variety of special circumstances. The long-term pattern of investments is easier to identify.

The analysis by the Canadian Embassy in Tokyo (1991) notes that "removal of the effects of those major projects in the transportation and lumber/pulp sectors reveals a pattern of increased investment flows in other sectors, led by investment in real estate businesses (including resorts and hotels), other manufacturing, and financial service businesses (such as the establishment of offices of Toyota Credit, Nikko, Daiwa and Sanyo Securities and Tokai Bank, among others)."

Long-term projections for Japan indicate that Japan will continue to enjoy large current account surpluses. Labour shortages, expensive land, tightening environmental regulations and ongoing pressures from its major trade partners will continue to bring about restructuring in the Japanese economy and sustain outward FDI flows over the long run.

The major long-term prospects for Canada as a recipient of a significant share of this FDI depend on several factors. Controllable factors will include:

(1) the regulatory climate;
(2) the macro-economic environment and political stability of the country; and
(3) the productivity (and prospects for improved productivity) in target sectors.

Less controllable factors include:

(1) access to other markets; and
(2) Japanese economic relations with other countries.

The controllable factors affect decisions to invest in two ways. They enter directly into the calculations of costs and benefits that potential investors make. They also affect general perceptions of the investment climate that stimulates or inhibits an interest in a country when searching for investment opportunities. Not surprisingly, Japanese investors are more familiar with, and pay more attention to, the U.S. as a potential host for investment compared to Canada, which has a significantly smaller market. Removal of regulatory location advantages brought about by the North American Free Trade Agreement (NAFTA) (e.g., removal of protective tariffs) could bring about more or less investment depending on the perceptions of Japanese investors with regard to the risks and benefits associated with investment in each country under the NAFTA. These include perceptions regarding the access NAFTA will provide foreign affiliates in each economy and the probability that certain aspects of NAFTA will change over time. The regulatory climate and costs, the competitiveness of the fiscal environment and stability of the macro-economic and political environments will be important factors in deciding where to invest. Indeed, Canada's size and dependence on the U.S. may mean higher risks that must be compensated by some advantages. Higher productivity (or at least the prospect of achieving higher productivity) and/or the availability of certain unique advantages in the supply of resources (human and natural) are, therefore, important factors in attracting FDI.

The Morohashi Mission (October 1989), a mission of Japanese businessmen, in its report "Canada: A Partner Challenging the World," highlighted relatively cheap energy costs, abundance of land and other natural resources, moderate labour costs complemented by high labour quality and a stable social and political climate, as the important advantages for FDI in Canada. While their Canadian hosts attempted to emphasize the advantages brought about by the Free Trade Agreement (FTA) of open access to the sizeable U.S. market, the members of the mission concluded that the effects of the FTA on foreign affiliates were uncertain. A secure access to the U.S. market and a less welcoming environment for investment in the U.S. would likely divert investment to Canada. Conversely, the lack of guarantees for sustained market access (e.g., the frequent use of nontariff barriers and "fair trade" measures, tight constraints on "domestic" content) and a more welcoming environment for investment in the U.S. would likely reduce significantly the perceived benefits for Japanese firms of investing in Canada.

A report of the Business Council on National Issues Perspectives entitled "Beckoning Opportunities: Toward a Stronger Canada-Japan Economic Relationship" (1991, p. 19) summarizes: "From the Japanese viewpoint, secure access to the markets and production facilities of North America is crucial. Although the bulk of Japanese investment in North America likely will continue to flow to the United States, there is a compelling case for viewing Canada as a key access point to the continent, now that the Free Trade Agreement has given Canadian products improved access to the United States market. Canada is rare among advanced economies in having no significant frictions with Japan. Both countries stand firmly in opposition to the United States' protectionist policies. To this can be added the fact that Canada's economy is for the most part complementary to Japan's rather than in direct competition. Canadians do not feel threatened by Japan's industrial success. The political climate in Canada generally is more receptive to a Japanese economic presence than is the case in the United States." There is, however, a danger that as Japan and the U.S. negotiate a new relationship, Canada's interests will be largely ignored by the two giants (see e.g., McMillan, 1988). NAFTA may also affect FDI flows to Canada. While NAFTA clarified some of the uncertainties in the FTA with respect to rules of origin, it increased the requirements for minimum North American contents. By increasing protection of FDI, NAFTA is likely to also result in a reduction of the political risk associated with investment in Mexico, and thus strengthen the competitive position of Mexico in attracting FDI. Mexico will thus provide an alternative base from which Japanese multinationals can export to the U.S. market.

## The Impact of Japanese Affiliates in Canada

Japanese affiliates in Canada employed 39,490 Canadian workers and 866 Japanese workers in 1992.* These figures compare with 541,245 local workers (17,276 Japanese workers) in the U.S., 54,804 local workers (1,147 Japanese workers) in Australia, 39,178 local workers (337 Japanese workers) in Mexico, 53,837 local workers (2,438 Japanese workers) in Germany, and 82,519 local workers (3,349 Japanese workers) in the U.K. The distribution by industry of employees working for Japanese direct investment operations in Canada in 1992 is given in Table 7.6.

In addition to the Japanese affiliates in Canada that are engaged in production, many are involved in the distribution, assembling, and servicing of products imported from Japan. Analyzing the largest Japanese affiliates in 1989, Rugman (1990) observed that 24 ranked among the top 500 Canadian companies. Six of these were the largest trading houses; seven were in auto and auto or motorbike wholesaling; seven were in technology, consumer electronic or electrical goods; two were in forest products; one was in wholesaling and services; and one was in computer and office equipment.

* These numbers are for Japanese-affiliated enterprises in Canada in which Japanese firms have at least 10% ownership.

**Table 7.6** Employment by Japanese Affiliates in Canada, 1992[a]

| INDUSTRY | LOCAL WORKERS | WORKERS FROM JAPANESE PARENT FIRMS |
|---|---|---|
| All | 39,490 | 866 |
| Agriculture/Fishery | 8 | 6 |
| Mining | 5,190 | 17 |
| Construction | 13 | 5 |
| Manufacturing | 23,367 | 275 |
| Food | 194 | 3 |
| Textile | – | – |
| Lumber/Furniture | 574 | 4 |
| Pulp/Paper | 5,378 | 37 |
| Printing | – | – |
| Chemicals | 161 | 5 |
| Petroleum/Coal | 1,497 | 1 |
| Rubber/Leather | 177 | 6 |
| Pottery/Ceramics | 250 | – |
| Iron/Steel | 462 | 9 |
| Nonferrous Metal Products | – | – |
| Metal Products | 409 | 9 |
| General Machinery | 948 | 28 |
| Electric Equipment | 1,724 | 26 |
| Transport Machinery | 2,505 | 47 |
| Auto | 8,549 | 80 |
| Precision Instruments | 156 | 1 |
| Other Manufacturing | 383 | 19 |
| Commerce | 7,281 | 415 |
| Finance/Insurance | 904 | 59 |
| Securities and Investment | 86 | 20 |
| Real Estate | 337 | 13 |
| Transportation | 522 | 29 |
| Service | 1,752 | 20 |
| Stockholding, Other | 30 | 7 |

SOURCE: Toyo Keizai, *Japanese-Affiliated Firms Overseas* (1993).

[a] These numbers are for Japanese-affiliated operations in Canada in which Japanese firms have at least 10% ownership.

He noted that the two forest firms produced lumber, plywood, pulp and paper. Three of the seven auto-related firms manufactured or assembled cars in Canada while the other four were engaged in distribution only. Of the five electronic firms, four had some Canadian manufacturing facilities. They also had distribution operations for their entire product line. The fifth electronic firm engaged only in distribution.

There is evidence that Japanese affiliates tend to have a high propensity to import components and parts from Japan and export raw materials to Japan. There is a shift towards a higher level of processing in Japanese resource imports, as the Japanese restructure their industry and move domestic production to higher value-added and knowledge intensive sectors. In the long run, the labour shortages in Japan are also likely to decrease the propensity of Japanese companies in Canada to import intermediate goods from Japan.

As we have previously observed, the prime motives for Japanese foreign direct investment in Canada are to develop product markets and resource supply sources. While there are some advantages that Japanese investment offers to Canadian exports in the resource sector—in particular, knowledge of how to satisfy Japanese market demand (e.g., quality requirements in particular market niches)—there is little that distinguishes Japanese investment from other sources of capital in the resource sector. A more pronounced and uniquely Japanese contribution can be found in the automobile sector. The experience of the Japanese investment in the automobile industry in Canada demonstrates both the potential for transfer of managerial innovation from Japan to Canada and the bottlenecks existing in Canada that constrain the degree to which diffusion of innovation takes place. The Japanese production management system of small-lot continuous-flow production has received a great deal of attention in North America where mass production systems dominate. The Japanese production system has been credited with significant increases in productivity and product quality. The introduction of a tiered supply structure, in which only a small fraction of the supply base deals directly with the vehicle maker, helped the Japanese reduce product development time as well as development costs (Wolf and Taylor, 1990).

In response to growing North American protectionism and the rising value of the yen, Japanese automobile producers shifted some of their production to North America in the mid and late 1980s. Canada has about 17% of the Japanese transplant assembly capacity in North America but has proportionally fewer Japanese parts plants (about 5%).

Wolf and Taylor (1990, p. 15) describe the "learning" that took place in the Canadian Japanese transplants whose operations are essentially replicas of plants in Japan. "North American labour had to accept a fundamentally different relationship with management which called for a new type of flexible organization. Each of the transplants developed recruiting and selection procedures to identify employees who would be best suited (in terms of attitudes and skills) to working a Japanese-style production system." Of the three Japanese assembly plants in Canada, only CAMI is unionized. The contract with the union, however, was negotiated to ensure job flexibility. Extensive training, including the sending of Canadian team leaders to Japanese plants, was undertaken. (Twelve percent of the work force spent at least one month in Japan in training.) Similar training programs took place in other Japanese transplants, with longer time commitments where technical training was received. Continuous on-the-job training with Japanese trainers has been the primary means used to implement the Japanese system of labour management relations. Note that since much of the training does not confer credentials, and is thus more valuable to the company that provides the training than to outsiders, the externalities of the training process are limited (and so is the mobility of the trained labour).

The presence of successful Japanese transplants in the North American scene, however, provides the impetus for their North American competitors to learn through imitation. The process of adopting Japanese production management innovation encountered resistance from the unions. In the U.S., the United Auto Workers eventually relented and joined manufacturers in creating a process to introduce a wide range of work place innovations. However, in Canada the Canadian Auto Workers (CAW) rejected the use of Japanese production methods in general in 1989. It issued a policy statement that specifically rejects "the use of continuous improvement and employee involvement. The CAW rejects the basic premise of international competitiveness, because it forces Canadian workers to compete with workers in countries whose real wages and living standards are much lower. Competitiveness between plants within the same corporation is viewed as pitting union members against union members. Nevertheless, when it found itself competing for the mandate to produce the new F cars against a GM plant in the United States, the CAW local at the St. Therese plant was willing to accept a reduction in job classifications, flexible overtime, and changes in training of staff in new technology. The CAW also sanctioned the use of the Japanese production system at the CAMI plant, without which Suzuki would not have established its plant in Ontario" (Wolf and Taylor, 1990, p. 23).

Transfer of technology is enhanced when Japanese and North American manufacturers enter into joint ventures. Domestic sourcing by Japanese transplants creates opportunities for parts manufacturers who are willing to make the effort to meet Japanese requirements. To assist these suppliers, the Japanese transplants engage in intensive information dissemination, publicizing their needs and requirements. They are willing to inspect plants of potential suppliers and provide recommendations for improvement. They also create technology linkages with their suppliers in Japan, encouraging the formation of joint ventures. In the U.S., the effect of these Japanese activities has been judged by suppliers to have increased production efficiency, quality control and product and process improvements, according to a U.S. General Accounting Office (1988) study. It reported that "some suppliers said they now felt more competitive and some were now demanding more from their own suppliers as well" (pp. 39–40).

While resource and market seeking are the major motives of Japanese FDI, there are a few examples where Japanese investment was motivated by opportunities to acquire technology. The major question is whether the Japanese, by acquiring Canadian companies, appropriated Canadian technologies without adequate compensation ("fire sale" buying) and benefit to Canadians. Typically, this concern arises when capital market failures in Canada create opportunities for Japanese multinationals to acquire high-technology Canadian companies that face difficulties in raising sufficient funds to remain viable.

One example is the purchase of Lumonics, a major supplier of laser equipment. The company operated successfully for about 20 years before it was acquired in 1989 by Sumitomo Heavy Industries Ltd. Lumonics needed to expand from its less than CAN$100 million sales volume in order to sustain its R&D effort and world marketing programs. It could not obtain the capital necessary for the expansion in the Canadian capital market where short-term concerns led to undervaluation of the company's prospects. Sumitomo, which had marketed Lumonics laser systems since 1986 in Japan, could provide both the marketing channels and the capital for Lumonics' growth. In March 1989, the directors of Lumonics announced the acceptance of a bid from Sumitomo at a premium of about 35% over the market price at the time. Globerman (1990), analyzing the case in terms of its impact upon Canadian interests, concluded that there was no basis to infer that Sumitomo obtained Lumonics for what it believed to be a bargain price. He observed that the relatively small number of large, Canadian-owned high technology companies may make it necessary for smaller Canadian-owned companies to seek larger partners outside of Canada. In this particular case, the advantages that Sumitomo had in marketing in Japan considerably enhanced the value of the company to Sumitomo.

Another example of a Japanese acquisition of a high-technology Canadian company was the purchase of Moli Energy by a consortium led by Mitsui. Moli, which was successful for a while in raising capital in Canada, had developed one of the most advanced rechargeable power batteries. Flaws in the product (fire hazards) led to a financial crisis in 1990. The only candidates to bail out the company were the members of the Japanese consortium led by Mitsui. Though the price paid by the consortium was significantly lower than the book value, it was judged to be a fair market value. The government of British Columbia, the only secured investor, will receive a royalty from future sales made by the company. In addition, the consortium agreed to invest a minimum of CAN$10 million in R&D to correct the flaws in Moli's technology. It also agreed to keep research and manufacturing in the province for at least five years. Again, Japanese "patience" versus Canadian "short termism" was the ingredient necessary for the survival of the Canadian company.

Indeed, one must view the fact that Japanese or other foreign investors are willing to buy Canadian high-technology corporations, rather than let them disappear, as a positive factor in ensuring development of Canadian technological capabilities. It increases the incentive for Canadian entrepreneurs to continue to invest in technology despite the fact that in the long run domestic capital markets have not always proved willing or able to provide sufficient support to allow the companies that are founded to mature and grow.

Perhaps the most potentially controversial type of Japanese FDI is that associated with investment in real estate. A significant part of this investment is associated with the tourist trade from Japan. In 1988, Japanese tourism abroad totalled 8.4 million people, about double the 1984 figure. Canada was one of the preferred destinations of tourists and enjoyed a rapid rate of growth in Japanese visitors. According to Statistics Canada, the number in 1989 was 454,000 visitors compared to 139,000 in 1985. To serve these flows, Japanese investors engaged in a series of significant purchases of hotels and resorts in Canada. In British Columbia alone seven hotels and resorts were bought by Japanese companies in 1987–1989. Edginton (1990) observed that a growing concern in the province was the loss of local business revenue because of vertical integration of tourist services by Japanese conglomerates. He noted that there is a perception that Japanese companies in the hospitality industry tend to dedicate their services to tourists from their home country. It is believed that little benefit accrues to local enterprises if Japanese tourists book their travel through Japanese wholesalers, stay in Japanese-owned hotels and shop in Japanese-owned businesses. However, this perception, reflected in many media reports, ignores benefits which may accrue from taxes, and externalities in labour markets and infrastructure development.

The Japanese have also invested, but to a much lesser extent, in commercial property. The largest single Japanese investment in Canada was the purchase by Sun Enterprises of the Bank of Hong Kong building for CAN$130 million in 1989. Such investment should be discouraged only if it is obvious that market failures resulted in a "fire sale." There is no evidence for market failures of this sort in the property market. Infusion of Japanese capital may free Canadian capital for investment in other real estate projects or in other sectors of the economy.

## Canadian Direct Investment in Japan

The Ministry of Finance of Japan reports that, in 1989, 1990 and 1991, Canadian FDI in Japan amounted to 83 cases (US$35 million), 53 cases (US$142 million) and 38 cases (US$764 million), respectively. In 1992, Canadian-affiliated firms* in Japan employed

* These numbers are for firms which are at least 40% owned by Canadian parent firms.

about 15,600 workers, with 9,918 workers working in nonferrous metals (e.g., Alcan operations). The sales by Canadian affiliates in the manufacturing industries exceeded 900 billion yen in 1992. Before tax and after tax profit margins for these Canadian firms' operations in Japan were 4.7% and 2.3%, respectively, which was lower than the profit margins for U.S. affiliates (7.3% and 3.8%) but higher than the profit margins for E.C. affiliates (4.2% and 1.9%). In general, the profit margins for foreign affiliates were considerably higher than those for domestic Japanese firms.

These Canadian subsidiaries imported at least 114.6 billion yen worth of goods and services from Canada, of which 67 billion yen was for nonferrous metals and 47.2 billion yen was for retail and wholesale goods and services. These figures are quite small compared to the import figures for U.S. firms' subsidiaries in Japan which were at least 1,808 billion yen for all industries, and 655 billion yen for manufacturing excluding petroleum.

The Canadian firm with the largest presence in Japan is Alcan which has three subsidiary firms listed on the Tokyo Stock Exchange (see Table 7.7).* These Alcan subsidiaries produce many well-known brand name aluminum products and operate essentially as Japanese firms. They reflect Alcan's global business strategy in Japan and Asia of providing anchors for an international network of a second level of subsidiaries. Toyo Aluminum, which has by far the largest market share in Japan for auto aluminum products, has subsidiaries in South Korea, France and the U.S. Nippon Light Metal has almost 20 overseas subsidiaries (1 in South Korea, 3 in China, 1 in Hong Kong, 2 in Thailand, 3 in Singapore, 2 in Malaysia, 1 in the U.K., 2 in Canada and 3 in the U.S.). Shin Nikkei has one subsidiary in Thailand and another in Singapore. Many of these subsidiaries are joint ventures between Alcan and its three Japanese affiliates and appear to take advantage of, among other things, Alcan's skill in aluminum production, the low cost of electricity in Canada, the capabilities of the subsidiaries in manufacturing aluminum building products and auto parts, and the customers the subsidiaries have developed over time (e.g., Japanese automakers).

Table 7.8 provides information about other subsidiaries of Canadian manufacturing firms. Like the subsidiaries of Alcan, some of these companies have also located operations outside of Japan in Asia and elsewhere. For

---

* The following company data are as of December, 1992.

**Table 7.7** Alcan's Subsidiaries in Japan

| SUBSIDIARY | MAJOR SHAREHOLDERS AND SHARE | NO. OF SHAREHOLDERS | SALES (BILLION YEN) | AFTER-TAX PROFIT (BILLION YEN) | NO. OF WORKERS[a] |
|---|---|---|---|---|---|
| Nippon Light Metals[b] | Alcan, 45.3%<br>Daiichi-Kangyo Bank, 3.8%<br>Industrial Bank of Japan, 3.5%<br>Asahi Life Insurance, 3.5% | 46,381 | 289 | 6.3 | 4,982 |
| Toyo Aluminum[c] | Alcan, 48.7% | 3,429 | 44 | 0.64 | 967 |
| Shin Nikkei[b] | Nippon Light Metal, 66.9%<br>(Alcan, 30.3%) | 6,068 | 267 | 8.7 | 6,068 |

SOURCE: Company reports.

[a] December 1992.
[b] Sales and profit for year ending March 1992.
[c] Sales and profit for year ending December 1992.

example, Singer Nikko has subsidiaries in China, Hong Kong and the U.S.; Toppan Moore has subsidiaries in at least 12 countries (1 in South Korea, 4 in China, 5 in Hong Kong, 1 in Thailand, 2 in Singapore, 1 in Sri Lanka, 1 in Taiwan, 2 in the U.S., 1 in the U.K., 1 in Australia and 1 in Germany). In addition to the production subsidiaries noted in Table 7.8, some firms have established distribution operations for their products in Japan. For example, Falconbridge markets specialized metals from Canada; McCain Foods (Japan) markets frozen potato products from Canada; and MacMillan Bloedel imports and sells Canadian lumber, paper and pulp.

There are several important impediments to Canadian investment in Japan (assuming that Canadian firms indeed have some ownership advantages that cannot be exploited through arm's-length sales or licensing):

(1) The costs of "foreignness" in Japan, which is higher than in most other developed countries. Significant cultural differences in the way of doing business, language problems, different consumer perceptions and habits, the difficulty of penetrating the traditional distribution and servicing networks, and imperfect labour markets, are some of the barriers to the establishment of foreign businesses (even when formal barriers are removed).

**Table 7.8** Other Subsidiaries of Canadian Firms in Japan

| SUBSIDIARY | MAJOR SHAREHOLDERS AND SHARE | SALES (BILLION YEN) | AFTER-TAX PROFIT (BILLION YEN) | NO. OF WORKERS[a] |
|---|---|---|---|---|
| Kirin Seagram[c] | Kirin Brewery, 50%<br>Seagram, 45%<br>Chivas Brothers, 5% | 51 | 4.2[b] | 550 |
| Singer Nikko[c] | Int'l Semi-Tech Microelectronics, 50%<br>Nihon Seikosho, 50% | 26 | 0.14 | 700 |
| Daido Inco Alloys[c] | Inco, 50%<br>Daido Tokushuko, 50% | 11 | 0.26[b] | 37 |
| Tokyo Nickel[c] | Inco, 45%<br>Sumitomo Metal Mining, 16%<br>Daido Tokushuko, 16%<br>Mitsui Co., 16%<br>IBJ, 5% | 39 | 0.6 | 53 |
| Toppan Moore[d] | Toppan, 55%<br>Moore, 45% | 159 | 4.8 | 3,050 |
| Nippon Diversity[c] | Molson, 100% | 3.6 | 0.1[b] | 178 |
| Baco[e] | Bata Industries, 50%<br>Achilles, 50% | 1.7 | n.a. | 116 |

SOURCE: Company reports.

[a] December 1992.
[b] Before tax profit.
[c] Sales and profit for year ending December 1992.
[d] Sales and profit for year ending March 1993.
[e] Sales and profit for year ending December 1991.

(2) An extensive informal regulatory system of administrative guidance which imposes high transaction costs upon all new businesses, but especially foreign ones.
(3) The high cost of land.
(4) The ability of domestic rivals to appropriate ownership advantages through imitation and learning.

When one considers the costs and risks for a Canadian company that is considering direct investment in Japan versus investment in markets such as the U.S. and the U.K., it is clear that only very high and well-defined benefits will be sufficient to attract significant Canadian foreign direct investment to Japan. Such opportunities exist in specific niches. Thus, for example, in the banking sector a niche in the loan market was created by Japanese regulatory provisions concerning foreign exchange loans (impact loans). The benefits associated with reputation and information gathering, and the ability to exploit certain types of technological advantages, ensured that the major Canadian banks continued to operate in Japan (the profitable niche of impact loans disappeared with the liberalization of the Japanese banking markets).

## Technology

Japan is becoming a major leader in technology development and technology exports (see Table 4.6). Its firms possess outstanding capabilities not only to develop new technologies, but also to employ and augment their technological capabilities for successful market introduction of new products and production processes. Canada lags behind in its R&D investment intensity and must rely on foreign technology which it can acquire through direct purchases, by importing technologies embodied in machines and goods, and through intra-company technology transfers associated with foreign direct investments. If technology is to be efficiently accumulated, then the appropriate absorptive capacity must exist. Such capacity depends on existing domestic technological capabilities.

In 1990, Canada paid 5,300 million yen for technology imports from Japan, and received 1,200 million yen for technology exports to Japan. These import and export figures are much lower than the import and export figures for the U.S. Indeed, Canadian imports of technology from Japan are only 4.9% of the imports of technology from Japan to the U.S., while the exports of technology from Canada to Japan are a mere 0.6% of the exports of technology from the U.S. to Japan. Given the potential benefits that can be derived from technology linkages between Canada and Japan, the relative weakness of the links that actually exist indicates a market failure. Indeed, it is in the area of technology that the greatest effort has been expended in developing new types of Japanese-Canadian bilateral programs.

8

## Canadian Policies Towards Japan

### Trade-Related Policies

The Canadian approach to securing market access in Asian countries consists of simultaneously working through the GATT while continuously negotiating on specific issues that arise in bilateral relationships. The relationship with Japan requires further monitoring of the bilateral negotiations and relations between Japan and the U.S. Indeed, pressures from the U.S. on Japan may result in a shift in Japan's position which favours the U.S. at the expense of Canada. U.S.-Japan negotiations to remove "structural impediments to trade" may open some new opportunities for Canadian exports but clearly the focus of the U.S. is on the opening of trade opportunities for U.S. business. In general, Canadian trade relations with Japan in the past two decades have been relatively harmonious, which is not surprising given the complementary nature of the Canadian comparative advantage in natural resources and the relative scarcity of natural resources in Japan. Both countries have a stake in preventing protectionist moves in their major market—the U.S.

Some issues, however, have arisen in specific sectors. For example, in the mid 1980s voluntary export restraints were negotiated with Japan in an attempt to protect the Canadian automobile industry from small, fuel-efficient Japanese cars. Similar restraints were also negotiated with Korea.

Estimates of the cost per job protected by these voluntary restraints were between $179,000 and $226,000 in 1985.

Significant increases in direct investment by Japanese automobile manufacturers in Canada during the 1980s created new opportunities for trade, but led to the emergence of new trade issues: in particular, those that concern local content requirements. This issue was particularly important in the context of the Free Trade Agreement (FTA) and the ability of the Japanese transplants to export to the U.S. cars assembled in Canada which contain parts produced outside the U.S. or Canada. Under the FTA, cars were entitled to enter the U.S. duty-free if at least 50% of their value originated in North America. The FTA contained ambiguities which allowed different authorities to assess North American content in different ways. The disputes that arose from these ambiguities threatened FDI flows to Canada. For example, the U.S. Customs Service claimed that Honda cars assembled in Canada did not meet this content requirement, while Honda claimed that 69% of all expenses in producing the car were incurred in North America. The U.S. Customs Service made Honda liable for approximately U.S. $16.5 million in back duties for the first 15 months after the FTA went into effect.

Later, the Customs Service issued guidelines to help companies calculate North American content figures. These rules, however, discriminated against Canadian plants and were likely to affect future investment decisions of Japanese companies in Canada that were motivated by the access to the U.S. market promised by the FTA. The NAFTA has removed some of the uncertainties with respect to rules of origin and strengthened the protection afforded to foreign subsidiaries in North America. However, the minimum North American content requirements were increased. The economic power of the U.S. relative to its partners in NAFTA, and its tendency to interpret rules so as to reflect only U.S. interests, is a source of concern to those contemplating investing in Canada. Only more favourable experience can reduce this concern.

Some specific sectoral trade impediments exist because of product standards, questions of certification or consumption habits. For example, for a long-time Japanese building codes and product standards impeded the export of processed lumber from Canada to Japan. Most of these differences have been resolved, largely through bilateral negotiations. Negotiations with regard to forest product trade in 1992 focused on obtaining official Japanese acceptance of the construction of three-storey timber frame apartment buildings, and of Canadian grades of machine stressed lumber and finger-jointed timber. In response, the Japanese government did modify building codes to allow the construction of wooden three-storey apartment buildings in nonurban areas.

Some sectoral trade irritants stem from historical circumstances. For example, Canada faces a discriminatory tariff on some of its lumber in the form of a relatively high tariff on spruce, pine and fir lumber which are important species in Canada. The U.S. lumber exports (mainly of other species) largely escape the higher tariff and enjoy an advantageous competitive position. Thus while GATT rules are not violated legally, sometimes they are violated in terms of their intended meaning.

The formal resolution of "trade" conflicts does not solve the problem of barriers to market access that stem from the structure of the Japanese marketing system (which inhibits direct access) and Japanese buying habits. Perhaps as importantly, it cannot solve problems with the flow of market information to Canadian exporters. To improve bilateral trade relations, the report of the Canada-Japan Forum 2000 recommended that the Japanese government should make an effort to improve market access by publishing the details of Japanese standards and regulations for imports. It also pointed out that "Canadians must make a greater effort to inform themselves of Japanese requirements and business culture. Canadian business should keep abreast of demand side changes in Japan which are creating dynamic growth opportunities for exporting higher value-added products." The report singled out the role that the Canadian media could play in providing timely information about trade opportunities from a Canadian perspective. It also recommended the establishment of a dispute settlement mechanism to resolve trade disputes between Canada and Japan.

The government of Canada, through its trade commissioners and consulates, attempts to facilitate contacts between Canadian exporters and potential Japanese buyers. The effort includes a variety of trade promotion mechanisms involving the organization and funding of trade fairs and exhibitions, the funding of trade missions, the provision of advice, and the facilitation of contacts. The Department of External Affairs, through its Pacific 2000 program, provides funding for training of business executives in the

Japanese language and culture, as well as other educational and cultural activities aimed at increasing awareness of Japan (and other Pacific Rim countries) and reducing the cultural gap and information barriers to trade. Clearly some of these activities will provide benefits only in the long run.

**Investment Policies**

Globalization is leading nations around the world to liberalize rules for foreign investment policies. Canada has led many Western countries in terminating some of its more restrictive programs to control and direct foreign investment. The elimination of the National Energy Program and the replacement of the Foreign Investment Review Agency (FIRA) with Investment Canada marked a new era in which investment promotion is receiving a higher priority than attempts to target or mould investment through government regulation. Whereas FIRA reviewed all foreign investments (including both takeovers and new investments), Investment Canada reviews only major foreign takeovers and foreign investments in sensitive sectors such as culture. Investment Canada has also been charged with promoting foreign direct investment in Canada. Its major review functions are focused upon improving terms of acquisition by obtaining undertakings such as assigning R&D functions or international product mandates to Canadian affiliates. Historically, the main preoccupation of the government was with investment from the U.S. and, to a lesser degree, Europe. The focus of attention broadened in the mid 1980s to include Japan and other Asia Pacific Rim countries. This was motivated by the recognition that Japanese direct investment offers special opportunities for access to Japanese technology and management know-how.

In 1986, the Canadian government adopted a new approach to Japan that sought to build on the many consultative mechanisms that already existed between the two countries. The government began its Pacific 2000 initiative in the hopes of heightening Japanese awareness of Canada as an attractive destination for Japanese investment. This program emphasizes investment cooperation as a means of enhancing Canada's presence and competitiveness in the Pacific Rim. Expanded linkages with Japan are considered a key element of the strategy.

The Canadian approach was to emphasize the advantages that Canada offers the Japanese in accessing the North American market at a time when some U.S. legislators have been raising questions about the desirability of foreign investment, and Japanese investment in particular. A series of meetings at the prime ministerial level and high level missions of business executives sponsored by both governments took place to increase awareness in the private sector of both opportunities and concerns that the business communities had in each country. The report of the 1989 Japanese investment study mission to Canada sponsored by Keidanren and MITI (Morohashi, 1990) indicates that the FTA was viewed less as offering opportunities for the Japanese to produce in Canada and sell in the U.S., and more as offering opportunities to "cover the Canadian market through investment in the U.S." (p. 21). Rugman (1990) observed that the Morohashi Mission Report made favourable comments regarding the investment environment in Canada in the long run but had little to say about short-run investment. Canada reassured Japan that the country was open to other types of FDI besides that from the U.S. and that the FTA was favourable for Canada. The major advantages of the FTA for Canada, as explained to mission officials, were the open access to the sizable U.S. market and the perceived increases in efficiency of Canadian industry that would follow from the implementation of the FTA. However, Japanese mission officials were not fully convinced and they concluded that "the effects of the FTA on third party investment in Canada were uncertain." As the Honda experience indicates, they were correct.

Mission members noted that the advantages that attract investment to Canada include relatively cheap energy costs and the abundance of land. Indeed, provincial policies and actions to promote investment are perhaps just as important as those initiated by the federal government. Attractive tax concessions, displays of regulatory flexibility, the award of secure access to cheap raw materials (e.g., wood fibre in Alberta), and low energy prices were among the means used to attract Japanese investment to Canada. The question that must be asked is whether the costs incurred by the provinces to attract investment were justified in light of the expected benefits. It is also necessary to consider whether attempts to attract investment may violate international agreements. The NAFTA has heightened Japanese concerns regarding a possible "North American fortress," despite assurances from Canada and the U.S. that it represents opportunities for trade creation rather than trade diversion. Many of the Japanese reservations and concerns about the FTA are also reflected in their perceptions of the NAFTA. The report of Task Force II (economics) that was established as part of the Canada-Japan Forum 2000 included the advice from the Japanese side to Canada to consider taking steps to eliminate barriers to investment including discriminatory taxation policies, federal-provincial jurisdictional disputes, and labour/management conflicts. The specific recommendation was for the two governments to commit themselves to policies designed to encourage bilateral corporate investment, joint ventures and other forms of economic partnership (Canada-Japan Trade Council, 1993).

## Technology-Related Policies

Responding to criticisms from Western countries that Japan exploited technologies and scientific discoveries while making few original contributions, the Japanese government in 1986 developed the "General Guidelines for Science and Technology Policy." This policy committed Japan to carrying out an extensive program of fundamental R&D. The guidelines prescribed an amount of R&D spending that would represent 10% of the world's total spending on R&D (about equal to Japan's share of world GNP). The Japanese government has entered into a number of bilateral Science and Technology Agreements with the major industrialized countries including the U.S., Canada, Germany, France, Italy and Australia.

In May 1986, the "Canada-Japan Science and Technology Agreement" was signed. The agreement mandated cooperative activities relating to mutually agreed on fields such as meetings of experts, exchange of information, exchange of scientists, implementation of cooperative projects and so on. The agreement called for the establishment of a Joint Committee on Scientific Technological Cooperation. The functions of the committee were:

(1) to exchange information and views on scientific and technological policy issues;
(2) to review cooperative activities and accomplishments under the agreement; and
(3) to provide advice to the contracting parties with regard to the information of the Agreement and the orientation of the cooperative activities.

In 1988, a complementary study was commissioned by Prime Ministers Mulroney and Uno. The study group was headed by Dr. Geraldine Kenney-

Wallace and included four Japanese and four Canadians. The study was concluded in 1989 and included the following recommendations:

(1) that the governments of Canada and Japan publicly and quickly commit themselves to a new, imaginative, and enhanced program of bilateral R&D activities which builds upon the existing bilateral S&T (science and technology) agreement. The key characteristics of the program that need support are:
- dedication to excellence;
- emphasis on young researchers;
- concentration on creative ideas and "frontier" science and technology.

(2) that Canada and Japan immediately pursue a program of enhanced cooperation in the following broad "umbrella" areas of science and technology. These areas of equal importance are:
- advanced materials and biomaterials;
- biotechnology and biosciences;
- oceanography and ocean engineering;
- space science, technology and cosmology.

In 1989, the government of Canada published its new international strategy entitled "Going Global." The strategy prescribed an integrated approach to international trade, science and technology, and investment. One of the initiatives of this policy was the Pacific 2000 program. Under the program, funds were made available for a variety of activities including the establishment of the Japan Science and Technology Fund (JSTF), with an initial funding level of $25 million over five years. The Fund, jointly managed by External Affairs and International Trade Canada and Industry, Science and Technology Canada, was developed in collaboration with the National Sciences and Engineering Research Council. Its objectives include:

(1) increasing the participation of Canadian scientists and engineers in relevant world-class Japanese research-and-technology development programs and projects;

(2) training highly qualified personnel in state-of-the-art Japanese research facilities and thereby filling identified gaps in Canada's scientific and technological capabilities;

(3) facilitating access to Japanese technologies and industrial laboratories considered important to the competitiveness of Canadian industry; and

(4) collaborating in research, standard setting and similar initiatives to facilitate exports to Japan.

The program is very active. A major initiative concerning climate change studies is underway. The major problem with the program is the strong emphasis on government-to-government relationships with little industry initiative or participation.

The Japanese government views Japan's technological relationship with Canada in terms of intergovernmental cooperation with little emphasis on industrial collaboration (outside the scope of government initiatives). Another problem in the collaborative relationship with Japan stems from the fact that, in Canada, scientific basic development activities are mainly conducted in universities that are well funded for research while in Japan university research is relatively poorly funded. In contrast, industry laboratories are well funded in Japan but not in Canada. In the light of the unequal funding positions, developing collaborative university-to-university or industry-to-industry research is difficult. Negotiations are now taking place to ensure that the Japanese Ministry of Education better supports university researchers who participate in international collaborative projects.

The depth and success of the collaborative relationship depends to a large extent on Japanese intentions and moves in the fields of science and technology. The Japanese interest in international collaboration is based on their desire to forestall criticisms of "free riding" in the area of funding basic research and development activities, and their recognition that Japan has reached a level of technology development at which only a major advance in basic research can provide the necessary impetus for another "take off." The Japanese government has initiated several major collaborative projects in which Canada has an interest. A significant program with funds reaching into the billions of dollars is the 10-year Human Frontier Sciences Program. Japan is committed to funding the program fully. It has invited the U.S. and the E.C. countries as partners and recruited U.S. and E.C. scientists. The program focuses mainly on the basic life sciences. Canada was invited to join the project in its third year and now has a representative in the project secretariat in Europe. Canadian researchers were encouraged to prepare proposals with seed funds and organization funds from the Japan Science and Technology Fund. The Japanese have modified their original stand in committing to fund 100% of the project and are now requesting that participating countries provide funds for 50% of the project outlays (this request is being negotiated at the time of writing).

A second initiative of great interest to Canada is the Japanese "Intelligent Manufacturing Systems" program. The objective of the program is to develop "smart" technologies to automate manufacturing. The program attempts to combine the strength of Germany in the development of precision tools, the strength of the U.S. in software development and the Japanese expertise in systems integration. Canada was invited to join the project management as an observer in November 1990. More recently, Canada joined the project as a full member.

In addition to these megaprojects there are other Japanese initiatives that offer potential for international collaboration, but without formal government-to-government relationships and coordination. In August 1990, for example, MITI announced a number of projects mainly aimed at Japanese scholars, but with an invitation for international participation. These projects are advertised in *Nature* and individual scientists are invited to apply. The short lead time makes it almost impossible for individual scientists to meet the deadlines without the support of a large firm. Indeed, some large firms employ liaison officers in MITI and thus can anticipate project announcements and are in a better position to win in the competition. The Canadian Department of External Affairs is negotiating with the Japanese to route information through it to facilitate Canadian participation.

The Japan Research and Development Corporation (JRDC) also has a number of collaborative initiatives (recently an agreement amounting to $5 billion was signed with the U.S.). Currently the National Research Council and JRDC are negotiating a collaborative agreement with a relatively small financial commitment. The process employed by JRDC is one that provides maximum advantage to the Japanese partners. JRDC decides on a priority field (e.g., energy) and on the total funding and then identifies a Japanese scientist to lead the project. The project leader is given the funds to form a team but must find an international partner. The international partners must secure the funds for their research from other sources. Research results will be shared by all nations. The Canadian Embassy in Tokyo will be the focal information source for interested Canadian scientists.

The importance of Japan in the area of technological development and the barriers (of language, transaction costs and information) that exist in accessing and transferring Japanese science and technology require constant monitoring of the development and facilitation of contacts. The Canadian Embassy in Japan has the largest science and technology group of any Canadian embassy (a group of two Canadian and five local officers and one scientific translator). However, without the extensive presence of Canadian private enterprises, these efforts, while extremely beneficial, would fail to provide sufficient access to Japan's technology and science community.

9

## Lessons and Opportunities for Canada

In the long run, despite the current recession and despite expected future labour shortages, it is likely that the Japanese economy will grow at an average rate of above 3% per year for the next few decades. Such economic growth may be achieved by government policies to encourage shifts in the industrial structure so as to place stronger emphasis on value-added commodities, expansion of offshore sourcing and substantial investment in infrastructure and housing. This will imply, among other things, that:

(1) imports of both manufactured and nonmanufactured goods will increase;
(2) Japanese FDI will continue to increase, given that the ratio of overseas production to total production is still quite small for Japanese manufacturers compared to their U.S. and German counterparts (though it is expected that a significant share of the future FDI will flow to Asia);
(3) the increasing income level of Japanese households will provide markets for differentiated products; and
(4) raw material imports for industry use will continue to decline, but material imports for housing (e.g., lumber), public construction projects and household items (clothing and furniture) will continue to grow.

Our analysis has indicated that Canadian exporters are not well positioned to benefit from the forecasted growth in exports. A change in the industrial profile in Canada emphasizing a higher degree of resource processing and a shift to manufacturing, if accompanied by productivity growth in these sectors, may help maintain Canada's overall share in the Japanese market for imports.

While many of the formal barriers to exports are likely to be removed in the near future, as a consequence of international pressures, structural impediments will continue to constrain market entry to Japan by foreigners. Joint ventures and the use of intermediaries (e.g., trading companies) provide a partial solution to market failures resulting from lack of know-how and the generally high transaction costs which face many foreign exporters in Japan. These are also probably the lowest cost and the lowest risk approaches to entering the relatively closed domestic distribution system in Japan and for forming linkages with Japanese industrial groups. Japanese FDI, and the potential for intra-firm trade that it brings with it, may also facilitate Canadian exports to Japan.

The ability of Canadian governments to correct these market failures (through the provision of subsidies, services, promotion and information) is limited by international agreements and resource constraints. Investments in cultural and linguistic education to increase the understanding of Japanese ways and tastes and the ability to communicate in Japanese are essential for developing and maintaining Canadian skills for exporting to Japan. Canadian government leadership is needed in these areas.

However, adjustment of Canada's industrial structure is best left to market forces. Government's role should be the dissemination of market information, the facilitation of transitions, and most importantly, the preservation and expansion of market access. Canada, a relatively small economy, must ensure that U.S. or E.C. pressures on the Japanese in trade negotiations do not result in disadvantageous changes for Canadian exporters. In particular, with respect to nontariff barriers (e.g., codes, product standards, etc.) the government of Canada must ensure that, as barriers are removed because of third-party negotiations and lobbying (e.g., codes are modified and standards changed), the new regulatory regime does not erode Canada's competitive advantage.

On the financial side, it is possible that the Japanese savings rate will gradually decline. This fact and the gradual decline in current surpluses towards zero, as some government policy makers hope to see, may result in reduced amounts of capital being available for the development of overseas markets. This could have serious implications in the long run for the sale of bonds by the Canadian and also the U.S. governments. In the short run, the large Canadian bond holdings by Japanese insurance companies should be a cause for worry for Canada. A shift in portfolio structures by some of the major Japanese insurance companies could have serious short-term destabilizing effects on the Canadian dollar. There is a need to maintain the confidence of these investors in the long-term stability of the Canadian macroeconomic environment and the prudence of government policy. (Japanese "patience" may be an important factor helping to ensure the stability of the holdings of Japanese insurance companies, but this patience should not be stretched too far.)

To achieve stable economic growth over the next two decades, despite expected labour supply constraints, Japan will continue to pursue aggressive technology policies aimed at achieving substantial labour savings and hence higher levels of labour productivity.

Canada must continue to encourage technology transfers from Japan. Some of the cooperative programs now in place (mostly involving government to government relationships) have been outlined here. Clearly there is a need for more industry exchanges. Joint ventures and alliances may provide Canadian firms with opportunities to access Japanese technologies. However, for the full benefits of technological transfer to accrue, a capacity to absorb technology must be actively promoted in Canada. This requires the enhancement of Canadian technological R&D capabilities.

Finally, there are policy lessons that can be drawn from Japan's experience. Japan's post-war economic history suggests that industrial policy can be successful as long as it does not attempt to stifle competition and as long as governments stay small and allow room for private initiative. Japan's experience suggests that government pursuit of a vision does not necessitate higher levels of government spending. Government industrial policies can play a role in enriching the perspectives of private entrepreneurs, but probably should not override private sector decision making. Indeed the government policies should be disciplined by markets. One particularly important lesson to be learned from the Japanese experience is that comparative advantage can be created—a nation does not need to rely solely on its inherited advantages. The Japanese experience also provides an example of how crises (which sometimes are manufactured) can permit a government to take the lead in pushing for important structural changes needed for adapting to new environmental conditions.

There are some major differences between Japan and Canada that lead us to be less than enthusiastic advocates of government industrial policy development for Canada. A government industrial policy is likely to end in failure if it is not sensitive to long-term market forces. An industrial policy must be subjected to some market discipline. There must be a societal consensus about the primacy of economic development. Rent-seeking must play only a very limited role in the society and in the formulation of the long-term vision underlying the industrial policy. Synergistic linkages must exist between governments and private sector entrepreneurs. Governments must have an arsenal of policy tools in order to create winners. The federal structure of Canada, the lack of consensus on the primacy of economic development objectives, the prevalence of rent-seeking behaviours and a variety of constraints on policy instruments (both domestic and those imposed by international commitments) all increase the chance of government failure. Furthermore, the small Canadian market requires an "open economy" where multiple experiments in international and domestic markets provide a more effective guiding hand than government intervention is likely to provide.

# References


Abramovitz, Moses. 1986. "Catching Up, Forging Ahead, and Falling Behind," *Journal of Economic History* XLVI, 385–406.

Aoki, Masahiko. 1988. *Information, Incentives, and Bargaining in the Japanese Economy.* New York: Cambridge University Press.

Balassa, Bela, and Noland, Marcus. 1988. *Japan and the World Economy.* Washington, D.C.: Institute for International Economics.

Baldwin, Richard, and Krugman, Paul R. 1986. "Market Access and International Competition: A Simulation Study of 16K Random Access Memories," NBER Working Paper.

Barro, Robert. 1991. "Economic Growth in a Cross Section of Countries," *The Quarterly Journal of Economics* 106, 407–43.

Brander, James A. 1986. "Rationales for Strategic Trade and Industrial Policy," in Paul R. Krugman (ed.), *Strategic Trade Policy and the New International Economics.* Cambridge, MA: MIT Press.

Canada-Japan Trade Council. 1993. *Newsletter,* January-February.

Canadian Embassy, Tokyo. Various years. *Japanese Portfolio Investment in Canada.*

———. 1991. "Briefing note on Canadian Exports to Japan."

Cass, David. 1965. "Optimum Growth in an Aggregate Model of Capital Accumulation," *Review of Economic Studies* XXXII, 233–40.

Caves, R., and Uekusa, M. 1976. *Industrial Organization in Japan.* Washington, D.C.: The Brookings Institution.

Clark, R. 1979. *The Japanese Company.* New Haven, Connecticut: Yale University Press.

Contractor, F.J. 1990. "Ownership Patterns of U.S. Joint Ventures Abroad and the Liberalization of Foreign Government Regulations in the 1980s," *Journal of International Business Studies* 21, 55–73.

Daly, Donald J. 1991. "International Competitiveness of Japanese Manufacturing," *Managerial and Decision Economics* 12, 93–102.

———. 1993. "The Recession in Japan: Productivity, Costs and Profits," paper presented at the Japan Studies Association of Canada, Montreal, October.

Dore, R. 1973. *British Factory-Japanese Factory.* Berkeley, CA: University of California Press.

Dowrick, Steve. 1992. "Technological Catch Up and Diverging Incomes: Patterns of Economic Growth 1960–88," *The Economic Journal* 102, 600–610.

Edginton, D.W. 1990. "Recent Trends in Japanese Investment in Canada," paper presented at the Canadian Association of Geographers' Annual Meeting, Edmonton, May.

External Affairs and International Trade Canada. 1991. *Protecting Intellectual Property: An Introduction to Japan*, Ottawa.

Fruin, W. Mark. 1983. *Kikkoman.* Cambridge, MA: Harvard University Press.

———. 1992. *The Japanese Enterprise System.* Oxford: Oxford University Press.

Fuss, M., and Waverman, L. 1990. "The Extent and Sources of Cost and Efficiency Between U.S. and Japanese Motor Vehicle Producers," *Journal of the Japanese and International Economies* 4.

Galbraith, John K. 1987. *Economics in Perspective.* Boston: Houghton-Mifflin Company.

Gerlach, Michael L. 1992. *Alliance Capitalism.* Berkeley, CA: University of California Press.

Glazer, Nathan. 1976. "Social and Cultural Factors in Japanese Economic Growth," in Hugh Patrick and Henry Rosovsky (eds.), *Asia's New Grant: How the Japanese Economic Works*, 813–96. Washington, D.C.: The Brookings Institute.

Globerman, S. 1990. "Foreign Acquisitions of Canadian High Technology Firms," paper presented at the Conference on Foreign Investment, Technology and Economic Growth, Ottawa, September.

Goldin, C. 1988. "Marriage Bars: Discrimination against Married Women Workers, 1920's to 1950's," NBER Working Paper No. 2747.

Goto, A., and Wakasugi, R. 1988. "Technology Policy," in R. Komiya, M. Okuno and K. Suzumura (eds.), *Industrial Policy of Japan*, 183–204. San Diego, CA: Academic Press.

Grier, Kevin, and Tullock, Gordon. 1989. "An Empirical Analysis of Cross-National Economic Growth, 1951–80," *Journal of Monetary Economics* 24, 259–76.

Helliwell, J.F. 1989. "Some Comparative Macroeconomics of the United States, Japan and Canada," in R.M. Stern (ed.), *Trade and Investment Relations Among the United States, Canada and Japan*, 35–80. Chicago: University of Chicago Press.

Higuchi, Yoshio 1991. *Japanese Economy and Employment Behaviour* (Nihon Keizai to Shugyo Kodo). Tokyo: Toyo Keizai Shimposhi.

Imai, K. 1988. "Industrial Policy and Technological Innovation," in R. Komiya, M. Okuno and K. Suzumura (eds.), *Industrial Policy of Japan*, 205–29. San Diego, CA: Academic Press.

Ito, M. 1992. "The Japanese Distribution System and Access to the Japanese Market," in P. Krugman (ed.), *Trade with Japan: Has the Door Opened Wider?* 175–87. Chicago: University of Chicago Press.

Japanese Economic Planning Agency. Various years. *White Paper on the Economy* (in Japanese), Tokyo.

———. Various years. *Summary of Economic Statistics.* Tokyo.

Japanese Ministry of Finance. Various years. *Handbook on Subsidies.* Tokyo.

Japanese Ministry of Industry and International Trade. 1990. *Japanese Firms' Overseas Business Activities.* Tokyo.

Japanese Ministry of Labour. 1987. *Long-Term Forecasts for the Supply of and the Demand for Labour* (in Japanese). Tokyo.

———. 1991. *Labour Statistics Annual.* Tokyo.

———. 1993. *Labour Statistics Annual.* Tokyo.

———. 1992. *White Paper on Labour.* Tokyo.

———. 1993. *White Paper on Labour.* Tokyo.

Japanese Science and Technology Agency. 1991. *White Paper on Science and Technology.* Tokyo.

———. 1993. *Indicators of Science and Technology.* Tokyo.

Johnson, C. 1978. *Japan's Public Policy Companies.* Washington, D.C.: American Enterprise Institute for Public Policy Research.

———. 1982. *MITI and the Japanese Miracle: The Growth of Industrial Policy 1925–1975*, Stanford, CA: Stanford University Press.

———. 1983. "Interview, Close Up," *Journal of Japanese Trade and Industry* 2(3), May/June, 37–40.

———. 1984. "The Industrial Policy Debate Re-Examined," *California Management Review* 27, Fall, 71–89.

Keidanren. 1993. "International Competitiveness of Japanese Companies Towards the 21st Century," *Keidanren Review of the Japanese Economy.*

Keizai Koho Center. Various years. *Japan: An International Comparison.* Tokyo: Keizai Koho Centre (The Japan Institute of Social and Economic Affairs).

Komiya, R. 1988. *Modern Japanese Economy* (Gendai Nihon Keizai). Tokyo: University of Tokyo Press.

Koopmans, Tjalling C. 1965. "On the Concept of Optimal Economic Growth," in *The Econometric Approach to Development Planning.* Amsterdam: North-Holland.

Krafcik, J.F. 1988. "Triumph of the Lean Production System," *Sloan Management Review,* Fall.

Krasner, S. 1978. *Defending the National Interest: Raw Materials Investment and U.S. Foreign Policy.* Princeton, NJ: Princeton University Press.

Krugman, Paul R. 1984. "The U.S. Response to Foreign Industrial Targetting," *Brookings Papers on Economic Activity,* 77–131.

———. "Introduction: New Thinking about Trade Policy," in Paul R. Krugman (ed.), *Strategic Trade Policy and the New International Economics.* Cambridge, MA: MIT Press.

Landefeld, J. Steven, Lawson, Ann M., and Weinberg, Douglas B. 1992. "Rates of Return on Direct Investment," *Survey of Current Business,* August, 79–86.

MacLean, Brian K. 1992. "Japan's Growth Experience: Lessons Galore, Limited Lessons, or the Lessons at All," *Review of Income and Wealth* 38, 99–108.

Marvel, H.P. 1993. "Contracts and Control in Japanese Distribution," *Managerial and Decision Economics* 14, 151–62.

Mason, M. 1992. *American Multinationals and Japan.* Cambridge, MA: Harvard University Press.

Mauer, P.R. 1989. *Competing in High-Tech Japan* (Nihon Shijo deno Kyoso). Tokyo: Simul Press.

McFetridge, Donald G. (ed.) 1985a. *Canadian Industrial Policy in Action.* Toronto: University of Toronto Press.

———. 1985b. "The Economics of Industrial Policy," in Donald G. McFetridge (ed.), *Canadian Industrial Policy in Action.* Toronto: University of Toronto Press.

McMillan, C.J. 1988. "Bridge Across the Pacific: Canada and Japan in the 1990's," Canada-Japan Trade Council, Ottawa.

———. 1989. "Investing in Tomorrow: Japan's Science and Technology Organization and Strategies," Canada-Japan Trade Council, Ottawa.

Morck, Randall, and Nakamura, Masao. 1993. "Banks and Corporate Control in Japan," Working Paper, Faculty of Business, University of Alberta, Edmonton.

Morgan, James C., and Morgan, J. Jeffrey. 1991. *Cracking the Japanese Market.* New York: The Free Press.

Morohashi, S. 1990. *Report of the Japanese Investment Study Mission to Canada, October 22 - November 3, 1989.* Tokyo: Keidanren.

Mutoh, Hiromichi. 1988. "The Automotive Industry," in Ryutaro Komiya, Masahiro Okuno and Kotaro Suzumura (eds.), *Industrial Policy of Japan*, 307–68. San Diego, CA: Academic Press.

Nagatani, Keizo. 1991. *Political Macroeconomics.* Oxford: Oxford University Press.

———. 1993. "On a Recent Trend in Japanese Capital Markets," paper presented at the Japan Studies Association of Canada, Montreal, October.

Nakamura, A., and Nakamura, M. 1985a. *The Second Paycheck: A Socio-economic Analysis of Earnings.* New York: Academic Press.

———. 1985b. "Dynamic Models of the Labor Force Behavior of Married Women Which Can Be Estimated Using Limited Amounts of Information," *Journal of Econometrics* 27, 273–98.

———. 1985c. "A Survey of Research on the Work Behavior of Canadian Women," in C. Riddell (ed.), Royal Commission on the Economic Union and Development Prospects for Canada Report Vol. 3, *Work and Pay: The Canadian Labour Market*, 171–218. Toronto: University of Toronto Press.

———. 1992. "The Econometrics of Female Labor Supply and Children," *Econometric Reviews* 11, 1–71.

Nakamura, M. 1991a. "Japanese Direct Investment in Asia-Pacific and Other Regions: Empirical Analysis Using MITI Survey Data," *International Journal of Production Economics* 25, 219–29.

———. 1991b. "Modeling the Performance of U.S. Direct Investment in Japan: Some Empirical Estimates," *Managerial and Decision Economics* 12, 103–21.

———. 1993. "Japanese Industrial Relations in an International Business Environment," *North American Journal of Economics and Finance* 4, 225–51.

Nakamura, M., and Hübler, O. 1993. "Is Variability in Flexible Wages Compensated?: Evidence from Germany, Japan and the U.S.," working paper, Commerce, University of British Columbia, Vancouver.

Nakamura, M., and Nakamura, A. 1989. "Inventory Management Behaviour of American and Japanese Firms," *Journal of the Japanese and International Economies* 3, 270–91.

———. 1991. "Risk Behavior and the Determinants of Bonus Versus Regular Pay in Japan," *Journal of the Japanese and International Economies* 5, 140–59.

Nakatani, Iwao. 1984. "The Economic Role of Financial Corporate Grouping," in Masahiko Aoki (ed.), *The Economic Analysis of the Japanese Firm*, 227–58. Amsterdam: North-Holland.

Nelson, Richard R., and Phelps, Edmund S. 1966. "Investment in Humans, Technological Diffusion, and Economic Growth," *American Economic Review Proceedings* LVI, 69–75.

Nemetz, P.N., Vertinsky, I., and Vertinsky, P. 1985. "Japan's Energy Strategy at the Crossroads," *Pacific Affairs* 4, 553–76.

Oi, W. 1983. "The Fixed Employment Costs of Specialized Labor," in J.E. Triplett (ed.), *The Measurement of Labor Cost*, 63–122. Chicago: University of Chicago Press.

Okimoto, D.I. 1989. *Between MITI and the Market: Japanese Industrial Policy for High Technology*. Stanford, CA: Stanford University Press.

Ordover, J.A. 1991. "A Patent System for Both Diffusion and Exclusion," *Journal of Economic Perspective* 5, 43–60.

Patrick, H. 1977. "The Future of the Japanese Economy: Output and Labor Productivity," *Journal of Japanese Studies* 3.

Peck, Merton J., and Tamura, Shuji. 1976. "Technology" in Hugh Patrick and Henry Rosovsky (eds.), *Asia's Giant: How the Japanese Economy Works*, 525–86. Washington, D.C.: The Brookings Institute.

Rebick, M. 1993. "The Persistence of Firm-Size Earnings Differentials and Labor Market Segmentation in Japan," *Journal of the Japanese and International Economies* 7, 132–56.

Ries, J.C. 1993. "Voluntary Export Restraints, Profits and Quality Adjustments," *Canadian Journal of Economics* 26, 688–706.

Rugman, A.M. 1990. "Japanese Direct Investment in Canada," Canada-Japan Trade Council, Ottawa.

Samuels, R.J. 1981. "The Politics of Alternative Energy Research and Development in Japan," in R.A. Morse (ed.), *The Politics of Japan's Energy Strategy*. Institute of East Asian Studies, University of California, Berkeley, CA.

———. 1983. "State Enterprise, State Strength, and Energy Policy in Transwar Japan," Working Paper MIT EL 83–010, Massachusetts Institute of Technology, Boston, MA.

Samuelson, Paul A., Nordhaus, William D., and McCallum, John. 1988. *Economics*, 6th Canadian Edition. Toronto: McGraw-Hill Ryerson.

Sarnat, Marshall, Thibault, François, Ursacki, Terry, and Vertinsky, Ilan. 1992. "Foreign Banks in Japan: A Study of a Japanese Deregulation Process," *Asia Pacific Journal of Management* 9, 15–37.

Saxonhouse, G.R. 1983. "What Is All This About Industrial Targetting in Japan?" *World Economy* 6, 25–73.

———. 1985. "What's Wrong With Japanese Trade Structure," Discussion Paper 160, Department of Economics, University of Michigan.

Saxonhouse, Gary R., and Stern, Robert M. 1989. "An Analytical Survey of Formal and Informal Barriers to International Trade and Investment in the United States, Canada, and Japan," in Robert M. Stern (ed.), *Trade and Investment Relations among the United States, Canada and Japan*, 293–353. Chicago: University of Chicago Press.

Sazanami, Yoko, 1989. "Trade and Investment Patterns and Barriers," in Robert M. Stern (ed.), *Trade and Investment Relations among the United States, Canada, and Japan*, 90–126. Chicago: University of Chicago Press.

Schmitz, Andrew. 1989. "Trade in Primary Products: Canada, the United States, and Japan," in Robert M. Stern (ed.), *Trade and Investment Relations among the United States, Canada and Japan*, 141–67. Chicago: University of Chicago Press.

Scott, Bruce R. 1985. "National Strategies: Key to International Competition," in Bruce R. Scott and George C. Lodge (eds.), *U.S. Competitiveness in the World Economy*, 71–143. Boston: Harvard Business School Press.

Sekiguchi, S., and Horiuchi, T. 1988. "Industrial Adjustment Policy," in R. Komiya, M. Okuno and K. Suzumura (eds.), *Industrial Policy of Japan*, 369–93. San Diego, CA: Academic Press.

Sheard, P. 1991. "The Role of Firm Organization in the Adjustment of a Declining Industry in Japan: The Case of Aluminum," *Journal of the Japanese and International Economies* 5, 14–40.

Shimada, 1981. *Earnings Structure and Human Investment*, Keio Economic Observatory Monograph No. 4, Kogakusha, Tokyo.

Shinjo, K. 1988. "The Computer Industry," in R. Komiya, M. Okuno and K. Suzumura (eds.), *Industrial Policy of Japan*, 333–65. San Diego, CA: Academic Press.

Shinohara, M. 1982. *Industrial Growth, Trade and Dynamic Patterns in the Japanese Economy*. Tokyo: University of Tokyo Press.

Solow, Robert M. 1956. "A Contribution to the Theory of Economic Growth," *Quarterly Journal of Economics* 70, 65–94.

Trebilcock, M.J. 1989. "Comment," in R.M. Stern (ed.), *Trade and Investment Relations among the United States, Canada and Japan*, 213–18. Chicago: University of Chicago Press.

Trezise, P. 1983. "Industrial Policy Is Not the Major Reason for Japan's Success," *Brookings Review* 1, Spring, 13–18.

Tsurumi, H., and Tsurumi, Y. 1993. "Product Life Cycle and U.S.-Japan Automobile Trade," *Journal of Econometrics* 23, 193–210.

Tsurumi, Yoshi. 1984. *Multinational Management*. Cambridge, MA: Ballinger.

Tsurumi, Y., and Tsurumi, H. 1991. "Value Added Maximization Behavior of Firms and the Japanese Semiconductor Industry," *Managerial and Decision Economics* 12, 123–34.

Tsuruta, T. 1983. "The Myth of Japan Inc.," *Technology Review* 86, 45.

Ursacki, Terry. 1992. "The Internationalization of the Japanese Pulp and Paper Industry: Implications for Canada," FEPA Research Unit Working Paper 172, University of British Columbia, Vancouver.

Ursacki, Terry, and Vertinsky, Ilan. 1992. "Choice of Entry Timing and Scale by Foreign Banks in Japan and Korea," *Journal of Banking and Finance* 16, 405–21.

U.S. Department of Commerce. 1980. *Benchmark Surveys*. Washington, D.C.

———. 1985. *Benchmark Surveys*. Washington, D.C.

U.S. General Accounting Office. 1988. *Report to Congressional Requesters: Foreign Investment, Growing Japanese Presence in the U.S. Auto Industry*. Washington, D.C.

Vernon, Raymond. 1966. "International Investment and International Trade in the Product Cycle," *Quarterly Journal of Economics* 80, 190–207.

Vertinsky, I. 1986. "Economic Growth and Decision Making in Japan: The Duality of Visible and Invisible Guiding Hands," in R. Wolff (ed.), *Organizing Industrial Development*, 41–57. Berlin: Walter de Gruyter.

———. 1987. "An Ecological Model of Resilient Decision Making: An Application to the Study of Public and Private Sector Decision Making in Japan," *Ecological Modelling* 38, 141–58.

Wade, R. 1990. *Governing the Market: Economic Theory and the Role of Government in East Asian Industrialization*, Princeton, NJ: Princeton University Press.

Wakasugi, R. 1989. *Trade, Direct Investment and the Japanese Industrial Organization* (in Japanese). Tokyo: Toyo Keizai Shimposha.

White, M., and Trevor, M. 1983. *Under Japanese Management: The Experience of British Workers*. London: Heineman.

Wolf, B.M., and Taylor, G. 1990. "Employee and Supplier Learning in the Canadian Automobile Industry: Implications for Competitiveness," paper presented at the Conference on Foreign Investment, Technology and Economic Growth, Ottawa, September.

Yamawaki, Hideki. 1988. "The Steel Industry," in R. Komiya, M. Okuno and K. Suzumura (eds.), *Industrial Policy of Japan*, 281–306. San Diego, CA: Academic Press.

———. 1991. "Exports and Foreign Distributional Activities: Evidence on Japanese Firms in the United States," *Review of Economies and Statistics* 73, 294–300.

Yoshioka, K., Nakajima, T., and Nakamura, M. 1993. "Sources of Total Factor Productivity for Japanese Manufacturing 1964–1988: Scale Economies or Technical Progress?" paper presented at the European Econometric Society Meeting, Uppsala, Sweden, August.

Ziemba, William T., and Schwartz, Sandra L. 1991. "The Growth in the Japanese Stock Market, 1949–90 and Prospects for the Future," *Managerial and Decision Economics* 12, 183–95.

# *Index*